French Armies of
the Thirty Years' War

French Armies of the Thirty Years' War

Stéphane Thion

LRT Editions

Little Round Top Editions
95, allée de Pierras
31650 Auzielle
www.lrt-editions.com

Printed in Singapore
First publishing

Contents

INTRODUCTION

The three musketeers, Cyrano de Bergerac, Louis XIII, Richelieu, Condé, Turenne, La Rochelle, Rocroi...these few words sum up the literary and historical representations most people are able to associate with the tumultuous events of the first half of the seventeenth century. We're not complaining ~ it's a good start!

Portos by Jean Adolphe Beaucé (1818-1875), in A. Dumas "The three musketeers"

This book begins in 1617, the year that Louis XIII really took power by distancing the queen mother and ordering the assassination of Concini (24 April 1617), and ends in 1648 ~ five years after the death of Louis XIII ~ the year of the Westphalia Peace Treaty (24 October 1648). This period was mostly dominated by the personality and works of Richelieu, who entered the king's Council in April 1624. He gave the king an ambition: *"to procure the ruin of the Huguenot party, humble the pride of the great, reduce all subjects to their duty, and elevate your majesty's name among foreign nations to its rightful reputation"*. By the time of his death, on the 4 December 1642, this programme had been accomplished.

The first military action of this period, called the 'Drôlerie des Ponts de Cé' was the uprising of the nobility who supported the queen mother against the king in August 1620. In reality the rebels were roundly defeated by the king's armies, but very few units actually fought. In his memoirs, Richelieu, who at the time was on the queen's side, gives a detailed analysis of this defeat. In particular, he drew from it principles that he was to follow throughout his life: *"I realised on this occasion that any party composed of many entities that have nothing in common other than their lightness of spirit ~ which makes them approve the present government constantly, and makes them desire change without knowing why ~ does not have great subsistence. I also realised that that which is held only by a precarious authority does not last long; that those who fight against a legitimate power are already half-defeated by their own imagination; that their thoughts ~ that not only are they exposed to the risk of losing their life through arms but, what is more, by the paths of justice if they are captured, representing for them the hangman at the same time that they affront the enemy ~ renders the contest most unequal, there being few men brave enough to ignore these thoughts as well as if they had never come to their mind"*. These political beliefs gave Louis XIII and Richelieu a powerful instrument that was to emerge transformed from the Thirty Years' War.

The army that Marie de Medici left to Henri IV's heir was small and inexperienced, but the Wars of Religion at the beginning of Louis XIII's reign, combined with Richelieu's actions, gave the French kingdom an increasingly efficient army. Commanded by great captains such as the Duc de Rohan, the Viscomte de Turenne and the Prince of Condé, the army was highly successful, as shown by the long list of French victories: Avins and the Valtelline in 1635, Tornavento in 1636, Leucates in 1637, La Rota in 1639, Casale and Turin in 1640, Wolfenbüttel in 1641, Kempen and Llerida in 1642, Rocroi in 1643, Friburg in 1644, Allerheim (or Nördlingen) and Lhorens in 1645, Zusmarchausen in 1647, and Lens in 1648.

This book is illustrated by a large number of reproductions, both contemporary and non-contemporary of this period, and the text is enriched with many passages from the memoirs or accounts of the great men of the century. This helps the reader to experience the daily life of Louis XIII's soldiers and the battles at that time through the eyes of witnesses to these events – or, to be more precise, through their own words. Although these testimonies have the advantage of transcribing perfectly the atmosphere of the period, their objectivity in some cases may be dubious: their authors were mostly concerned with receiving honours for their own actions, even if it meant embellishing them a little. This can easily be seen by comparing the battles of Friburg and Allerheim as recounted by Turenne and Gramont, or the different accounts of the battle of Rocroi. The author nevertheless defends this approach as there is infinitely more risk involved in interpreting events that are nearly four centuries old with the mentality of the twenty-first century. In any case, have a good trip through the heart of the seventeenth century!

7

CHAPTER I

CONTEXT :
THE THIRTY YEARS' WAR

Cardinal Richelieu, Philippe de Champaigne (1602-1674). Palais de l'Institut, Paris.

The Thirty Years' War should never have been a French war. It was originally a religious conflict between the Catholics and Protestants of the Habsburg Empire. When France became involved in 1635, the Thirty Years' War was theoretically over... This terrible conflict began in Bohemia, the Czech Republic of today, during "counter-reform" operations carried out by the Catholics, at the instigation of Emperor Ferdinand II of Habsburg, who was trying to reconquer lands lost to the Protestant church. In his *Letter of Majesty for Religious Liberty* published on the 9 July 1609, Rudolf II granted his Bohemian subjects the privilege that *"each party may practise freely and fully the religion in which he believes he may find his salvation..."*. The Czech Protestants also enjoyed political advantages, as well as special arrangements that meant religious buildings could be used by different faiths. This *Letter of Majesty*, accorded reluctantly by Rudolf II, was a thorn in the side of both the Catholics and the Habsburgs, headed up by the completely new emperor and king of Bohemia, Ferdinand II. The Catholics mobilised all their energy to regain control of Protestant parishes. Whenever possible, royal (Bohemian) or imperial (on the lands of the Emperor) power intervened in favour of the Catholics in issues opposing the two faiths. It was the brutal resolution of such an issue in favour of the Catholics that resulted in the "Defenestration of Prague" on the 23 May 1618. From 1618 to

From the origins of the war to the end of the Swedish Period

1635, Ferdinand II was forced to constantly reestablish imperial power and the preeminence of the Catholic faith within the Empire. To do this, he was obliged to nullify the "illegal" secularisation of Catholic property by the Protestants wherever possible.

The Bohemian states revolted, and gave the crown of Bohemia to the Elector Palatine Frederick V. On the 7 November 1620, the imperial army under Tilly defeated the combined armies of Mathias Thurn, von Mansfeld and Christian of Anhalt at the Battle of White Mountain, a few miles away from Prague. Christian of Brunswick later suffered a total defeat against Tilly at Stadtlohn on the 6 August 1623, and the many imperial successes between 1620 and 1624 began to be of grave concern to the European powers: the United Provinces, the Protestant States of North Germany, England, Denmark and Sweden, but also to France. At this time, the United Provinces were at war with Spain and were unable to intervene; Sweden was at war with Poland; and France was trying to suppress Protestant rebellions. It was therefore Christian IV of Denmark who came to the rescue of the Protestant cause in June 1625, a cause supported in Northern Germany by the Electors of Brandenburg and Saxony. However, on the 26 April 1626, Wallenstein - who had entered the service of the Emperor - defeated von Mansfeld at the battle of Dessau Bridge, and Tilly crushed Christian IV's army at Lutter-am-Barenberg on the

11

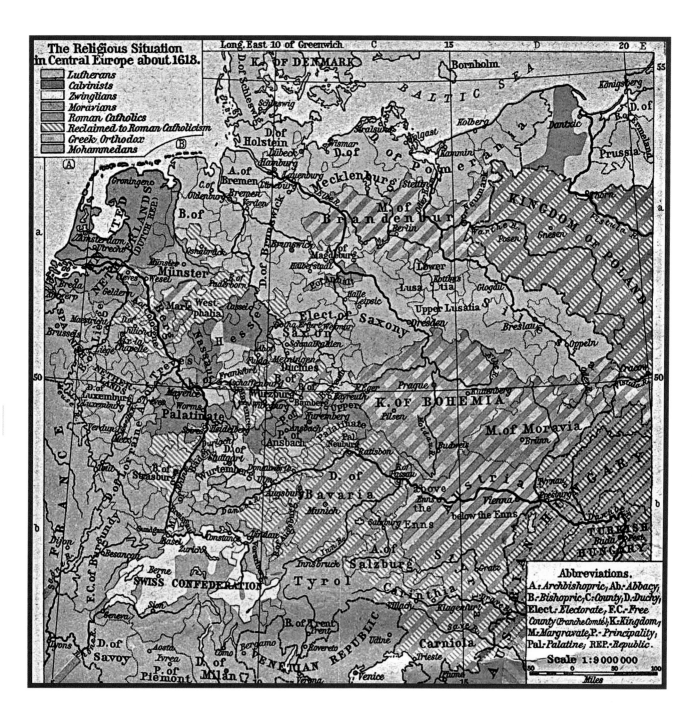

The religious situation in central Europe circa 1618, William R. Shepherd's The historical atlas (1923)

26 August of the same year. 1627 and 1628 saw the capture of territories from Christian IV and his allies in Northern Germany, followed by a religious re-organisation of these conquered lands. The peace treaty of 7 June 1629 put an end to the Danish inter-vention in the Thirty Years' War; Ferdinand II now had his hands free to issue his Edict of Restitution in February 1629, which called into question the abusive secularisation that had taken place since

1555. The time of conflict appeared to have passed, but plotting was at its height. Wallenstein aroused much enmity within the empire, especially that of Duke Maximilian of Bavaria, and Tilly. Encouraged by his entourage and Richelieu's agents, the Emperor Ferdinand II dismissed Wallenstein on the 13 August 1630. Fearing the victory of Ferdinand II, the French contributed to the Emperor losing his right-hand man just before the Swedish intervention.

At the same time, the combination of the success of Ferdinand II, French diplomacy and French subsidies encouraged Gustavus Adolphus of Sweden to intervene in North Germany, which he did on the 6 July 1630. Tilly, fearing the arrival of the Swedish army, ordered an assault on Magdeburg, in which the entire population of the town was massacred on the 20 May 1631. Gustavus Adolphus' victory over Tilly at Breitenfeld on the 17 September 1631 encouraged the Emperor to recall Wallenstein. He abandoned Duke Maximilian's Bavaria, leaving it to be ravaged by Swedish troops, while Tilly died of an injury at the end of April 1632. Gustavus Adolphus was defeated by Wallenstein at the walls of *Alte feste*, a fortress close to Nuremberg, in July 1632, but he in turn defeated Wallenstein at the battle of Lützen on the 16 November 1632. This victory came with a heavy price – the death of the king of Sweden, the 'Lion of the North'. Encouraged by the king of France, Louis XIII, and the Swedish Chancellor Oxenstierna, the Swedish generals Baner, Horn and Torstensson, and the German general Bernard of Saxe-Weimar, continued the war, despite the lassitude of the population. Wallenstein defeated the Swedes at Steinau in September 1633, but Bernard of Saxe-Weimar entered Donauwörth, then Ratisbon on the 14 November 1633. The storming of Ratisbon, the town of the Imperial Diet, had a significant impact in that it incited Duke Maximilian of Bavaria to plot once again against Wallenstein. The duke's hatred of Wallenstein led to the assassination of the Generalissimo during the night of the 25-26 February 1634. But this heinous crime did not help the Swedes – on the 6 September, Marshal Horn suffered a heavy defeat at Nördlingen. The Swedes abandoned Bavaria and Bernard of Saxe-Weimar returned to Alsace. On the 23 November, the preliminaries for peace were negotiated between Ferdinand II and the Electors of Saxony and Brandenburg. A peace treaty was then signed in Prague on the 30 May 1635 between the Elector of Saxony and the Emperor, a treaty which was extended to all German princes who wished to join, and which was approved by the Elector of Brandenburg on the 6 September.

Presumed painting of the White Mountain battle, near Prague (1620), Pieter Snayers (1592-1667). Louvre Museum, Paris.

Siege of la Rochelle,
Claude Gellée
("Le Lorrain", 1600-1682).
Louvre Museum, Paris.

14

With the coalition between Gustavus Adolphus of Sweden and Richelieu of France severely damaged, Germany was now on the point of regaining peace, even if many Protestant princes and free towns of the empire remained hostile to it. But Chancellor Oxenstierna had no interest in peace in Germany: his strategy was to take control of the continental coast of the Baltic, by establishing a protectorate over the Protestant states of North Germany. Nor did Cardinal Richelieu have any interest in the cessation of the war; he feared that Spain would be able to use imperial troops liberated by the end of conflict to threaten French interests. Spain's strategy was to establish a route of free passage for her armies from Milan to the Spanish Netherlands; Richelieu's strategy was to do everything possible to hinder this plan. In his memoirs, he gives us the opinion he gave to the king on the subject at the beginning of 1629; he suggests that to defend the frontiers of the kingdom, France should protect the small frontier states of Germany and Italy, and control the access routes to these zones, namely from the Rhine through Lorraine and Alsace, and from Italy through the Savoy: '*A constant attempt to halt the progression of Spain was necessary; and, to prevent this nation from increasing its domination and extending its frontiers, France had to think only of her own fortification, and construct and open gateways to all the states of her neighbours, and be able to protect them from the oppression of Spain, when the occasion so required; for this, the first thing that needed to be done was to become powerful on the sea, which gives entry to all the states of the world; after this it was necessary to fortify at Metz, and, if possible, to advance up to Strasburg to have an entry to Germany; which needed to be done over time, with great discretion, and in a subtle and secret manner; a large citadel was needed at Versoix to gain importance in the eyes of the Swiss, to have a point of entry, and to put Geneva in a state of being one of the allies of France; we could also consider obtaining from Maréchal de Longueville the sovereignty of Neufchâtel, which, being in Switzerland, gives a greater foothold and more reason for France to be considered sovereign by men of little value, who respect only that which is before their eyes; and it was with these foreigners that His majesty needed to maintain alliance most carefully, both because they separate Germany from Italy, and because, as they are ready for war, it is important to have them on our side and to deprive the enemy of them; it was necessary to consider the Marquisate of Saluce, either for an entente with Maréchal de Savoie.... or by making use of the poor relations between the subjects of the Marquisate and himself, and reconquering it; (...) to be even more in a position to be feared in Italy, it was necessary to maintain thirty galleys; Navarre and the Franche-Comté could still be considered as belonging to us, being contiguous to France, and easy to conquer whenever we so wished; but he did not speak of it, and it would be imprudent to think of it if, on the one hand, what is written above had not succeeded, and on the other hand, we would not be able to do so without provoking open war with Spain, which was to be avoided as far as possible.*'

The war in Germany and Bohemia began through internal troubles, and France was not spared troubles of its own. After a revolt of the nobility supporting Queen Marie de Medici, which culminated in the battle of the Ponts de Cé near Angers on the 7 August 1620, Louis XIII had to face a number of Protestant rebellions. An expedition of the young king to Bearn, aiming to restore certain temporal rights to the Catholic Church (here we find the same motivations as those that triggered the Thirty Years' War in Bohemia), irritated the Protestants. The Protestants met at La Rochelle on the 24 December 1620 and decided to assemble their own military organisation. This same assembly demanded that Louis XIII retract the measures he had taken in Bearn. Each side hardened its positions, until a Huguenot party seized Privas in February 1621. The king himself took command of the army on the 18 April, and besieged Saint-Jean d'Angély on the 16 May; the town surrendered on the 23 June 1621. This was followed by the storming of Pons on the 28 June, Clairac on the 4 August and Nérac on the 9 July. The siege of Montauban began on the 17 August, but the royal troops were not able to take the town and lifted the siege on the 10 November. The population of Monheurt, a small village between Agen and Marmande, was massacred by frenzied royal troops on the 12 December. On the 21 March 1622, the king once again took command of his army, and fought in the battle of Riez in Lower Poitou on the 16 April 1622, blockaded La Rochelle at the end of that same month, stormed Nègrepelisse on the 10 June, where the entire population was massacred, and then Saint-Antonin on the 21 June 1622. The king entered Béziers on the 18 July. On the 2 August, Praslin besieged Lunel, and Sommières was taken on the 17 August. The royal troops arrived at Montpellier in September, but the siege went on until October without them being able to take the town. Lesdiguières negotiated peace with the Duc de Rohan, who surrendered on the 10 October. The peace of Montpellier, signed on the 18 October 1622, renewed the Edict of Nantes.

In January 1625, the Huguenots rebelled once again: Soubise seized 7 vessels at La Rochelle and the Duc de Rohan raised a revolt in Languedoc, after complaining to Louis XIII of non-compliance with the clauses of the Treaty of Montpellier. Soubise landed his troops on the Isle of Rhé at the beginning of September 1625; Toiras and La Rochefoucault landed on the 14 September to oust them. Soubise fled to the Isle of Oléron; on the 18 September, the last Protestants surrendered to Toiras. Peace was signed on the 5 February 1626 with England's help. But at the instigation of the Duke of Buckingham, high admiral of the fleet,

Storming of Privas, Louis XIII and Cardinal Richelieu arrive into town, May 28th, 1629. French school. Galerie du Château de Richelieu. Châteaux de Versailles and Trianon, Versailles.

15

English diplomacy became more sympathetic to the French Protestants; Charles the 1st feared in particular the rising power of the French fleet. On the 26 July 1626, the English fleet landed an army on the Isle of Rhé, which was being defended by Toiras. On the 2 August, the English and the emigrants laid siege to Saint-Martin de Ré; on the 15 August, Gaston of Orléans besieged La Rochelle. On the 8 November 1626, Toiras, with the reinforcement of troops brought by Schomberg, forced the enemy to retreat from the island, ending the English expedition. On the 12 November, Richelieu launched the construction of a dyke that was to isolate La Rochelle, but the town held out until the 28 October 1628. Rohan led the rebellion in the south of France; Louis XIII sent the Prince de Condé against him, who arrived at Saint-Affrique on the 28 May 1628. As he was unable to take the town, he authorised widescale destruction, giving his soldiers free rein to pillage, burn, rape and kill. However, Rohan remained in charge of the Languedoc; the peace signed between France and England on the 14 April 1629 allowed Louis XIII to concentrate new resources against him. On the 12 May 1629, the

Duc d'Estrées took Calvisson and the royal army took Privas on the 27 May, massacring the inhabitants. All the towns in the Cévennes then surrendered to the Duc de Montmorency. Rohan sought clemency from the king, and on the 27 June 1629, The Edict of Grace put an end to the Protestant uprising in Languedoc. This act allowed Richelieu to assert at the beginning of 1630 that: *"For the six years that the Cardinal has been in office, France, regaining vigour, opposed the multiple usurpations of Spain, which had largely increased since the death of the king, but with the disadvantage that most of her forces were occupied either with other wars abroad, or her own civil wars. Now that France has obliged England to make peace, and has quashed the heretic rebellion, she has all her forces available to use them in Italy to prevent Spain from invading the other states, and all the more so because Spain does not believe France to be powerful enough to halt the course of its unjust enterprises."*

P. 17 :
The Musketeer's Tale (1897), Adolphe Alexandre Lesrel (1839-2929). Private Collection. London.

The town of Montauban surrenders to Louis XIII and Cardinal Richelieu, August 21st, 1629. French school. Galerie du Château de Richelieu. Châteaux de Versailles and Trianon, Versailles.

France enter the war

Before 1635, France only intervened occasionally and indirectly in the war that shook Central Europe, but when it did so it was always in the spirit of the opinion given to the king in January 1629.

François-Annibal, marquis de Coeuvres, duc d'Estrées, Maréchal de France in 1626 (1572-1670) by Paulin Jean-Baptiste Guérin (1783-1855). Châteaux de Versailles and Trianon, Versailles.

In July 1620, the Catholic Grisons of the Valtelline revolted against their Protestant overlords. Spain took the opportunity to intervene through the intermediary of the Governor of Milan, occupying the valley and building forts. The Pope intervened in 1621, obtaining the replacement of Spanish garrisons by papal troops, but this agreement did nothing to hinder the the movement of Spanish troops through the Valtelline. The high Adda valley, between the Palatinate, Milan, the Tyrol and Austria, was an important Spanish communication point. On the 7 February 1623, France signed an alliance with the Duchy of Savoy and the Republic of Venice. This treaty prepared for a French intervention in the Valtelline. In October 1624, François Annibal d'Estrées penetrated Grison territory and ousted the imperialists from the region in February 1625. Charles-Emmanuel of Savoy requested military aid from France to attack Genoa, a Spanish ally. Richelieu readily agreed, and Lesdiguières arrived

at Turin on the 1 February 1625 and at the walls of Asti on the 4 March, between Genoa and Milan. After storming Capriata, Novi and Rossiglione, Lesdiguières decided to slow his pace, preferring to lay siege to Gavi, against the advice of the Duke of Savoy. Gavi surrendered on the 22 April, but it was too late to take Genoa. In the Tyrol, an imperial army was preparing to intervene in the Valtelline, while the Spanish under the Duke of Feria prepared an army to come to Genoa's aid. The Spanish took Acqui then marched on Casale, reclaiming Gavi and Novi, while Lesdiguières beat a retreat to the Piedmont. Charles-Emmanuel of Savoy, joined by Créqui, who replaced Lesdiguières as he had returned to the Dauphiné, entrenched his army at Verrua and the Duke of Feria was stopped on the 5 August 1625 at his lines of defence. On the 17 November 1625, the Duke of Feria lifted the siege of Verrua and Lesdiguières took his troops back to the Dauphiné. A truce was signed on the 5 February 1626 between Louis XIII and Spain, which resulted in the Treaty of Monçon of the 5 March 1626; the Valtelline was returned to the Vatican.

Vincenzo Gonzaga, Duke of Mantua, died in 1627. Charles Gonzaga, Duc de Nevers was the closest direct heir. His property – the duchy of Mantua and the Marquisate of Montferrat – were both fiefdoms of the Empire, and Ferdinand II was given trusteeship at the request of Sapin and Savoy. In February 1629, the Spanish besieged Casale; as soon as La Rochelle had been taken, Louis XIII and Richelieu led an army to bring aid to Casale, crossing the Alps at Mont-Genèvre, and taking Suse on the 6 March. During the night of the 15-16 March, the Spanish lifted the siege of Casale. After sending an army to the Grisons on the 5 June 1629, Emperor Ferdinand II ordered the French to evacuate his Italian property. In September, he sent a second army to Mantua, and a third to besiege Casale. Richelieu and the Royal Army left on the 29 December 1629 for Suse, fighting off Charles-Emmanuel of Savoy, now his enemy, and took Pignerol on the 21 March. On the 12 May 1630, the king began his conquest of Savoy. Chambéry opened its gates on the 17 May; Prince Thomas, second son of the Duke of Savoy, retreated to Bourg-Saint-Maurice and was defeated by Châtillon on the 6 July 1630 at the battle of Séez. The storming of Montmélian on the 19 July 1630 ended the campaign. The Duc de Montmorency, who had been given the task of taking the Marquisate of Saluces, crossed Mont Cenis on the 7 July and defeated Charles-Emmanuel of Savoy on the 10 July between Saint Ambroise and Avigliana. Charles-Emmanuel died of an apoplexy a few days later, on the 26 July. His successor, Victor Amedeo the 1st, brother-in-law of Louis XIII, was more favourable to the French, but this war had to be ended. On the 17 July, the imperialists stormed Mantua by surprise, taking Charles Gonzaga and the Maréchal d'Estrées prisoner. Louis XIII asked the Duc de Montmorency to help Casale, which was being held by Toiras. He took Carignan on the 6 August 1630. Victor Amedeo managed to escape, but the exhausted and diminished French did not push on until Turin and Casale. Louis XIII sent Schomberg to the Piedmont, clearing the route from Suse to Turin. Schomberg's army, now reinforced by the armies of La Force and Marillac, arrived at Casale on the 26 October. Opposing them were the Spanish under the Marquis of Santa-Croce and Spinola. But the battle never happened: mediation by Pope Urban VIII put an end to hostilities and led to the Treaty of Cherasco on the 26 April 1631. Charles Gonzaga, Duc de Nevers, could now take possession of the Duchy of Mantua and the Marquisate of Montferrat.

At the beginning of 1632, Richelieu said to the king that *"...to resolve the situation rapidly, it was necessary to consider that, given current state of affairs in Germany, one could only act in one of these four manners:*

- ⬦ *1. either to join with the king of Sweden to wage open war against the house of Austria;*
- ⬦ *2. or come to an agreement with the emperor and Spain to wage war against Sweden and the Protestant princes;*
- ⬦ *3. or try to make the Catholic Electors accept neutrality in the terms proposed by the king of Sweden, if he did not wish to consent to better terms, and let him continue war in Germany without becoming involved, but only to maintain a few troops on the border to use when necessary;*
- ⬦ *4. or also take possession of Alsace, Brisach and passages of the Rhine held by the Catholic Electors, and to have there an army to use on occasions of necessity (...)"* But he rejected the second method, reminding the king of *"the little trust we can have in the Spanish, the danger of allowing the House of Austria to grow to the extent that it becomes a formidable force for France, and forces us to a very long war to defend ourselves against Austria or against other enemies, both external and internal, that they could enkindle in this event"*. But the king chose neither the first nor the second scenario, as he did not want war and wanted to avoid severance with both the king of Sweden and the House of Austria. He therefore opted for neutrality, but events were to push him to intervene in the Lorraine.

In the Lorraine, Duc Charles IV had regularly welcomed enemies of Richelieu or Louis XIII since 1629, and sided in the war with Tilly against France's Swedish allies. As Charles IV had authorised the occupation of fortresses from Nancy to Strasburg by imperialist troops, Louis XIII, assisted by Maréchal d'Effiat and Maréchal de La Force, led the army to the Lorraine in December 1631. A treaty was signed on the 6 January 1632 between Louis XIII and Charles IV, but Charles IV soon resumed his active alliance with Ferdinand II, leading to other interventions by the armies of Maréchals d'Effiat and de La Force in 1632 and 1633. Charles IV surrendered on the 20 September 1633 and the French army entered Nancy on the 25 September. The Duc de Lorraine abdicated on the 19 January 1634, leaving power to his brother.

Charles de Schomberg, duc d'Halluin, Maréchal de France in 1637, viceroy of Catalonia in 1648 (1601-1656) by Jean-Sébatien Rouillard (1789-1852). Châteaux de Versailles and Trianon, Versailles.

Alsace had been occupied by the Swedes, under Horn, since August 1632. The Alsatian cities, weary of pillaging, asked for help from Louis XIII. A convention negotiated on the 9 October 1634 between France and Sweden, followed by a treaty signed on the 22 October, authorised Maréchal de La Force to occupy Alsace. Under the orders of Maréchal de La Force, the Viscomte de Turenne fought the imperialists in Lower Alsace from December 1634, in coordination with the army of Bernard of Saxe-Weimar who occupied the opposite bank of the Rhine. While Maréchals Brézé and de La Force battled with the imperialists in Alsace, Prince Thomas of Savoy, at the head of a Spanish army, invaded the Electorate of Treves in March 1635 and took prisoner the Elector Archbishop, who was under the protection of Louis XIII. The dice were cast. Richelieu, sensing that war was inevitable, reinforced his alliances with the United Provinces (8 February 1935) and Sweden (28 April 1635).

At the beginning of 1633, Richelieu once again persuaded Louis XIII to finance the war in Germany and Holland, fearing that *"if peace is made in Germany and a truce in Holland, or one of the two, France will have to support alone a defensive war, which could spread to her own territory, with no means of avoidance...".* Early 1635, he justified France's intervention by saying: *"After having long fought against war, which has been the ambition of Spain for the last few years, and their bad will towards this State, which, like a mountain that hinders the flow of an impetuous torrent, has prevented their monarchy from inundating all Europe; after having spent much time protecting ourselves from their traps and continuous enterprises against this kingdom, which we have, with God's blessing, happily remedied by indefatigable vigilance; finally, this year it is now impossible for us to withdraw further, and we are obliged to enter into open war with them, a war which we declare, but which we will not be first to begin, as it is they who attack us and force our hand by so many hostilities, so many insults, and so many preparations they began long ago to oppress us all at once, which, in order to defend ourselves, we are obliged to declare that we no longer wish to suffer the covert war that they inflict on us, and that they disguise to the world under the misleading name of peace, a peace which, all things considered, has never been the case since the Treaty of Vervins imposed the end of the rupture between themselves and Henri IV."*

At the beginning of 1635, Louis XIII had armies in Champagne, Picardy (under Maréchals Brézé and Châtillon), Lorraine (under Maréchal de La Force), as well as one on the Sarre under Cardinal de La Valette, who could count on aid from Bernard of Saxe-Weimar and the Weimarians, and an army in the Valtelline under the Duc de Rohan. He also had the support of the army of the Duke of Savoy in the Alps. The army in Picardy was to cross the Meuse and join up with the army of Stathouder Frederick Hendrick of Nassau. The French army encountered and defeated the Spanish army of Prince Thomas of Savoy on the 22 May 1635 at Avins. The combined French and Dutch armies marched on Brussels, but, decimated by typhus, they could but withdraw to their bases. During this time, the Spanish and imperial armies

20

Casale rescue, 26 October 1630. Galerie du Château de Richelieu. Châteaux de Versailles and Trianon, Versailles.

P. 21 : Les chanteurs, Adolphe Alexandre Lesrel. Private collection.

of Cardinal-Infante and Piccolomini occupied the Duchy of Cleves. In September 1635 the imperialists occupied Frankfurt and the Croats of Gallas harassed the rear of the armies of Cardinal de la Valette and Bernard of Saxe-Weimar along the Rhine up to Metz. On the 2 October, Louis XIII and the army of Champagne retook the town of Saint-Mihiel from Charles IV, but at the end of 1635, he was firmly entrenched in the Franche-Comté while Gallas held Alsace.

During this time, Duc Henri de Rohan led a successful campaign in the Valtelline, aiming to cut Spanish and imperial communications between Northern Italy and the Palatinate. Rohan entered Switzerland at the end of March 1635; although he was in a poor position, on the 27 June 1635 he forced Fenarmont's imperialists to retreat into the valley of Livigno, fought them on the 3 July 1635 at the bridge of Mazzo and seized Fort des Bains and Sainte-Marie on the 17 July. At the same time, the town of Valenza was besieged by the Duke of Savoy, the Duke of Parma and Maréchal de Créqui. On the 31 October, Rohan ousted Fenarmont from the Valtelline with a victory at Val di Fraele. The following day the armies of the Duke of Savoy, the Duke of Parma and Maréchal de Créqui abandoned the siege of Valenza and timidly entered Piedmont. On the 10 November at Morbegno, Rohan defeated the Spanish army of the Governor of Milan, and seized his camp. However, 1635 ended to the overall advantage of Habsburg, and the war, which could have lasted only 16 years, was set to last another 14.

In 1636, Baner's Swedish armies were in Pomerania and Mecklemburg; French armies were in the Lorraine, the Valtelline and Pignerol; the armies of the Duke of Savoy were in the confines of Milan; the Spanish armies occupied Franche-Comté, the Electorates of Treves and Cologne; and the imperial armies occupied the Lower Palatinate and Alsace. In February 1636, the Spanish invaded the Duchy of Parma, and Maréchal de Créqui, impatient with the hesitations of the Duke of Savoy, took the lead of an army of 6,000 French soldiers present in Casale. But he was defeated by the Marquis de Leganez, Governor of Milan, at Vespolate on the 27 February. On the 3 June, the Duke of Savoy relaunched the offensive and crossed the Po with de Créqui in the vanguard and reached Boffalora in the Ticino on the 16 June. On the 22 June 1636, Maréchal de Créqui, supported belatedly by Victor Amedeo of Savoy, fought off the Marquis de Leganez at the battle of Tornavento.

The Prince de Condé, Governor of Burgundy, was entrusted with an army of 20.000 infantrymen and 8,000 horsemen to conquer the Franche-Comté, and laid siege to Dôle on the 29 May 1636; but the Cardinal-Infante launched an attack on Picardy. On the 2 July, Prince Thomas entered Picardy leading 30,000 infantrymen and 12,000 horsemen. The town of La Capelle surrendered on the 9 July, and the Spanish took Le Catelet and Bray-sur-Somme before arriving at Corbie, twelve or so miles from Amiens. The country was in danger. The army of Champagne under the Comte de Soissons was rein-

Strength of France: Louis XIII and Gaston d'Orléans on horseback, circa 1627, by Abraham Bosse (1602-1676). Rothschild collection, Louvre Museum, Paris.

forced by the army of Maréchal de Brézé, who had returned from Holland. Prince Thomas attacked, while at Bray Maréchal Brézé resisted; but the Comte de Soissons decided to retreat along the Oise, leaving the Imperial cavalry of Johann von Werth free to harass the rear. Corbie surrendered on the 15 August while Louis XIII and Richelieu succeeded in raising a new army of 30,000 infantry and 12,000 horsemen by decreeing a *levy en masse*, thus making good use of the hesitations of the Cardinal-Infante. Faced with this sudden increase, the Cardinal-Infante took his army back to the Netherlands, fearing a counter-attack by the Dutch under Prince Frederick Hendrick of Nassau. Paris was saved ~ but the war had come to French territory. At the beginning of October, Louis XIII and Richelieu laid siege to Corbie, which was taken on the 14 November. On the 15 August, the Prince de Condé lifted the siege of Dôle, threatened by the armies of Charles IV and Gallas who had crossed the Rhine. The imperialists crossed the Saône, entered Burgundy and laid siege to Saint-Jean-de-Losne, which resisted heroically. The siege was lifted on the 4 November, thanks to the aid of the Franco-Weimarian army under Cardinal de la Valette and Bernard of Saxe-Weimar. This army was supposed to prevent the meeting of Gallas' imperial army and the Spanish army of Prince Thomas of Savoy, who was still in Picardy.

In March 1636, Baner's Swedish army invaded Saxony and devastated the lands of the Elector of Saxony, who was guilty of signing the treaty of Prague. During a bloody battle near Wittstock on the 4 and 5 October 1635, Baner defeated an imperialist and Saxon army sent to the rescue. Baner then laid siege to Leipzig in January 1637, but imperial and Saxon forces forced him to retreat to Torgau, where he remained until June. Emperor Ferdinand II died on the 15 February, and on the 15 April 1637, the French fleet commanded by Cardinal de Sourdis retook the Isles of Lérins in Provence, occupied by the Spanish for the previous 2 years. At the beginning of June the army of Cardinal de la Valette launched the offensive in Flanders. Cateau-Cambrésis fell on the 21 June, Landrecies on the 22 July and La Capelle on the 15 September; the cavalry of La Valette, commanded by the Vicomte de Turenne, dealt a heavy defeat to the cavalry of Piccolomini, but a counter-offensive from Cardinal-Infante forced the French to retreat south of Maubeuge. The Spanish, fighting on two

fronts, where unable to prevent the storming of Breda by the Dutch on the 10 October 1637. The army of Champagne under Maréchal de Châtillon, who was aiming to take Luxemburg, was unable to oust the occupying Spanish and imperialists. The army of Bernard of Saxe-Weimar had launched an offensive in the Franche-Comté in May and dealt a defeat to the imperial army of Charles IV, Duc de Lorraine, on the 22 June at Ray sur Saône. Bernard then returned to Alsace, but, faced with the threat of an offensive by Piccolomini, left for Mulhouse in September to take up his winter quarters. A second French army under the Duc de Longueville took Lons le Saulnier on the 25 June 1637 then withdrew to Burgundy. Finally, in the Valtelline a revolt from the Grison leagues had erupted on the 18 March 1637 and the Duc de Rohan had to flee at the beginning of May with his army, joining up with the army of Bernard of Saxe-Weimar in Alsace. On the 8 September Victor Amedeo of Savoy died, and with him the French alliance. At the end of August, the Spanish tried to land at Leucates, in Roussillon,

Storming of Landrecies, July 26th, 1637 (1836) by Hippolyte Lecomte (1781-1857). Châteaux de Versailles and Trianon, Versailles.

P. 24-25 :
Louis XIV welcomes the Grand Condé in Versailles, after Rocroi, Jean Léon Gerôme (1824-1904). Orsay museum, Paris.

23

but they were beaten back on the 28 September by the Duc d'Halluin, governor of Languedoc, with the support of the region's Protestants.

On the 6 March 1638, France renewed its alliance with Sweden. A few weeks earlier, Bernard of Saxe-Weimar had set out to travel up the Rhine towards Austria, taking a number of forest towns. He was surprised on the 28 February at Rheinfelden by imperialists under Savelli and Johann von Werth, a battle in which the Duc de Rohan was fatally injured, but he dealt them a terrible defeat on the 3 March with a night attack on their camp, taking Johann von Werth prisoner. Aided by Guébriant and Turenne, he then left for Brisgau, took Freiburg on the 11 August, and laid siege to Brisach, defeating the Duc de Lorraine and the imperialists Lamboy and Goetz who tried to flee the town at the end of October; he finally took Brisach on the 18 December after a 4-month siege. From their bases in Pomerania, the Swedes launched raids against Gallas' imperialists and ravaged the countryside of Mecklemburg and Brandenburg. In Italy, Maréchal de Créqui was killed on the 17 March, cut in half by a cannonball while he tried to come to the aid of the besieged town of Bremen. Leganez took advantage of the situation to retake Bremen, then Vercelli on the 6 July, thus closing the Piedmont border. Later, La Valette ousted the duchy of Montferrat and defeated the Spanish on the 7 October at Fellizano.

In Artois, the army of Picardy under Maréchals de Châtillon and de Brézé attempted to take Saint-Omer, but had to lift the siege, threatened by the back-up armies of Prince Thomas and Piccolomini; the two Maréchals took back Le Catelet on the 14 September 1638. In the Basque Country, Cardinal de Sourdis destroyed the Spanish fleet in the bay of Guéthary and landed reinforcements for the Cardinal de la Valette and the Prince de Condé who was heading up the Guyenne army. But the besieged Spaniards roundly defeated the French under Condé at Fontarabie on the 7 September.

The Swedes under Baner began the 1639 campaign by entering Saxony and defeating the Saxons and imperialists under Gallas on the 14 April at Chemnitz. Encouraged by this success, Baner travelled up the Elbe, arriving outside Prague in May then held his position in Bohemia. Bernard of Saxe-Weimar had returned to the Franche-Comté, taking Morteau and Pontarlier at the end of January and

the Fort de Joux on the 14 February. He then left for the Jura and returned to Alsace in June after ravaging the Franche-Comté. However, Bernard of Saxe-Weimar, who had become an embarrassment for Richelieu, died on the 8 July of the plague while preparing for an expedition to Bavaria to join Baner. During this time, Guébriant managed to convince von Erlach to retain the Weimarian army under the French colours.

In Italy, Prince Thomas of Savoy, who had returned to the Piedmont, laid siege to Turin on the 18 April 1639. Piedmont revolted against Queen Christine, ally of the French, while the Marquis de Leganez and Prince Thomas were now in control of Turin, with the exception of the citadel and the Po valley. The French still held Casale and Chivasso. Cardinal de la Valette, dead at Rivoli on the 27 September 1639, was replaced by the Comte d'Harcourt, with Turenne as deputy. Harcourt, whose cavalry was commanded by Turenne, took Chieri on the 4 November 1639, allowing him to reestablish communication with Casale, then forced Leganez and Prince Thomas to retreat to La Rotta on the 20 November.

In Champagne, June 1639 saw La Meilleraye besiege Hesdin, Feuquières and Thionville. Piccolomini came to the aid of Thionville, and dealt a severe defeat to Feuquières on the 7 June 1639, but La Meilleraye took Hesdin on the 29 June. In the Pyrenees, the Prince de Condé led the armies of Languedoc and Guyenne and seized the citadel of Salces on the 9 July, which was then taken back on the 24 December by the Spanish. 1639 ended badly for the Spanish, with a fleet of 77 vessels being destroyed on the 21 October by a Dutch squadron in the Channel.

1640 began no better for Philip IV of Spain, as the bad feeling between Prince Thomas and Piccolomini forced him to withdraw the imperial army from the Netherlands. Deprived of a maritime route after the disaster of Dover, and with no overland route since the loss of Brisach and the imperial reinforcements, the Spanish situation in Holland had become delicate. To crown it all, Catalonia refused to support the war effort and revolted on the 7 June 1640. This rebellion encouraged sympathies between the Catalans and Louis XIII's diplomats, and resulted in the signing of a treaty of fraternity with France on the 16 December 1640. This treaty led to a military alliance at the beginning of 1641. In the succession of disasters for the Spanish marine, the Marquis of Brézé destroyed the Indes squadron in the Bay of Cadiz.

In June 1640, the French relaunched the offensive in Artois and laid siege to Arras, taking the town on the 8 August. In Italy, the Spanish had taken Saluces from the French, but the Comte d'Harcourt once again beat Leganez and Prince Thomas at Casale on the 29 April 1640, then besieged Turin. Here he fought off Leganez who had come to the aid of the town on the 11 July. Leganez left for Milan, and Prince Thomas surrendered the town to the French. The Duchess Regent thus reclaimed possession of her Duchy, and Prince Thomas abandoned the Spanish alliance. To conclude this catastrophic year, Portugal, whose autonomy had been less and less respected by Spain, seceded on the 1 December 1640! Later on the 1 June 1640, the new king of Portugal, John IV, signed a Treaty of Alliance with France, followed by a truce with the United Provinces on the 12 June 1641.

Things were no better for the successor of Ferdinand II, Emperor Ferdinand III: he summoned a Diet on the 26 July 1640 to try to extend the Treaty of Prague to all princes who had not yet signed, but the new Elector of Brandenburg, Frederick-William, went back on the peace conditions and signed a separate peace agreement with Sweden. Baner's army, pursued by Piccolomini across Bohemia and Saxony, was now in difficulty.

Leading a diminished army, Baner died on the 20 May 1641 at Halberstadt and was replaced by Torstensson. On the 29 June 1641, Wrangel and Guébriant, who had come to the aid of Klitzing, the general of Brunswick, were victorious over the imperialists of Archduke Leopold and Piccolomini at Wolfenbüttel in Lower Saxony. But the badly-paid Swedish army rebelled and Torstensson was only able to restore the situation at the end of 1641.

In Italy, the Comte d'Harcourt ended his campaign by taking Coni on the 8 September, then Montecalvo and Demonte. At the same time, the kingdom of France also had its own troubles to face: Gaston d'Orléans had organised a new rebellion with the help of the Comte de Soissons, the Duc de Bouillon and the Duc de Lorraine. On the 6 July 1641, the discontented army, reinforced by the Imperialists of Lamboy, defeated Maréchal de Chatillon's army of Champagne at La Marfée near Sedan. After this defeat, Châtillon was replaced by Maréchal Brézé. La Meilleraye, who had seized

Cardinal Richelieu introduces Poussin to Louis XIII, in Rome (1640). Jean Alaux ("Le Romain", 1786-1864). Louvre museum, Paris.

27

Aire in desperation on the 27 July 1641, beat a retreat from the combined armies of the Cardinal-Infante, Lamboy and the Duc de Lorraine, leaving Aire in the hands of the Spanish on the 9 August 1641. Brézé's army of Champagne then joined the army of Picardy under La Meilleraye; they took Lens, La Bassée and Bapaume in September.

At the beginning of 1642, Guébriant's Franco-Weimarian army was in Westphalia. Lamboy waited around Kempen for von Hatzfeld's Bavarian reinforcements to attack in Champagne, while the Spanish attacked in Picardy. Avoiding von Hatzfeld, Guébriant crossed the Rhine to Wesel then won a glorious victory over Lamboy's imperialists at Kempen on the 17 January 1642, which earned him his marshal's baton. Then, whilst the Weimarians were conquering the Duchy of Juliers, Guébriant left to defend Alsace against the Mercy's Bavarian army, which was occupying the Duchy of Bade. The Swede Torstensson had taken his troops in hand and left for Bohemia at the beginning of 1642, seizing Glosgow on the Oder. He defeated

Cardinal Jules Mazarin (1602-1661) - circa 1650. French school. Châteaux de Versailles and Trianon, Versailles.

28

the Saxon army on the 30 May 1642 at Schweidnitz, and went on to pillage Moravia. Piccolomini set off in pursuit of Torstensson who was threatening Vienna and besieging Glosgow. Torstensson then left for Silesia, liberated Glosgow and headed to Leipzig. He encountered the Imperialists of Archduke Leopold and Piccolomini, crushing them on the 2 November 1642 at Breitenfeld, then took Leipzig on the 4 December 1642.

In the Netherlands, the Cardinal-Infante died on the 9 November 1641 and Francisco de Melo took over as Governor of the Netherlands. He took back Lens from the French on the 19 April 1642 and La Bassée on the 13 May, while the Comte d'Harcourt, now in Picardy, was conquering Boulogne. The defeat of Harcourt and Honnecourt on the 26 May opened up the door to Champagne for Melo, but he preferred to head back towards Guébriant in the Rhine valley.

In the Pyrenees, La Meilleraye liberated Roussillon with Turenne's assistance. He took Collioure on the 13 April 1642 and Perpignan on the 9 September of that year, after Admiral Brézé had dispersed a Spanish fleet attempting to bring supplies to the town on the 30 June. But the Catalonian army under La Mothe-Houdencourt, supported by the fleet of de Sourdis, was unable to take Tarragona and lifted the blockade on the 20 August. Leganez besieged Llerida at the beginning of September while La Mothe-Houdencourt, recently made Maréchal, brought aid to Perpignan and dealt a new defeat to Leganez.

In Italy, the Duc de Longueville, supported by Thomas and Maurice of Savoy, entered Milan after storming Tortona on the 26 November 1642.

1642 ended the firm advantage of the French, Swedish and Dutch; Richelieu, who had played a large hand in French victories, died on the 4 December 1642. Louis XIII replaced his prime minister by his brilliant secretary, Cardinal Giulio Mazarin. Mazarin rapidly took affairs in hand: he sent Turenne to the Piedmont, reinforced Guébriant in Alsace, La Mothe-Houdencourt in Catalonia, and the army of Champagne, now commanded by the Comte d'Espenan, while La Meilleraye led the small army of Burgundy against the Franche-Comté. He then appointed Louis de Bourbon, Duc d'Enghien - then aged 21 - to lead the army of Picardy.

1643 began with other major changes at the head of warring states. In Spain, Olivarès was

removed from power on the 17 January 1643, followed by the death of Louis XIII on the 14 May
1643, leaving the kingdom of France under the
regency of Queen Anne of Austria, well supported
by Mazarin. In Germany, the various protagonists
worked hard for peace, but peace was slow in
coming. During this time, the Swedish Chancellor
Oxenstierna managed to bring Prince George the 1st
Ràkoczi of Transylvania into the Franco-Swedish
alliance through the Treaty of Stockholm, signed
on the 26 April 1643.

Governor Francisco de Melo intended to
sidestep the armies of Champagne and Picardy,
take Rocroi, descend on Reims then follow the
valley of the Marne to Paris; but he was roundly
defeated on the 19 May 1643 at Rocroi by the
young Duc d'Enghien, well-supported by Gassion
and Sirot. With Rocroi now liberated, Enghien led
the armies of Picardy, Champagne and Burgundy
to Thionville, which fell on the 8 September. On
the 28 May 1644, Gaston d'Orléans led the army of
Picardy, supported by Maréchal La Meilleraye and
Maréchal Gassion, and retook Gravelines from the
Spanish. In Italy, 1644 saw the siege of Santia by
Prince Thomas and Maréchal du Plessis-Praslin,
while on the other side of the Pyrenees Maréchal
de La Mothe-Houdencourt lost Llerida on the
31 July 1644.

Guébriant, leading the German army and reinforced by units from the army of the Duc d'Enghien,
crossed the Rhine in October and besieged
Rottweil. Rottweil was taken on the 24 November,
but Guébriant died that day from a cannon injury.
The same day, a Weimarian party commanded by
Rantzau was surprised and defeated in their siege
of Tuttlinge by the Bavarians under Mercy and
Hatzfeld. The Franco-Weimarian army withdrew
to Alsace, which it devastated before being taken
in hand by Turenne, who was promoted to Maréchal on the 3 December 1643. After wintering in
Lorraine, Turenne launched an offensive in January
1644, taking back Vesoul and Luxeuil. At the
beginning of May, he crossed the Rhine and took
Donaueschingen before returning to Alsace at the
end of June. The Bavarian von Mercy had taken
the initiative of storming Uberlingen on the 11 May,
then laying siege to Freiburg-en-Brisgau on the
27 June. D'Enghien and Turenne were defeated by
Mercy's defensive positions, notably in the bloody
assault of the 5 August, but they forced von Mercy
to retreat to Rothenburg on the 10 August. Turenne

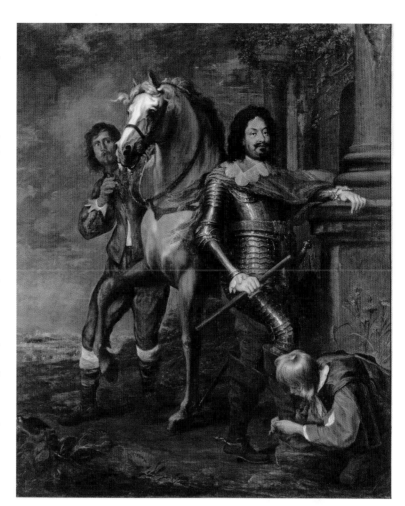

retook Philippsburg on the 9 September 1644 after
10 days of siege, then Worms, Oppenheim, Mentz,
and Landau before the end of September. This
brilliant campaign meant that the French held practically all the left bank of the Rhine.

In April 1643, the Swedes under Torstensson
were still in Moravia. But Christian IV of Denmark
had begun negotiations with Emperor Ferdinand III
who sent an imperial army commanded by Gallas,
to the North as support; Oxenstierna then recalled
Torstensson. Swiftly, the Swedish entered Holstein
then Schleswig and finally Jutland in January 1644,
while the Swedish armies under Wrangel and
Horn besieged Malmö. But with the Danes under
Frederick of Denmark and the imperialists under
Gallas and Hatzfeld threatening to encircle him,
Torstensson was forced to move south. The Swedes
under Königsmarck, chased from Mecklemburg
by Frederick of Denmark, severely defeated the
Imperialists under Gallas at Magdeburg, while von
Hatzfeld's army was defeated on the 23 November
1644 near Wittenberg. Peace was signed between

*Portrait of General Ottavio
Piccolomini* (1599-1656) by
Jan Gerritsz Van Bronckhorst
(1603-1662). Bonnat museum,
Bayonne, France.

Denmark and Sweden on the 23 August 1645 after long open negotiations in February.

Prince Ràkoczi of Transylvania entered the campaign in February 1644 but was defeated on the 9 April by the imperialists under Götz. Ràkoczi lost land throughout the rest of 1644, while Torstensson returned to Moravia in the spring of 1645, attracting imperialists to him anxious to protect Vienna. Torstensson won another bloody victory against Götz and Hatzfeld on the 6 March 1645 at Jankau, in Bohemia. The Swedes then besieged Brno, and Vienna at the beginning of April; Ràkoczi's army entered Hungary and joined with the Swedes at Brünn. On the 27 July 1645, Ràkoczi opened negotiations with Emperor Ferdinand III, which resulted in the Peace Treaty of Linz on the 16 December. In October, Torstensson decided not to pursue his attack on Vienna and went back to Saxony where, because of ill health, he left command of the army to Wrangel.

At the end of March 1645, Turenne led the Franco-Weimarian army in a new offensive; he crossed the Rhine on the 24 March and captured Rothenburg. But with his troops imprudently dispersed, he was defeated by Mercy on the 5 May 1645 at Mergentheim (or Marienthal). Mazarin then sent the Duc d'Enghien to Turenne's aid, and on the 6 August 1645 their armies encountered the Bavarians of Mercy and Werth at Allerheim, near Nördlingen. In October, the French returned to Philipsburg along the Rhine, escaped the combined armies of Archduke Leopold, Gallas, Hatzfeld and Johann von Werth, then retook Treves on the 23 November 1645.

In July and August 1645, Gaston d'Orléans, Gassion and Rantzau took many towns in Artois and Flanders including Bethune, Saint-Omer and Lens, while in Catalonia the Comte d'Harcourt and Plessis Praslin seized Rosas and Balaguer on the 20 October after defeating the Spanish at Lhorens.

In April 1646, Turenne was in Mentz; Wrangel left Bohemia, took Paderborn and arrived in Hesse. The two armies threatened Bavaria, joining up belatedly on the 10 August 1646; they crossed the Danube, seizing Aschaffenburg on the 22 August followed by the fortress of Rain, and laid siege to Augsburg at the beginning of October. They lifted the siege under threat from Johann von Werth. As winter had arrived, they took Landsberg by surprise, which served as a storehouse for arms and victuals for the Bavarians. The imperial army withdrew to Austria, and Duke Maximilian of Bavaria, tired of war, began negotiations with Mazarin. Turenne made do with a few incursions in Luxemburg after suppressing a Weimarian rebellion.

For Mazarin, there was still Spain to be dealt with. In the Netherlands, Gaston d'Orléans and the Duc d'Enghien had besieged Courtrai on the 15 June 1646, which surrendered on the 28 June before Piccolomini, Charles IV of Lorraine and Lamboy were able to come to their aid. Bergues was taken on the 29 July and Mardick was taken back on the 25 August. D'Enghien continued the conquest by taking Furnes on the 7 September, then by besieging Dunkirk on the 25 September 1646. Piccolomini, Beck and the Marquis of Caracena tried without success to break the siege. D'Enghien

Urbain de Maillé, Marquis de Brézé, maréchal de France in 1632 (1597-1650). Jérôme-Martin Langlois (1779-1838). Château de Versailles and Trianon, Versailles.

30

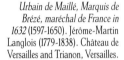

P. 31 : *Equestrian portrait of Louis XIII in armour*, attributed to Jean de Saint-Igny (circa 1600-1647). Châteaux de Versailles and Trianon, Versailles.

took the fort of Mardyck on the 24 August and Dunkirk surrendered on the 10 October.

To the North, the Dutch occupied the mouths of the river Escaut but, fearing a more and more probable proximity with France, they began negotiations with Spain - thereby ending the Franco-Dutch alliance. The Dutch negotiated a peace treaty in Münster on the 30 January 1648, taking advantage of the unhoped-for conditions. In the Netherlands, the Spanish also took advantage of the situation to launch a new offensive against Gassion and Rantzau: Armentières fell on the 31 May 1647, followed by Commines and Landrecies, then Dixmude on the 14 November. Gassion died on the 23 September during the siege of Lens. Mazarin then sent Turenne to the aid of Rantzau.

In Italy, Prince Thomas of Savoy and the fleet of Admiral Brézé besieged Ortebello on the 10 May 1646, while Maréchal du Plessis Praslin remained in the Piedmont to face Milan's Spanish army. However, Brézé was killed, cut in half by a cannonball in a battle with the Spanish fleet on the 14 May, which put an end to the intervention. Threatened by a Spanish army from Naples, Prince Thomas evacuated his army. Mazarin persevered: the armies of Plessis Praslin and La Meilleraye landed on the Isle of Elba, then seized Piombino on the 16 October 1646. Spain thus lost its outlying stations, and the Duke of Modena gave his support to the French cause. Maréchal du Plessis Praslin launched a new offensive and, with the help of the Duke of Modena, dealt a crushing defeat to the Marquis of Caracena on the 4 July 1647 on the banks of the Oglio river.

To complicate the Spanish situation in Italy, a revolt broke out in Sicily in the spring of 1647, followed by a similar revolt in Naples in June 1647. This Neapolitan revolt did not weaken over time, and negotiations were opened with France so that this new "Neapolitan Republic" would have a chance of survival. However, at the beginning of 1648, Spain finally retook control of the town.

Beyond the Pyrenees, the French were in Barcelona, but their presence was irritating for the Catalans. The Comte d'Harcourt fought off Leganez who tried to break through his lines on the 5 October at Llerida but Leganez then turned Harcourt's lines around, forcing Harcourt to retreat. The Spanish now held Llerida in addition to Tortosa and Tarragona. Mazarin entrusted command of the Catalonian army to the Duc d'Enghien. The prince entered Barcelona on the 11 April 1647 and relaunched the siege of Llerida on the 11 May 1647; but the besieged citizens defended themselves valiantly, and the Marquis of Aytona assembled a relief army. Condé gave in, and left for Barcelona on the 5 August, then for France on the 7 November, having forced back the Marquis of Aytona's army beyond the Ebre.

Turenne began the year 1648 by joining up with Wrangel on the 23 March 1648 in Hanau. They headed for Munich, forcing back Melander's Bavarians to Ingolstadt and Ratisbon as they advanced; the Bavarians, threatened by the Swedes, had resumed their alliance with the imperialists. On the 16 May, Turenne, Wrangel and Königsmarck crossed the Danube at Lautingen then dealt a heavy defeat to the Bavarian and imperialist armies of Mélander and Montecuccoli on the 17 May at Zusmarchausen. They then crossed the Lech at Rain and the Iser at Freizing, only to be stopped at the Inne due to a lack of boats. Piccolomini assumed command of the imperial army, forcing the retreat of Turenne and Wrangel up the Iser, and set up camp at Landau. While Turenne and Wrangel occupied Bavaria, Königsmarck left for Bohemia. On the 26 July 1648, his troops entered the outskirts of Prague; but the old town resisted until the Treaty of Westphalia.

Artois was to be decisive. In April 1648 Mazarin entrusted the army of Picardy to the Prince de Condé. He faced Archduke Leopold, now Viceroy of the Netherlands, who assembled a strong army around Lille. On the 13 May, Condé occupied Ypres and forced Dunkirk to surrender on the 27 May, while the Archduke took back Courtrai on the 19 May. Archduke Leopold then besieged Le Catelet on the 19 June. Condé arrived from Arras to come to the aid of the town, and the Archduke withdrew to Landrecies on the 30 June. While Condé received reinforcements from the Count of Erlach and his Weimarians, the Spanish retook Furnes on the 2 August. Archduke Leopold confidently began to make his way to Paris on the 12 August. On the 14 August there was an encounter between the cavalries of the two armies; the Spanish army arrived on the plain of Lens on the 18 August. The Archduke placed his army in a position that he believed to be unassailable, and awaited his adversary, who arrived on the morning of the 19 August. But Condé considered the Spanish positions too strong and refused the battle. *The rear left broke rank to march to the right* in the direction of Bethune. He hoped this manœuvre would make the Archduke leave his formidable position to attack

his moving army...and the Archduke fell into the trap. On the 20 August, after the French cavalry had forced open the two wings of the enemy cavalry, the two armies advanced towards each other. Beck, who commanded two *tercios viejos* in the centre, was injured, and his infantry routed. The Spanish defeat was total. Condé rested for 8 days, then joined Rantzau at the siege of Furnes.

The battle of Lens ended a war that had lasted thirty years. The armies of Turenne, Wrangel and Königsmark were threatening Vienna and Prague, Emperor Ferdinand's ally, Maximilian of Bavaria, fervently wanted peace and Philip IV had lost his main army. Ferdinand had no choice other than to make peace. He approved the propositions for peace from France and Sweden in Münster and Osnabrück; since 1641, talks had taken place between France and the Empire in Münster, and between Sweden and the Empire in Osnabrück. The definitive peace treaty, called the Peace of Westphalia, was signed on the 24 October 1648, ending the Thirty Years' War but not the war between France and Spain, which was to end with the Treaty of the Pyrenees on the 7 November 1659.

Europe in 1648,
Robert H. Labberton (1884)

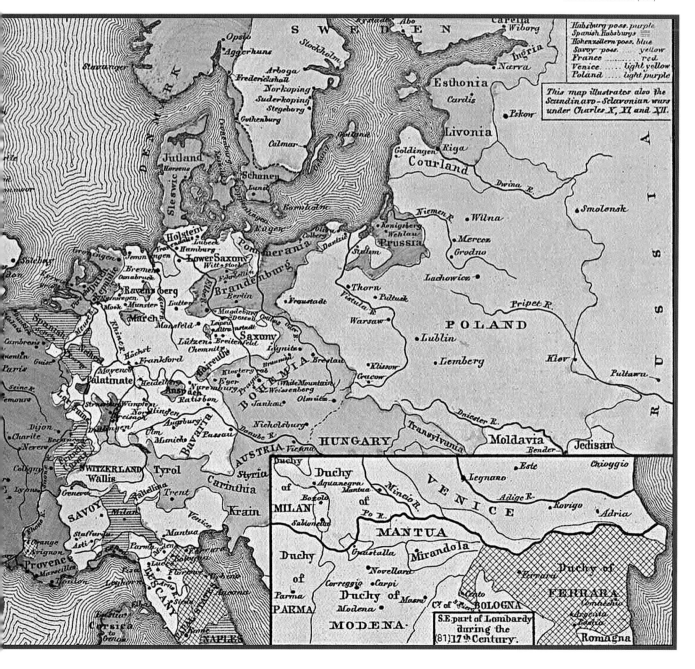

CHAPTER II

THE FRENCH ARMY BEFORE THE WAR

At the turn of the 17th century, French military commanders took inspiration from the Dutch and Spanish military theory, hoping to reproduce the manœuvre, shot techniques and discipline characteristic of these two armies. At the end of the Wars of Religion, Henri IV reorganised the French army based on the Dutch model; many Huguenot nobles had trained in warfare with the Dutch. This reorganisation of the army was to continue under Richelieu.

In 1600, Henri IV's army had decreased to less than 7,000 infantry and 1,500 cavalry. During the succession crisis of Cleves in 1610, the French army had 25,000 infantry and 5,000 horses, plus 12,000 foreign infantry and 400 shot, siege and campaign weapons. Sully estimated that an army of 50,000 infantry and 8,000 cavalry was needed to enter into war and this is why he strove to fill the State coffers. However, on the death of the king, this army was disbanded by the Regency. The army took up arms again under King Louis XIII in 1620, and had more than 50,000 men by the time it was disbanded by the *ordonnance* of 10 September 1620.

Between 1624 and 1635, main developments were in administration and the organisation of services. When Lesdiguières died in 1627 the office of Constable of France died with him, Richelieu thus demonstrating his desire for the centralisation of military affairs, which were passed into the hands of one of the four Secretaries of State: Beauclerc took on this responsibility from 1626 to 1630, followed by Servien from 1630 to 1636. With this

function now occupied by the *noblesse de robe*, the rights and duties of the soldiery could be formalised, in particular through the *ordonnance* of 1629, called the "Code Michaud", which aimed at increasing discipline in the French armies and controlling the condition of the troops. The objective of this section of the *ordonnance* of January 1629, Article 220, is worthy of note: *"With regard to order and discipline of the soldiery, both cavalry and infantry, because civil war has led most of them to spread disorder and because their actions resulted in much damage which the previous military ordonnances did not remedy, we consider it judicious for the good of our State, the policing of our soldiers and the relief of our people to remedy this situation by a new regulation, without modification on previous regulations and for which we determine, state, and dictate."*

In practice, this *ordonnance* legislated all aspects of army life: administration of the regiment; the number of annual musters; soldiers' pay and the appointment of captains and officers; salary increases and promotions for soldiers of merit; monetary loans to soldiers; supply of garrison bread; the various stationing locations throughout France; campaign hospitals; enlisting of soldiers and checks; duration of service (at least 6 months); regulation of routes and lodgings for the troops; the order of march for regiments; responsibility and the policing role of captains and officers on marches; responsibilities of the *mestres de camp* (colonels); organisation of the regiment guard; management of civilian complaints; supply of provisions to sol-

35

Henri IV king of France (1553-1610), Frans Pourbus the Younger (1569-1622). Louvre Museum, Paris.

diers; housing for companies; presence of *mestres de camp* and captains in their regiment or company; presence of lieutenants, ensigns and sergeant majors in their company; the organisation of drills; leave and dismissal of soldiers and officers; commissions given by the *mestres de camp*; the duties of the soldiery; and, finally, military justice. These subjects are addressed in a total of 123 articles. This somewhat fastidious inventory highlights the preoccupations of Louis XIII and Richelieu regarding the army: the restoration of authority, in particular by obliging *mestres de camp* and captains to be present in their units; recruitment of a high-quality, disciplined and less "volatile" army by fighting against desertion and *passe-volants*; and the protection of civilians. Finally, this *ordonnance* attempts to fight against the dishonest practices of captains and *mestres de camp*, practices highlighted by Richelieu himself in his memoirs in his account of an episode of the siege of La Rochelle

(1627): *"And because pay is the soul of the soldier and maintains his courage, which he seems to lose when he is not paid, and so that the soldier would always be paid on time, the Cardinal appointed one commissioner per regiment and ordered them to distribute pay directly to the soldier and not to their captains, which led to three major advantages for the army: the soldiers were actually paid, and because the captains could no longer steal their pay, they could no longer introduce passe-volants, and the king knew every week the number of soldiers he had in his army."*

As military generals had always tried to avoid royal legislation, the king appointed *maîtres des requêtes*, who later became *intendants*, whose task was to ensure the application of the king's orders, provide reports, supervise the commissioners and war controllers and assist the General-in-Chief. The position of *intendant* was made official by the Edict of May 1635.

36

Weaponry of horse arquebusiers, (1621). Musée de l'Armée, Paris.

The Dutch School

The Prince of Orange, Maurice, Count of Nassau, considerably influenced the military strategy of his era. Maurice of Nassau, son of William of Nassau and Anne of Saxony, became governor (*Stadthouder*) and Captain General of the United Provinces on the death of his father in 1584. His theories and many victories over the Spanish led him to be considered as one of the greatest captains of his time; he died in The Hague, on the 23 April 1625. To perfect his new infantry tactics, the Prince of Orange took inspiration from Roman and Byzantine authors, and created lighter and thereby more flexible formations. He was the mind behind the tactic of infantry units 10 rows deep – which he also implemented in practice – rather than the Spanish-inspired 40 – 50 rows that had been used up until that point. From 1594 he developed salvo fire, with the first row of musketeers firing simultaneously, then drawing back to reload, with the next row taking their place at the front. Each successive row took the place of the preceding row to fire. And although firepower now took precedence over hand-to-hand combat, Maurice de Nassau always maintained that it was the pikeman's duty to protect the musketeer and not the other way around. The role of the musketeers, placed in front of the pikemen, was to prepare the assault by firing at 30 *toises* (60 metres) - a quarter of the weapon's maximum range.

The works of Jean-Jacques Walhausen, captain of the Guard and the town of Dantzig, confirm the theories of Maurice of Nassau. His works include 8 books; the first, *L'art militaire pour l'infanterie* (1615) addresses the use of the pike and musket, drill for an infantry company, battle arrangements for a company and regiment, and military discipline of the infantry. The second book, *Kriegskunst zu Pferd* (1616) deals with the art of war for cavalry. The fourth book, *Archiley Kriegskunst* (1617), addresses artillery.

These works were written after *Les principes de l'art militaire*, written in French by Jean de Billon and published in 1613-1615, although it was written before the death of Henri IV (1610), probably between 1605 and 1610.

Frédéric Henri de Nassau, Prince of Orange and Stadhouder (1584-1647) by Gerrit Van Honthorst (1590-1656). Louvre Museum, Paris.

The French infantry from 1617 to 1634

Around 1602, Sully reorganised the French infantry into permanent and temporary regiments, which were raised only in the event of war. In March and April 1610, Henri IV set up 17 infantry regiments including 5 foreign regiments, bringing the army to 50,000 infantry. The *Gardes Françaises* (French Guards) now counted 20 companies of 200 men; the old regiments of *Champagne, Picardie, Piémont, Normandie and Navarre* had 20 companies of 100 men; other permanent regiments (*Bourg-l'Espinasse, Nerestang, Balagny, Sault, Deportes, Beaumont*) had 10 companies of 100 men; and the Lorraine regiments of *Vaubecourt* and *Nesmond* had 15 companies. The *Gardes*

Henri IV reviewing his soldiers by Charles Henri Pille (1844-1897). Musée national du château de Pau. Pau, France.

Suisses (Swiss Guard) were established in 1616, with 20 companies of 300 men.

In 1620, permanent regiments grouped together the regiments of the Guard (*Gardes Françaises* and *Gardes Suisses),* the five *Vieux Corps* (*Champagne, Picardie, Piémont, Normandie* and *Navarre)* and six regiments bearing the name of their colonel, the *Petits Vieux: Chappes, Rambures, Bourg-l'Espinasse, Sault, Vaubecourt* and *Beaumont.* As from 1616, these permanent regiments carried the *drapeau blanc.* In times of war, a large number of temporary regiments were raised, which made up the major part of the army; these regiments generally took the name of their colonel, and a colonel could raise a number of regiments. After the pacification of 1622, the newly-raised infantry regiments were disbanded. Others were raised in 1624 (*Diesbach, Schmidt* and *Siders*); a regiment from Liège, *La Hocquerie,* was raised in 1629 and *Vaubecourt,* raised in 1610, was from the Lorraine.

38

39

P. 39 :
A Sentinel, Time of Louis XIII
(1851). Jean-Louis Ernest Meissonier
(1815-91). The Wallace Collection,
London.

P. 40-41 :
The lost game,
Jean-Louis Ernest Meissonier,
(1815-91). By kind permission of
the Trustees of the Wallace
collection, London.

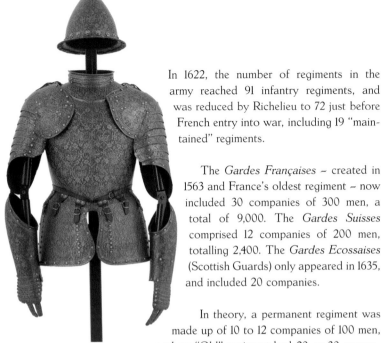

Half armour hand crafted by Maestro dal Castello, circa 1600-1620. Musée de l'Armée, Paris.

42

Drive in your pike (the first motion), plate from "Exercise of Arms", Jacob de Gheyn (1565-1629). Musée de l'Armée, Paris.

In 1622, the number of regiments in the army reached 91 infantry regiments, and was reduced by Richelieu to 72 just before French entry into war, including 19 "maintained" regiments.

The *Gardes Françaises* – created in 1563 and France's oldest regiment – now included 30 companies of 300 men, a total of 9,000. The *Gardes Suisses* comprised 12 companies of 200 men, totalling 2,400. The *Gardes Ecossaises* (Scottish Guards) only appeared in 1635, and included 20 companies.

In theory, a permanent regiment was made up of 10 to 12 companies of 100 men, and an "Old" regiment had 20 or 30 companies of 100 men; *Navarre* and *Champagne* had 30 companies, most often divided into 3 battalions. *Normandie* appears to have had only 2 battalions and 20 companies. A "temporary" regiment generally had 10 companies, as was the case of the *Bordeilles* regiment in February 1622, which had 10 companies and a total of 900 men.

In general, around 40% were pikemen and 60% were musketeers. On campaign, losses, illness and desertion rapidly reduced the numbers of the company to around fifty men per company, rarely more than 70 men, and regiments rarely exceeded 1,000. The two rebel regiments of the Duc de Retz, who fought in the Drôlerie des Ponts de Cé in August 1620, totalled only 1,500 men between them.

Henri IV had raised one foreign regiment before 1610, but this number rapidly increased to 7 under the Regency, and to 12 by 1625. Foreign regiments, notably the larger Swiss regiments, had 8 to 20 companies of 100 to 300 men: 3 Swiss regiments raised between 1610 and 1614 had between 2,100 and 3,000 men in companies of 300. However, in 1624, Annibal d'Estrée's 3 Swiss regiments (*Diesbach, Schmidt* and *Siders*) in Italy had 1,000 men each, in 5 companies of 200 men.

During this period preceding France's entry into the Thirty Years' War, the royal army was able to bring together all or part of its elite regiments on campaign. This was the case for the siege of Saint-Jean d'Angély in 1621 with the *Gardes Françaises*, the *Gardes Suisses*, *Picardie, Piémont, Champagne, Navarre, Normandy, Rambures, Chappes* and *Lauzières*. In Saintonge, 1622, there were 5 battalions from the *Gardes Françaises*, 2 battalions from the *Gardes Suisses*, 3 battalions from *Navarre*, 2 battalions from *Normandie, Picardie, Piémont*, and *Champagne* – left in La Rochelle – and many other regiments, including *Nerestang*. Maréchal de Montmorency's army at Carignan in the Piedmont, on the 6 August 1630, included the *Gardes Françaises, Champagne, Piémont, Picardie, Navarre, Normandie, Rambures, Sault, Vaubécourt* and 20 other regiments.

Fire, plate 11 from "Exercise of Arms", Jacob de Gheyn (1565-1629). Musée de l'Armée, Paris.

Man with a sword,
Jean-Louis-Ernest Meissonier
(1815-1891). Château de
Compiègne. Compiègne, France.

43

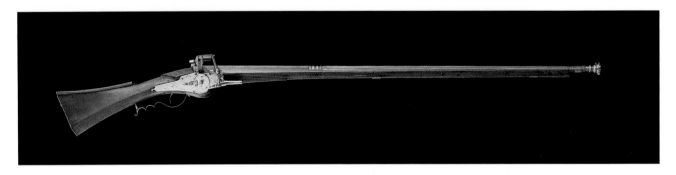

Wheel-lock arquebus circa 1610.
Musée de l'Armée, Paris.

However, when the "old" regiments were together, relations were soured by quarrels of precedence, which Louis XIII settled in 1620. The Marquis de Fontenay Mareuil gives this anecdote in his memoirs, a little before the Drôlerie des Ponts de Cé: *"It was on this occasion that he (the king) settled once and for all the differences that had so long divided the regiments of Piémont, Champagne and Navarre, and which on many occasions had nearly caused much ill, each of them claiming to have the right to pass before the other, and giving more importance to this advantage over the other than to fighting the enemy. The reasons they alleged were: for the regiment of Piémont, that it was the largest infantry regiment from beyond the mountains, as Picardie was the largest regiment below, and having always been on equal footing with Picardie when there were two colonels, and the fact that the two offices were now brought together in the person of Mr. d'Espernon, and all the infantry brought together in one same corps, could not lose it the place that it had kept for so long; and that although he ceded to Picardie when King Henri the Great called him from Provence to serve at his side, he had no other alternative, because the Baron de Biron was at the time the mestre de camp, and the Maréchal de Biron, who was his brother, commanded the army and had all power, obliged him to do so; this did not prevent him from preceding all the others. Champagne said that he was used to marching behind Picardie, and that nothing had ever come between them; and Navarre, having been the regiment of the Guards of King Henri the Great when he was but King of Navarre, would have preceded Picardie if the authority of the Maréchal de Biron had not prevented him; this is why he should at least march behind him. But the king, without taking account of all these reasons, ordered that in the future they would alternate, and that every six months they would each have preference in turn,*

having drawn lots in his presence, and before the army engaged in battle."

In his work of military theory, *Les principes de l'art militaire*, Jean de Billon recommends 2,600 men in 13 companies of 200 men in addition to the captain, the ensign, three sergeants, a drum-major, a fifer and a harbinger. But he specifies *"there are captains who support the idea that it is better that the companies be of 100 men, (...) 200 men being difficult to steer, to know well and to discipline. (...) A captain needs great resources to keep 200 men always well-armed, considering the large number of arms that are lost and broken."* Jean-Jacques Walhausen recommends a regiment of 3,000 men, including 1,000 to 1,200 pikemen, in 10 companies of 300 (including 100 to 120 pikemen).

Considering the size of the proposed regiments, these two theoreticians wrote their works before the beginning of the Thirty Years' War (1618). As we have seen, in France only the *Vieux corps* reached such numbers. At the end of the 1630's, the size of the regiments diminished sharply, and in his *Traité de la guerre* published in 1636, Duc Henri II de Rohan recommends regiments of 600 pikemen and 600 musketeers; in practice, a temporary regiment rarely exceeded 1,000 men. The regiment of *Bordeilles* in 1622 counted 900 men, and *Chamblai* and *Lèques*, the two regiments of the Duc de Rohan that accompanied him to the Valtelline in 1633, should theoretically have had 1,000 men each, but totalled only 1,200 men between them. In 1635, the Duc de Rohan brought 7 regiments into the Valtelline, with a total of 4,000 men - less than 600 men per regiment.

According to the *ordonnance* of 1629, the general staff of a permanent regiment comprised: one *mestre de camp*; one Sergeant-major; one Aide-major, one Provost of Justice (responsible for policing), one Conduct Commissioner (responsible for intendancy), one Quartermaster (who arranged the quartering of troops), one chaplain and one surgeon. The officers for a company of 200 men included: one Captain, one Lieutenant, one Ensign (who carried the flag in the regiment colours), two Sergeants, three Corporals, one harbinger, two drummers and a barber-surgeon. The rest of the company included 6 *anspessades*, 45 "appointees", 100 experienced soldiers and 37 cadets. As mentioned above, the combat unit, i.e. the battalion, was the combination of a number of companies, with the pikemen in the centre and the musketeers on the wings (the *manches de mousquetaires*) or in front of the first line of pikemen. The most senior of the company captains commanded the battalion. The sergeant-major took orders from the *mestre de camp* for the choice of position, battle array, alignment, and distances and intervals between the battalions.

The Colonel General, who reported directly to the Crown, maintained one company – the *colonelle* – in the *Gardes Françaises* and the five *vieux corps* (*Picardie, Piémont, Navarre, Champagne* and *Normandy*). This *colonelle* company carried the *drapeau blanc* of the Colonel General and was commanded by a Lieutenant Colonel appointed by the Colonel General.

The regiments were divided into battalions of 1,000 to 1,200 men, forming as many battalions as their numbers permitted – normally one to three, and at least five in the case of the *Gardes Françaises*, as in Saintonge in 1622. However, a battalion could only be constituted of a detachment of 5 companies, like the *Gardes Françaises* at the Pas de Suse in March 1629, or *Champagne* on the Isle of Rhé in 1627, and it was common to create detachments of 100 to 200 men from one or more companies.

In 1628, a battalion was formed from companies of the regiments of *Chappes* and *Navarre* within the Schomberg army which was to reinforce the Isle of Rhé (the other part of the regiment was at Fort Louis), two battalions were formed from the *Champagne* regiment, one from the regiment of *Rambures*, one from *Beaumont*, two from *Plessis-Praslin*, and two from the *La Meilleraye* regiment. The force of these battalions could not exceed 400 men; he strength of Schomberg's army, including the cavalry, totalled 4,000 men. In 1630, Schomberg's army in the Piedmont totalled 18,000 infantry from 14 regiments and 4 companies from *Champagne*, which were divided into 18 battalions of 1,000 to 1,200 men.

Theoretically speaking, in combat the battalion was deployed in ten rows with pikes in the centre and musketeers on the wings, following the Dutch model. In his writings, Jean de Billon describes a battalion of 200 men formed in 10 rows of 20 men abreast, with 10 files of pikemen in the centre and 5 files of musketeers on each side. In drill, each file and each row were spaced by 6 feet. A battalion such as this occupied a space of 104 feet in width and 54 feet in depth. For an experienced battalion, the rows and files could be spaced 3 feet or less, the battalion then occupying half as much surface area. But Billon specifies that the best strength for a complete battalion is 500 men, with 50 files and 10 rows. This battalion would then have 200 musketeers in 20 files, with 10 files on each flank, and 300 pikemen in the centre. Two battalions could then form a unit of 1000 men. But on campaign, where numbers diminished rapidly, battalions were more usually arranged in 8 ranks.

For combat, Billon stipulates that *"it is necessary to be the first in the field and to line up to await the enemy and see him arrive."* Then the battalion had to move with small steps, stopping 50 or 60 paces from the enemy, *"each man joining left shoulder to right shoulder, bending forwards, putting the weight on the right foot stretched behind"*, then to *"move forward only 5 or 6 large paces, pikes lowered for a stronger impact."* Finally, he specifies that *"if advancing on the enemy from afar, the advance should be with small paces also, stopping every hundred paces, or less, to straighten the files,*

Matchlock musket between 1610 and 1620. Musée de l'Armée, Paris.

Wheel-lock arquebus between 1620 and 1625. Musée de l'Armée, Paris.

then tighten the rows at the front, and prevent the files from approaching more than one and a half feet from each other, constantly shouting that they tighten the rows but not the files; it is necessary to consider what the enemy intends to do, and not march without reflection." With regard to the musketeers, he says, " It is necessary to cause as much

Pike drill, figures 3 to 21 of pike drill, in *L'Art Militaire pour l'Infanterie* [...] by Johann Jacobi von Wallhausen (16..-17..). Musée de l'Armée, Paris.

46

Musket drill, figures 84 to 143 of musket drill and figures 1 to 3 of pike drill, in *L'Art Militaire pour l'Infanterie* [...] by Johann Jacobi von Wallhausen (16..-17..). Musée de l'Armée, Paris.

damage as possible to the enemy with the musketeer troops before engaging in hand to hand combat," then suggests general fire from the musketeers on the flank of the battalion *"for which the musketeers should be doubled by half files to better fire without injury."* Finally, he suggests that the detached musketeer platoons fire on the flank then *"engage hand-to-hand by the flanks of the enemy."* Facing the cavalry, the pikemen advance with their *"pikes lowered,"* as did the regiments of the Duc de Rohan in July 1635 (*La Frezelière* and *Lèques)* against the German cavalry in the Val-Fresle.

On campaign, the battalions could be regrouped in battle corps (advanced-guard, main body, rear-guard) which could include up to 6 battalions, as was the case for the army of Maréchal Schomberg on the 17 October 1630 at Casale. Brigades are already mentioned in 1629, notably at the siege of Privas, during which *Champagne* and *Piémont* formed a brigade.

In his book, Billon already mentions three-battalion brigades: *"There are two facing that seem to be only one corps, and another behind these two. (...) Or one single battalion is placed in front and two others behind, and when it comes to hand-to-hand combat with the enemy they leave and charge the flank."* There seems to have been numerous possible battalion formations, and J.J. von Walhausen, like J. de Billon, suggests a wide variety. However, on campaign, formations and manœuvre described by the theoreticians would have rarely been applied; the experienced troops may have performed these manœuvres but the majority of combat units and the temporary regiments most probably would not have had time to train in such methods.

Soldiers were divided into pikemen and musketeers; Jean de Billon explains that *"Some foreigners observed that, with more senior soldiers, two thirds were pikemen and the other third musketeers. And if they were new soldiers, two thirds were musketeers and the other third were pikemen."* Among the soldiers, the *anspessades* were better paid and replaced the corporals when they were absent. The cadets were volunteers from good families. According to Billon, *"It is necessary therefore for each company to have one hundred musketeers or arquebusiers, for we are constrained to give arquebuses to the young cadets and gentlemen, who have not yet*

built up their strength. It seems to me that since we have found the way to carry short cannons as far as longer cannons, it would be good to make muskets in this form. (...) The bandolier for the army must be of good leather, and the charges of wood, so that they do not break. In Flanders, they carry large receptacles of horn hung from a leather flask pouch, for they hold much powder. (...) Swords must be short. And each soldier should have a roupille (cape) for the rain, and this should be a little large." And he adds, regarding the pikemen, *"After this, eighty or one hundred armed pikemen are required."* Their pikes should be *"strong and of good wood; and the iron squared and of the best quality. They also need short swords, roupilles for those who so wish, but fitted close to the body and not large, and the best pointed burgonets. Because the straps that support the doublet break most often, it would be well to attach the doublet to the corselet with two buckles of iron (...)."*

Helmets, morions or cabassets, and armour were given in priority to the corporals, *anspessades* and pikemen of the elite. The pikeman's full equipment was the *pot*, cuirasse, doublet, a sword and a pike more than 5 metres in length. But as the campaign advanced, pikemen had the tendency to lighten their equipment, in particular by replacing the corselet with a buff jerkin. Musketeers could wear a hat, a *boukinkan* or morion; they wore a cassock, or more rarely a buff jerkin, and were equipped with a sword and musket, which definitively replaced the arquebus in 1622.

The Duc de Rohan describes the equipment of the infantry just before France entered the war (1635): *"The most ordinary arms of the Infantry at the present time for defence are the pot, the cuirasse and the doublet; and for the offence the sword, pike and musket, which are by and large the arms of the Greeks and Romans (...) The battle corps is made up of pikes, which is a very proper arm to resist the cavalry, with many pikes together forming a solid corps, difficult to break at the head by reason of its length, four or five rows of pikes, the blades of which protrude past the front of the soldiers and always hold the cavalry squadrons at a distance of twelve or fourteen feet."*

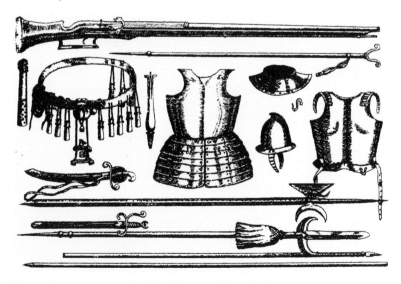

Pikeman and musketeer weaponry, from *L'Art Militaire pour l'Infanterie* [...] by Johann Jacobi von Wallhausen (16..-17..). BNF.

Swiss pikeman armour, hand crafted circa 1620-1630. Musée de l'Armée, Paris.

The French cavalry from 1617 to 1634

At the end of the Wars of Religion, the Catholic cavalry still followed its old organisation – with its origins in the Hundred-Year War – and still charged *en haie* (in a thin, extended line) 2 or 3 rows deep. The original *compagnies d'ordonnance* had 100 *lances*; a *lance* comprised a Gendarme bearing the lance, and two "archers", by this time called *chevau légers*. The Huguenots, inspired by the German and the Dutch models, rapidly adopted the pistol and reduced the weight of their armour. In 1620, there was only a part of the Gendarmerie left that still kept the full armour, and this became progressively lighter; the burgonet or capeline often replacing the visored helmet, and high boots in supple leather replacing greves. The Huguenots had also adopted a deep formation, but in contrast to the German model, they preferred the charge to the caracole. Because of this the Huguenot formation was less deep: 6 rows instead of the 10 rows of German formations.

Henri IV reformed the cavalry in 1600, and this organisation remained until Richelieu's new reform at the end of 1634. In 1603, the cavalry, with a total of 1,500 horses, included the king's Household and 19 companies of *gendarmes* and *chevau légers*, with 25 to 30 horsemen each. The king's Household was made up of 4 companies of *gardes du corps*: a Scots company, a company of the king's *chevau légers*, a company of *Gendarmes* and a troop of 100 arquebusiers and *carabins*. In 1609, cavalry numbers were brought up to 8,500 horses, but contrary to what was happening in the infantry, the nobility - who were the captains of the cavalry companies - held their resistance against the formation of large units until 1638.

During the Regency in 1615, "bands" of *carabins* were added to each company of light cavalry, armed with a carbine rather than the more cumbersome arquebus, and commanded by a lieutenant. However, in 1621, the *chevau légers* had practically all adopted the carbine, so the *carabins* formed a special corps commanded by a *mestre de camp des*

carabins, Arnauld de Corbeville. After the pacification of 1622, cavalry companies maintained by the governors of the provinces were reduced to fifteen, and the king increased his Household with a company of 100 musketeers recruited from gentlemen volunteers.

The Reverend Father Gabriel Daniel recounts Puysegur's version of the creation of this unit: *"After this (the storming of Montpellier in 1622), the king marched straight to Avignon and during his march he removed the carbines from the Carabins company, and gave them muskets, and gave command of the company, which had no leader after the death of the captain, to de Montalet, the grade of Lieutenant to de la Vergne and the Cornette to de Montalet, who bore the same name. (...) His majesty asked d'Espernon for six of his Guards to put in the company; he wished - and I can even say that he forced - me to take the cassock of the musketeer (...) His Majesty assured me (...) that he had decided to put only gentlemen in this company, which he would find among his Guards, as well as a few soldiers of fortune; but*

Gendarme armour hand crafted circa 1630. Musée de l'Armée, Paris.

P. 49 : Mousquetaire du Roi circa 1630, Suzanne Dana.

48

that he did not wish to take any who had not served, desiring after they had served a time in the company, to remove them and disperse them in the "vieux" and "petit" regiments, and even give them ensigns and lieutenancies in the guards (...)."

On the 3 October 1634, Louis XIII retook charge of the unit, thus becoming captain of the company of musketeers.

The king had his own company of musketeers which accompanied him everywhere; Richelieu also had his company of Guards. Gabriel Daniel reports that there was *"emulation between these two companies that went as far as jealousy, of*

Louis XIII's armour, between 1620 and 1630. Musée de l'Armée, Paris.

50

the sort that very often there were quarrels and combats between the king's musketeers and the cardinal's guards. It was a pleasure for the king to learn that the musketeers had mistreated the Guards and the Cardinal also applauded when the musketeers were dominated. Because duels were forbidden, the duels between the Musketeers and the Cardinal's Guards were passed off as 'encounters'. The Cardinal took the occasion to make a few attempts to break the company of musketeers, but did not succeed."* These words seem to be inspired by the memoirs of Monsieur d'Artagnan, captain lieutenant of the first company of the king's Musketeers: *"De Tréville had called all three from the South-West* (author's note: Porthos, Athos and Aramis were all three from Béarn) *because they had engaged in a few battles, which gave them much reputation in the province. What is more, he was most content to choose his men thus, because there was such jealousy between the company of musketeers, and that of Cardinal Richelieu's guards, that they fought each other every day. This was nothing, as it happens every day that men quarrel together, especially when there is aspersion cast on their reputation. But that which is somewhat surprising, is that the masters each boasted that they had men whose courage placed them above all others. The cardinal constantly boasted of the bravery of his guards, and the king tried constantly to diminish this bravery because he could see that His Eminence the cardinal sought only to elevate his company above his own. The minister had even posted men in the provinces with the order to bring him the combatants who had excelled in fighting. Thus it was at this time when there were rigorous edicts against duels, and even when some persons of great quality were punished by death, who had fought regardless of these edicts, he offered to these persons not only exile at his side, but also, most often, his favour."*

In his memoirs, Richelieu describes the impression that the king's musketeers must have made in an anecdote that occurred at the siege of La Rochelle in 1627: *"As the cardinal had, upon the order from the king, paid all the expenses of this embarkation (for the Isle of Rhé), all that remained was to await the wind. These troops had been so well chosen that they would have been capable to fight twice their number, and the musketeers alone, thirty-two of them that His Majesty had equipped with arms against mus-*

kets and halberds, were in such condition that they would have been able to reduce any army to pieces. But His Majesty did not content himself with this foresight and these arms; his main recourse was to God, and he ordered each man to make his peace with God, and in particular his musketeers, whom he ordered to confess and take communion before leaving."

As the king had absolute confidence in his musketeers, he demanded for the attack of the Pas de Suse on the 6 March 1629, that the musketeers join forces with the *enfants perdus* to force the barricades.

In 1627, the French cavalry included the king's Household in 7 companies (4 *Gardes du Corps* companies, one Scottish company and three French companies, 1 company of *gendarmes de la garde*, 1 company of *chevau légers de la garde* and 1 company of the king's musketeers*)*, the *gendarmerie de France* (16 companies recruited from the lower nobility), the companies of *chevau légers* under the command of a colonel general of the light cavalry, the *carabins*, forming a separate corps from the 1st April 1622, and the nobility of the *ban* and the *arrière-ban*, which were to serve personally, both on horseback and in arms, bringing with them a number of horsemen proportional to the size of their fiefdom. This nobility was difficult to control, and was not often employed. These formations were to be abandoned when the cavalry was reorganised into regiments.

There were two types of *gendarmerie* company: the companies of princes of the royal bloodline, and the companies of gentlemen, these latter including those of the maréchals de France, Lords or Gentlemen, after whom the company was named. Disputes were frequent over service and command, as Bussy Rabutin tells us in his memoirs: *"The Prince de Condé and the Duc d'Enghien wanted their lieutenants of chevau légers to command the lieutenants of the gendarmes of the gentlemen, and this was practiced when one and the other commanded the army, but in their absence if a maréchal de France commanded*

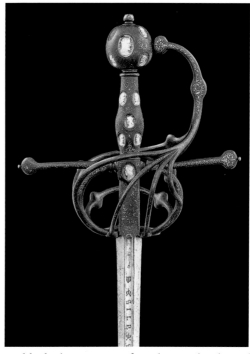

Louis XIII's sword (1614).
Silbestre Nieto, spanish craftman.
Musée de l'Armée, Paris.

and he had a company of gendarmes, he claimed that the lieutenant of this company commanded the lieutenants of the chevau légers d'ordonnance (...)"

The combat unit was the squadron, composed of 120 to 150 horsemen. One or more companies (or *cornettes*) were grouped together to form a squadron. The officers of a squadron were: one captain, one lieutenant, one sub-lieutenant, one *guidon* (for the gendarmerie) or a *cornette* (for the light cavalry), four quartermasters, three brigadiers and three trumpeters. The eldest of the captains commanded the squadron. After the siege of La Rochelle in 1628, Richelieu brought the companies together in squadrons of at least 100 horses. The companies barely reached 50 horses, or even half this number, and so two to four companies had to

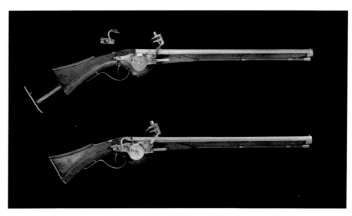

Wheel-lock and marchlock arquebus,
between 1610 and 1620.
Musée de l'Armée, Paris.

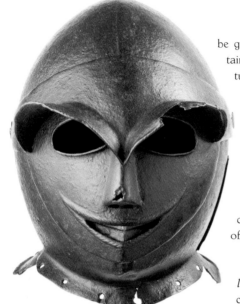

Savoyard "armet",
hand crafted circa 1620.
Musée de l'Armée, Paris.

52

be grouped together with the captains commanding the squadron in turn.

However, it was not before the 3 October 1634 that this practice was regulated: 91 squadrons of light cavalry and 7 carabins (Arnauld, Bideran, Courval, Du Pré, Harancourt, Maubuisson, Villas), of 100 horses each were created, each carrying the name of the commanding captain.

In his book *Les principes de l'art militaire*, Jean de Billon specifies that the rows of a squadron had to be of an even number, and he gives 8 or 10 as an example. He also specifies that a squadron must not have more than 400 horses. A squadron of 100 horses should be aligned 20 horses abreast (files) and 5 in depth (rows). The files and rows could be spaced by 6 feet or 3 feet, as for the infantry. In the first case, a squadron occupied a surface of 200 feet across and 80 feet in depth, whilst the second arrangement occupied half this surface. For 400 horses, Billon suggests 40 horses abreast and 10 rows deep. Billon also thinks that *"the most perfect number is one hundred men in each cornette (company), besides the leaders (...). In this way the three companies make three hundred men without the leaders, and each company will be divided into five brigades (...). And then, when desired, up to four cornettes can be joined together, which is a fairly large squadron (...)."*

In his *Traité de la guerre* of 1636, the Duc de Rohan himself suggests regiments of 500 horses, including 50 *carabins* and 50 arquebusiers. But all this remained theoretical; in the Valtelline in 1635, the Duc de Rohan still spoke of the 6 *cornettes* present in his army. These 6 *cornettes* combined totalled less than 400 horses, and less than 70 horsemen per *cornette*. From July 1635, the Duc de Rohan speaks of 3 squadrons (*Canillac, Saint-André* and *Villeneuve*) and no longer of 6 *cornettes*, apparently in compliance with Richelieu's *ordonnance*.

At the beginning of 1617, there were three classes of horseman: the *gendarme*, the *chevau léger*, and the *carabin*. The *gendarme*, already described at the beginning of this chapter, now had a lighter armour called *three-quarter* armour, comprising a

cuirasse, jointed elements protecting the shoulders, arms and the front of the thighs, a doublet protecting the kidneys, and a visored helmet, which would gradually be replaced by a burgonet or a capeline. The army museum has many Savoyard armet helmets, most probably worn by *gendarmes*, particularly in Italy and the Savoy. Arms included a strong sword, and two cavalry pistols. The *chevau légers* and *carabins*, identical since the adoption of the *mousqueton* (short-barrelled musket) by the *chevau légers*, wore a morion, soon replaced by the capeline or the burgonet, and a cuirasse or half-armour over a buff jerkin. They were armed with a *mousqueton* which replaced the arquebus in 1621, a strong sword and two cavalry pistols.

According to Billon, the horsemen *"...have the cuirasse for protection from the arquebus, doublet, leg armour, neck piece, brassats, gauntlets, and 'salade helmet, the visor of which lifts up. Besides this they have two pistols (...). The company of carabins shall be of sixty men (...). They shall have the protective cuirasse and a "pot" or "salade" helmet with no other defensive arms. And for offensive arms, a large wheel-lock arquebus of three feet or a little more, with a very large calibre, and the sword at the side, and a short pistol, as*

Horse armour said to be
Louis XIII's, circa 1630.
Musée de l'Armée, Paris.

53

The cavalier, portrait of
the Artist, 1872, Jean-Louis
Ernest Meissonier (1815-91)
Collection of the New York
Historical Society, USA.

Wheel-lock arquebus, between 1615 and 1630. Paris, musée de l'Armée

The four kinds of horse, in L'Art militaire à cheval [...] by Johann Jacobi von Wallhausen (16..-17..): lancer, cuirassier, arquebusier and dragoon. Paris, Musée de l'Armée

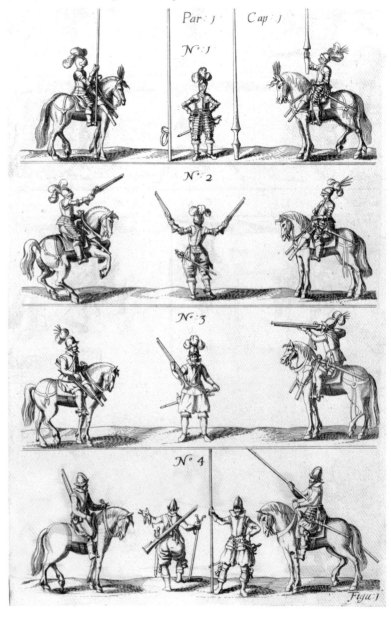

the king himself has instituted. (...) They shall wear, if they so wish, cassocks and gamaches instead of boots, for greater ease in walking when necessary. Thus covered and armed, they are able to combat on foot and on horseback, and to join with the cavalry." Through this account of the *carabins*, Jean de Billon provides us with a description of the future dragoons; but it was only in 1635 that dragoon regiments were actually created.

At the beginning of the 1630's, the Duc de Rohan described the horseman's equipment in the following manner: *"As for the offensive arms of the cavalry, we have five sorts; the lance, the pistol, the sword, the carbine and the matchlock; these first two are given to the heavily armed cavalry, which should have for defensive arms cuirasse, 'salade' helmet, brassats, doublets, leg armour and garde-reins, and it is not so long ago that horses wore bards; ...those that carry the carbines have the "pot" and the cuirasse; and for them to fight on horseback they should be well mounted; but those that carry matchlocks have no defensive arms; of the five sorts of offensive arms, there are no more than three in frequent use: the pistol, the sword and the carbine. Only the Spaniards still have a few companies of lancers that they retain more through pride than through reason; for the lance has no effect other than through the straight progress of the horse; and still there is only one row that can use it (...); the matchlock has also been as if abandoned because in the civil wars it ruined the infantry, encouraging them to steal. Nevertheless a few well disciplined troops of this type in an army are of great service; either for executions, or to win difficult passages, or to guard the cavalry quarters, or even for fighting on foot in combat like enfants perdus in front of the cavalry squadrons."*

54

55

*A Roundhead
on horseback,*
Ernest Crofts
(1847-1911) / Private
Collection.

P. 56-57 :
*Innocents and Card
Sharpers: a game
of piquet* (1861),
Jean-Louis Ernest
Meissonier (1815-91).
National Museum
and Gallery of
Wales, Cardiff

Artillery from 1617 to 1634

Sully, Grand Master of Artillery from 1599, compiled an arsenal of nearly 400 pieces, including around forty that were used on campaign, at a cost of 12 million *livres*.

Sully's artillery comprised six models: a cannon firing a 33-pound cannonball up to 1500 paces; the *long couleuvrine* with a 16-pound ball; the *bastard* cannon, with a 7½-pound cannonball; the *medium* with a 2½-pound ball; the *falcon* with a 1½-pound ball and the *falconet*, with a ¾-pound ball. These pieces were mainly forged at the Paris arsenal, and the equipment had not been renewed since.

Artillery personnel were as follows: for management and control, one lieutenant general, 3 general controllers, 18 provincial controllers, 2 treasurer-generals, 1 arsenal inspector, and 186 lieutenants and commissioners. Firearms and siege personnel were: 3 sap and mine captains, 67 cannon gunners, 182 gunners and 18 firers. Personnel for the construction and repairs of equipment included: 5 foundrymen, 3 gunsmiths, 11 saltpeter commissioners, 3 tentmakers, 11 wheelwrights, 5 carpenters, 1 ropemaker, 1 cooper and 10 blacksmiths. The artillery train comprised: 10 captain generals and cart drivers, 29 cart captains and 27 following officers. Accessory staff included: 1 bailiff, one lieutenant and his clerks, a doctor and surgeon, chaplains, and 20 officers.

Cannon with Cardinal Richelieu's coat of arms, before 1627. Paris, Musée de l'Armée.

58

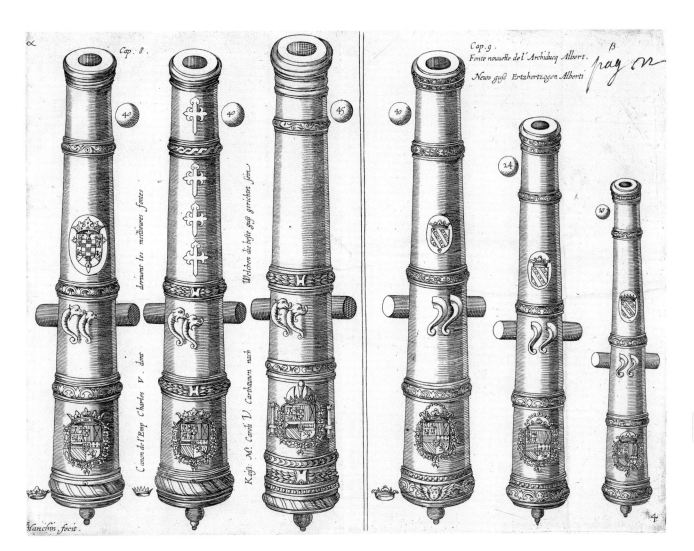

These are roughly the same posts as those mentioned by Jean de Billon in his *Principes de l'Art Militaire*: a grand master of artillery, one lieutenant general of artillery, lieutenants of artillery, commissioners, cart captains and munitions captains, marshals, master gunners, loaders, cannoneers, carters, blacksmiths and carpenters.

Artillery batteries were generally guarded by an infantry company, as was the case for the Pernes company of the Piémont regiment during the siege of Marsillargues in 1622 (*Mémoirs of the Marquis de Fontenay Mareuil*).

Henri II de Rohan assigns the use of artillery mainly to sieges: *"It is proper to speak of artillery after sieges, for it is mainly thanks to the artillery that towns are taken, and since it has been in use, none of these towns remain impregnable unless they are inaccessible; it has changed entirely the form and matter of fortifications."* He goes on to describe the constraints: *"(The Artillery) requires much equipment, needing one hundred artillery horses to pull a battery cannon over all types of terrain; and to be able to fire only one hundred shots; ...to use a piece of battery correctly, eighteen men are needed, besides a certain number of blacksmiths, wheelwrights, marshals and other workers to repair the gun carriages, carpenters to make the bridges, scouts to repair paths; in brief, an army which transports cannon can march only slowly and heavily, and that which has none cannot be efficient: this is why today artillery is essential to an army (...)"*

But the cannon also has its role on the battlefield, especially when an entrenched army needed to be dislodged, as illustrated by the Maréchal de Bassompierre during the attack of the Pas de Suse in 1629: *"We advanced also six pieces of six-pound cannon, pulled along using a hook...to force the barricades."*

Emperor Charles V's cannons, made from the best cast-iron. From Jean Théodore de Bry drawing (1561-1623). Paris, Musée de l'Armée.

Command

The King of France was the commander in chief of all armies. Below him in the hierarchy was the constable (until 1646), followed by the colonel generals who commanded the infantry, cavalry and the Swiss. On campaign, each army was commanded by one or more maréchals, most often highly experienced men of war, although by virtue of their social position princes of the royal bloodline could also take command of the armies. Superior command – princes and maréchals – were often of a very advanced age, and soured by rivalries and conflicts of precedence. Bassompierre recounts this in his memoirs (May 1629): *"Mr de Montmorency, whom Schomberg had allowed through forgetfulness or otherwise to take rank before him at the king's council, wished to do the same to me, which I did not accept. For this reason, the king refused to sit at the Council."* Richelieu shared the command of his armies among many generals, but this division of responsibilities was sometimes at the expense of their efficiency. Richelieu also appointed members of the clergy to lead armies – such as Sourdis or La Valette – with satisfactory results.

Nonetheless, the French elite had a sound training in warfare. Italian-inspired military academies had developed in France under the reign of Henri IV; a number of academies were set up in the suburbs of Saint-Germain. Turenne studied in one of these academies when he was 15, before completing his training in Holland with his uncle Frederick-Hendrick of Nassau. Many Frenchmen – Huguenots and Catholics alike – went to study warfare in the Netherlands. Richelieu himself was interested in the school of Nassau; in 1636 he undertook the foundation of a military academy for the young nobility on the old Rue du Temple. The Duc d'Enghien, future conqueror of Rocroi, studied there in 1637; this keen general interest meant that France had an ample supply of great military thinkers.

During this first period, the most remarkable "captain" and thinker was without doubt the Duc de Rohan. Rohan published *Le parfait capitaine* in 1631, followed by his *Traité de la guerre* in 1636.

However, besides being a theoretician, the Duc de Rohan was above all an excellent "captain". The Duc d'Aumale said of him in 1886: *"He (Rohan) was not only the leader of the insurrection of the South; he was its soul; he had inspired, prepared, organised and directed it down to the smallest detail. The resistance he encountered did but stimulate his genius. In this theatre of so many bloody battles, he invented and practiced a type of warfare without precedence (...) We can understand that a true captain such as Rohan knew how to use a mountain range, a few valleys and a curtain of rock to either show himself or hide to take his adversaries unawares, to keep them in ignorance, to sow troubles in their combinations, and knew how to join groups of insurgents, quartered at the extremities of the Languedoc, separated by large distances, and a veritable mass of hostile populations; how he could, with a few bands of hastily disciplined peasants, hold out against the power of the royal household for two years."*

What is striking in reading Rohan's memoirs is the care he takes in describing the geopolitical situation of the region in which he was operating. In an introduction to the chapters on his intervention in the Valtelline, he dedicates 5 pages to the geographical situation of the Grisons, and the entire first book (around sixty pages) to the political, diplomatic and strategic situation of the region; the entire third book chronicles the timeline of events in the Grisons. The rest of the book details the evolution of this context. On Rohan's death in April 1638, Maréchal de Bassompierre said: *"This same month the Duc de Rohan died, without doubt a great loss for France; for he was a very great personage and more experienced than any other man of our times."*

Like J.J. von Walhausen and Jean de Billon, Rohan theorised all aspects of warfare - but he did so as the great captain that he was. His *Traité de la guerre* addresses a great many military issues: the selection of soldiers and arms, military discipline, marches, encampment and entrenchment, battles, fortresses, surprise attacks and musters, sieges, defence of town squares, artillery, baggage and pioneers, spies and guides, supplies, general duties of an army and their functions, attacks adapted to the strengths and situation of a region as well as its defences, the means to ensure a conquest, and the way to aid an ally. He also discusses the nature of the commander – the prince or his lieutenant – who should be able to turn both the war and his reputation to his favour.

The Duc Henri de Rohan insists on the importance of the conduct of the men, and like many others before him, he gives seven clear principles in his chapter on battle:

◈ Never be forced into battle against your will;
◈ Choose a battlefield best suited to your army;
◈ Array your army for battle in such a way as to be at an advantage;
◈ Have a good general staff and a efficient chain of command (in three infantry corps and two cavalry corps);
◈ Respect distances between the different units in such a way that a disrupted unit does not disorganise the one behind;
◈ Put the most valiant soldiers on the wings of the army and engage battle on the strongest wing;
◈ Forbid pursuit and pillage before the enemy is fully defeated.

In his chapter on arms, Rohan regrets that the Prince of Orange did not pursue his idea of reintroducing the targe and sword in infantry equipment. He praises the merits of the pike and the musket, but, taking the example of the Romans, considers that a unit of soldiers armed with targes and swords can defeat a unit of pikemen. He therefore recommends that each battalion be accompanied by a hundred or a hundred and twenty targes to charge the flank, specifying that the infantry regiment should have 1,440 men, made up

of 600 pikemen, 600 musketeers, and 240 targe bearers. This recommendation is in agreement with his own practices – in 1628, alongside Montpellier, he divided his advanced-guard of 1,500 men into six troops: *"The first three were each of thirty armed men, chosen from volunteers, and the best men chosen from the cavalry with halberd and pistol, and eighty half pikes, half muskets; each dozen of armed men had an officer in charge, and they carried with them a few revolvers and ladders (...) The three other troops were of four hundred men each, who were to support the first; after came the Duc with his armed men, and was followed by all the rest of the battalions, of which the largest was not more than four or five hundred men."*

As explained above, the cavalry regiment was supposed to have 500 horses, with 400 gendarmes, 50 *carabins* and 50 arquebusiers. In this same chapter, he considers that an army should comprise 25% cavalry in open country (8,000 horsemen for 24,000 infantry) and 1/6th cavalry on rugged ground.

In the following chapters he expresses his dislike of fortresses, which hindered the mobility of an army.

Richelieu's ideas were similar to those of the Duc de Rohan. He did not wish to multiply the strongholds, and therefore pushed to destroy

Louis XIII's hall in the Musée de l'Armée. Paris, Musée de l'Armée

those that were useless. Like the Duc, he favoured the offensive, saying *"It is better to attack when one can do so without temerity"*, and considered that this was better suited to the French temperament, whose natural impatience was *"unsuited to defence"*. And, like the Duc, he thought that a military engagement should be prepared down to the smallest details, which postponed France's entry into this war until 1635.

An army could be commanded by the king, the cardinal or a prince, but as a general rule it was commanded by one to three maréchals de France and one to three field marshals. Until his death, the king gave the title of lieutenant general to his army general: this was the title borne by the Maréchal de Turenne when he replaced Guebriant at the head of the army of Alsace, and by the Maréchal de l'Hôpital at the battle of Rocroi. Richelieu summarises command of an army as follows: *"In this event, command should be swiftly sent to the troops that are to obey and advance, money should be sent to pay them and also the necessary officers, to whit: field marshals, an intendant and two army marshals, and the necessary money should be sent for the pay of this army (...)"*. This passage takes place the last days of the year 1628. Later in his memoirs, he describes the arrangements of Louis XIII at the beginning of 1633: *"(...) This meant arranging with the Prince of Orange the conquests that would be made, and giving him the leadership and command of all arms. The king was required simply to send and maintain one maréchal de France and two or three field marshals, twelve thousand infantry, two thousand horses and everything else required by an army; that in this way the war would be easy, because all that would be required of the king would be to maintain another army corps in Alsace, under the command of two maréchals de France and two carefully chosen field marshals"*. It should be noted that the cardinal suggested this eventuality the same year because he considered that *"the difficulty to be considered in this affair was the small number of people capable of making war in France"*. He already had a somewhat acerbic view of the conduct of the maréchals, as he had had for the soldiers a few years earlier during the attack of the Pas de Suse (March 1629): *"It can be said in truth that all did well on this occasion; however all the order that had been desirable, and that had been decided upon, was not able*

to be maintained, as much through the difficulties of the terrain which was harsh and narrow, separated every hundred paces by low drystone walls, which broke the battalions, as through the nature of the French, which has always been considered more courageous than wise, and which led each man to march as he wished, which could greatly prejudice the service of the king. In consideration of this, Maréchals de Créqui, de Bassompierre and Schomberg, and the field marshals were all together at the head of the volunteers, contrary to reason which would have placed them separately in diverse locations, to give orders in all places." It was normal at the time for the maréchals to advance to the middle of the battlefield, carrying their sword in hand. Witness accounts describe them at their post in the line of battle most often accompanied by a *cornette*, company or squadron of their guards, gendarmes or *chevau légers*. They could thus intervene at any moment in the battle, as in the golden days of chivalry.

There were many levels in the chain of command between the maréchals and company captains: field marshals, battle marshals, battle sergeants, *mestres de camp*, and colonels.

In his *Histoire de la milice française*, Gabriel Daniel tells us: *"The field marshal is one of the leading and most important officers of the troops: it is he who, together with the general, orders the encampment and lodgings of the army, and who, when the army decamps, scouts ahead to assess the lie of the land so that the troops may march in safety. After the field marshals have determined the form and size of the camp, they leave the apportioning of the terrain to the quartermaster general and the major-general: it is one of the functions of the field marshal himself to post a large guard in an advantageous position, around half a league from the camp. It is they who oversee the quartering of the troops and their departure, etc. They are called field marshals because they have the authority to order the arrangement of the camp, in the same way as the maréchal de France over the entire army."* Under Henri IV, and at the beginning of the reign of Louis XIII, there was one single field marshal per army. In 1630, a maréchal de France could be served by a number of field marshals, most often two, each responsible for one of the army corps. During the battle, the maréchal or

62

field marshal commanded the reserve corps or one of the wings of the army.

The office of battle marshal appeared at the end of the reign of Louis XIII, towards 1643: *"The battle marshals were officers the main function of whom was to lead the army into battle according to a plan given to them by the general, and as we name field marshal he who presides over the arrangement of the troops in the camps, in the same way we name battle marshal he who, following the order of battle addressed to him, assigns to each officer and each corps the post that he should occupy in the arrangement of the army,"* explains Gabriel Daniel.

The field marshals – and later the battle marshals – were assisted in their tasks by the battle sergeants: *"In the absence of field marshals, the battle sergeant should take command, for his office is above all others; for he sits on the council, and he may enter the garrisons when the troops are garrisoned, and arrange the troops for battle, and know the number of soldiers and if they are well armed; for he must report to the king, the general and even the war secretary during wartime and sometimes even in peacetime; for such is the function of the battle sergeant; before they had twenty four ordinary guards, who went to visit by the frontiers instead of the commissioners that are sent there. Thus, they should be men chosen for their high capability and bravery."*

In 1630, each army corps commanded by a maréchal de France sent to the aid of Casale had one or two field marshals: Maréchal de Schomberg had Field Marshals Feuquières and Frangipani as well as two aides-de-camp; Maréchal de Marillac had Field Marshals Brézé and Chastelier-Barlot and two aides-de-camp; and Maréchal de La Force had Field Marshal Arpajou and two aides-de-camp. In 1633, the general staff of the *"Powerful army of the king"*, an army of Germany under the command of Maréchal de la Force, is listed as: three field marshals, the Marquis de La Force, the Vicomte d'Arpajou and Hebron (Scottish); one battle sergeant (d'Espenan); three aides-de-camp; one intendant; one quartermaster; one lieutenant of artillery and one general of army supplies. The Duc de Rohan describes the chain of command in his *Traité de la guerre* of 1636: *"The field marshal general receives them (the orders) from the general then goes to his quarters; here the commissioner for the cavalry receives the orders for the cavalry; the battle sergeant for the infantry, who then sends them to the sergeant majors of the brigade; for the artillery, the quartermaster, and for supplies his own quartermaster. In brief, by speaking to these four persons the field marshal general gives orders to the entire army. All orders and commands have to be given in writing."*

The *mestres de camp* were originally officers *"the function of whom was to assign, in a camp, the quarters of the bands or companies that compose a corps of troops, after taking the order from the field marshal."* However, in the time of Louis XIII the mestre de camp was the commander in chief of a cavalry, infantry, or dragoon regiment. Gabriel Daniel provides us with the following anecdote: *"Before, that is to say in the time of Louis XIII, it would have*

Henri, Duc de Rohan (1617-38). French school (17th century). Château de Beauregard, France.

HENRY · DVC · DE · ROHAN

been improper to refer to a colonel as mestre de camp: for example, Maréchal de Bassompierre, who in his remarks on the history of Dupleix, where Monsieur Arnault is called colonel of the carabins, refers thus to this historian: *"You are an idiot. He was never mestre de camp, and the carabins are not only under the colonel of the light cavalry, but also under the mestre de camp of the chevau légers."*

He goes on: *"there were no cavalry regiments in France until seventy years after the institution of the infantry regiments: for these were instituted by Henri II, and the cavalry was only regimented in this kingdom in the year 1635 under the reign of Louis XIII. When the cavalry regiments were instituted, by the same reason the same title of mestre de camp was given to the commanders of these corps, the colonel general of the cavalry alone bearing the title of colonel, so that there were mestres de camp of the cavalry and mestres de camp of the infantry."* The office of colonel general of the infantry was disconti-

Savoyard "armet", hand crafted circa 1620-1630. Paris, Musée de l'Armée.

64

nued by Louis XIV in 1661. *Mestres de camps* had many responsibilities: *"The mestre de camp has the right to expel the captains and the junior officers of his regiment for misconduct, and to have them arrested. The justice of the regiment is performed in his own name and in the name of the king; he presents the officers for the offices of his regiment to the State war secretary; but they are not always approved, and sometimes others are appointed. The king always appoints the captain and the cornette."*

The title of colonel, according to the Duc d'Aumale in his book *Histoire des Princes de Condé*, *"was given to the leaders of certain corps, of the cavalry in particular, recruited abroad or coming from foreign service, or corps organised from the infantry of foreign troops. The title of mestre de camp was that borne generally by the leaders of the corps."* According to Gabriel Daniel, writing at the beginning of the eighteenth century, the title of Colonel *"...is given to the commander of a regiment of infantry or dragoons: for the dragoons are an infantry corps. It is also given to the commander of a regiment of foreign cavalry, and to the commander of a regiment of 'milice bourgeoise' in a town."* But as d'Artagnan says in his memoirs, *"There was one among them (regiments from Champagne) of which the colonel was very young, because at that time, as in this, the standing of a person was of more importance in their obtaining such a position than their services, and indeed it is not without reason that one has always been held in higher esteem than the other, because one of the essential qualities for a colonel who wishes to have a good regiment is to provide a good table."*

Raising a company was very costly: not only did captains have to enlist men; they also had to pay for their upkeep. The money paid by the king for the levy was most often used to equip these men – they were not the owners of their arms and equipment. To remain within the budget, captains who left the service demanded a "handover" from their successor, thereby setting the bases for venality of office. For the levy or new regiments, the king gave commissions to *mestres de camps*, who in turn gave commissions to the captains; these commissions were subject to the approval of Louis XIII. However, venality of office had the advantage of establishing ownership of the regiment, and therefore heredity of the office; the Estates General of 1614 had condemned the principle of venality of office, as the upper echelons of society wanted military service to be the only route to enter the nobility.

The term "officer" in the sense of military officers only entered common usage at the beginning of the seventeenth century. J.J. Walhausen speaks of "major" officers (colonel, lieutenant-colonel, the captain of the guards of the regiment, *quartenier* of the regiment, the major and the provosts), officers (captains, lieutenants and ensigns), and "minor" officers (sergeants, corporals and *anspessades*). The Wars of Religion created many career openings, and soon the high-level ranks were no longer exclusive to the nobility, legitimising the term "officer". In his memoirs, D'Artagnan recounts an event that took place in 1640, telling how officers plotted against their young colonel who had much enthusiasm but little experience: *"It is not that the colonels, at this time, did not have a great authority over their captains, but when the captains were recognised for their bravery, and they had friends, if the colonel happened to wish to undertake something against them, they all leagued against him; most often he was repudiated by the court, because the court did not wish to remove good men from their positions to satisfy the caprice of one man."*

In 1633, the king's powerful army (the army of Germany under Maréchal de La Force), also included field marshals, the battle sergeant, the quartermaster and aides-de-camp in the list of officers.

A *cavalier*, time of Louis XIII (1874),
Jean-Louis Ernest Meissonier (1815-1891)
Paris, Orsay museum.

65

On campaign

The armies of the time never had more than 30,000 men. The Genoese army in 1625 had 23,000 men, while the army of Savoy in 1630 had a little over 20,000, reinforced by 6,000 Swiss troops. Armies deployed to repress Protestant rebellions rarely exceeded 10,000 men, and this is also the case of the army sent to the Valtelline in 1635. The proportion of cavalry remained low in the armies of the first third of the seventeenth century: 600 horses for a little under 9,000 men at the Ponts de Cé in 1620; 3,000 horses for 26,000 men in the Piedmont in 1629; and 3,750 horses for 21,750 men in Schomberg's army in 1630. This is equal to an average of 6 to 12% cavalry, with a peak of 17% in 1630. With entry into the Thirty Years' War, these proportions were greatly exceeded, although there were of course exceptions, such as the small army of the Duc de Mayenne in Montauban on the 26 July 1621, which had 6 companies of cavalry, 4 companies of *chevau légers* and 6 *carabin* companies for only one infantry regiment and 6 cannons. The total would have been somewhere around 4,000 men: this was therefore an army corps rather than a full army.

At the beginning of a campaign, the preoccupations of the administration were to control troop numbers and reduce *passe-volants* ("invisible men"). The Code Michaud set out that muster rolls should be much more precise than before: they should now show the first name, surname, and *nom de guerre* (nickname), age, place of birth, status and physical description of the soldier. Misinformation was heavily sanctioned, regardless of whether it was the *passe-volant*, captain of the company or the war commissioner who was found to be accomplice to this practice. Actual company numbers were penalised by this, and the king even conceded to the accordance of a bonus to captains whose companies reached 70 men! It was on the occasion of these musters that pay was advanced: they were termed loans. Captains, commissioners and controllers were obliged to attend these musters in person; the *mestre de camp* was only required to attend twice a year.

The *ordonnance* of January 1629 specifies the amount of pay: 6 *sous* per day for the soldiers, 10 for the cadets, 12 for the experienced soldiers, 15 for drummers, surgeons and harbingers, 17 for *anspessades*, 20 for corporals, 30 for sergeants, 45 for *appointés*, 73 for ensigns, 100 for lieutenants, 300 for captains and 500 for the *mestres de camp*. For the regiment's general staff, daily pay was 30 *sous* for the chaplain and surgeon, 60 for the quartermaster, 100 for the aide-de-major and the conduct commissioner, 300 *sous* for the sergeant major and 360 for the provost and his officers. The number of musters was established at *"ten months of musters for each year, one month being 36 days;"* the simple soldier could therefore hope for a loan of 216 sols per monthly muster. Nevertheless, numbers dwindled rapidly on campaign and the Comte du Plessis, who was part of Schomberg's army in 1630, recalls that: *"Regiments were strongly diminished through Plague, which had lasted throughout the campaign, and had near destroyed them: but it is a fact that, despite this ravage, the company of the Comte de Plessis had still eight hundred men in twelve companies; and that it was far from ruined at the end of the campaign unlike the last comers, through the extraordinary care taken by the mestre de camp, who applied himself with much determination to maintain it and discipline it well ..."*

Soldiers unfit for active service ~ whether through injury or old age ~ were sometimes sent to strongholds as the garrison, under the authority of the governor: they were called the *"mortes payes"* ~ dead pay. War cripples and invalids previously benefited from *oblatus* pensions, paid by the Christian *Maison de la Charité* since 1604. Beneficiaries were designated on the rolls drawn up by the constable and the colonel general of the infantry. An edict of November 1635 founded the Commanderie de Saint-Louis at Bicêtre ~ an establishment for the care of invalid soldiers ~ with the aim of replacing religious establishments; this extended

P. 67 :
The Musketeers 1626,
Eugène Chaperon (1857-1938),
exhibit at the *Salon des Artistes
Français de 1908.*

the obligation of the abbeys of France set out in the Edicts of March 1624 and May 1630 to pay a pension of 100 *livres* to crippled soldiers in priories with a high income. The Code Michau specifies in Article 231 that *"...those captains and officers, who through age or injury have become incapable of service and reside at their expense, we shall pay or provide any other requital for the rest of their lives, for which they shall be obliged to voluntarily deliver their charge into the hands of those we deem competent; and for crippled or invalid soldiers, we shall give them a place as a lay monk, 'morte paye' or other provisions sufficient for their upkeep."* Then in Article 232: *"hospitals shall be maintained to take care of sick or injured soldiers."*

The *ordonnance* of January 1629 lays out the routes, stages and lodgings of armies on campaign. The "routes and stations" system dated back to an *ordonnance* by François 1st in 1549. The "routes" were shown in documents specifying the itinerary, and also served as "bonds" for local authorities. Declarations of the stations were sent to the governors and lieutenant generals of the places concerned. Article 252 of the Code Michau orders that *"...all soldiering troops, whether in regiment corps or companies that travel around our kingdom should always respect these routes according to the order that they shall be given. We most expressly forbid all captains, mestres de camp and other leaders of these soldiers to depart from or change these routes, or to take the liberty of expanding into neighbouring villages... We desire and order that all horse and foot soldiers in numbers of six hundred or more lodging in villages, armed or unarmed, without an order signed by us or our governors or lieutenant generals of the provinces or one of our field marshals, shall be considered as vagabonds and thieves (...)."* The *ordonnance* of 1629 sets out in Article 255 that *"...the regiments shall be ordered to march in two or three corps, both to avoid difficulty and confusion that could be encountered in the distribution of victuals to such a large number of men, and for the commodity of the places that give them quarters and receive them, and also because it is easier to discipline a reduced number of persons"*, and then in Article 260: *"We desire and order that all troops, both infantry and cavalry, travel through the kingdom in corps and in order, and that at*

the front of each corps it is forbidden under pain of torture for any soldier to leave his place in line or lose his flag from view."

This *ordonnance* provides legislation for a major bane of the times: the king's soldiers took what they needed to live off the land – sometimes through indiscipline, but mainly because they were not paid regularly. In the document entitled *La défaite des troupes de Monsieur de Favas, la Noue, & Bellay, au bourg de Saint Benoît en Bas Poitou, par Messieurs les Maréchal de Praslin, Duc d'Elbeuf & Comte de La Rochefoucault*, the author relates the wrongdoing of the troops of Favas, La Noue and Bellay: *"For their first exploit under arms, they profaned and pillaged the churches of Triaize and Saint Denis du Perrier, without sparing the bells. Luçon saved itself from their claws with five hundred écus and eighteen couples of oxen, which had to be given to pull their cannon."* In the same way, Jean-François Delors cites the following facts in his article *Fronton et les malheurs du temps: vers 1620-1630: "On the 2 February 1628, two companies of the Sainte-Croix regiment arrived in Fronton and left the following day in the direction of Fabas, where they stole an ox. 189 sols were given to them under the promise that they would create no disorder."* But *"... they committed much abuse, forgot to pay for their food, and borrowed carts for their cartage and oxen that they did not return. This did not stop 5 companies of the same regiment from returning on the 5th, despite the intervention of M. de Fénelon, a country squire. He received all the same twenty sacks of oats."* However, the villages of Triaize, Saint Denis du Perrier and Fabas did rather well all things considered: the massacring of entire populations, destruction of villages and the wasting of fields were frequent at the time.

The recruitment of soldiers was one of the captain's duties. The recruiters were assigned a region, either to complete the numbers of their corps or to raise a new regiment. Towns were the recruiter's preferred places for recruitment, especially as there were many miscreants and untrustworthy men of whom local authorities were keen to rid their town. From the end of the 15th century, recruitment was extended to foreigners – the Swiss in particular – and to the Germans during the Wars of Religion.

P. 69 :
Cavalier with riding crop,
from J.L Ernest Meissonier.
Reproduced by permission of the
Thomas Ross collection (UK).

70

On this point, the Duc de Rohan does not agree with Richelieu. The Duc thinks that *"The French and the German armies abound with good men, and manage easily without auxiliaries; but in no manner do their choose their soldiers, they use only those who wish to go voluntarily to war; England alone of all the States of our times may choose them and take who it wishes (...) The other kingdoms who do not have this right must incite the men of honour and ambition to enlist, as much in the hope to be advanced to other honours, embracing the profession of war-fare, as by the aim to succeed by means other than this; to refuse any office of the kingdom, or of the king's Household, or any leadership of sol-diery, to any who have not served as a soldier for a certain number of years in the bands; nor to appoint any man to the office of mestre de camp who has not been captain of the cavalry without having been officer in the cavalry (...) ; in brief, that none may advance in any office, who has not passed through the degrees of war; and as the hope to improve oneself is a strong incentive to encourage each man to exercise the profession of war, also the apprehension to find oneself poor and crippled after a long service is an unkindly means to retain them: this is why I would like to provide for them by establishing a fund for these people, so that they can live out the remainder of their days in comfort and with honour."* Concre-tely, Rohan thought that lack of promotion pos-sibilities was at the origin of the lack of vocation of the French, while Richelieu thought that *"it is near impossible to successfully enter major wars with the French alone. Foreigners are absolu-tely necessary to maintain the army corps, and although the French cavalry fights well, we cannot do without the foreign cavalry for the guards and to support all the fatigues of an army."* He gives the following explanation: *"Our nation, hot and ardent in battle, is not vigilant in defence nor suited to designs nor enterprises that cannot be achieved without difficulty."*

Any campaign aimed for victory by arms; the army therefore had to be both led and arranged on the battlefield. The Maréchal de Bassompierre gave this order of march for the royal army on the 15 April 1622 at the Isle of Riez: *"The rendezvous for all troops shall be at ten o'clock in the evening, and the infantry shall come and array for battle to the left of our quarters, on a plain that is there,*

and the regiment of the guards shall have 5 bat-talions that shall be in rhombus formation, and shall lead; behind this regiment shall be the Swiss with 2 large battalions, then 2 Normandie batta-lions and finally Navarre, with 3 battalions; I gave their positions to their sergeant majors, then gave them the order and sent them on their way. There were 7 corps in our cavalry, to whit: d'Esplans' carabins who were at the head on the right of my lodgings; then the company of the Roches Baritaut, followed by the chevau légers of the king's Guard; then the gendarmes; then 50 horses bearing gendarmes and chevau légers, which made up a squadron; behind them, the nobility of the queen mother who formed a squadron with a few volunteers; and finally the company of de Guise's chevau légers: and having given the order to the sergeant-majors, I sent them on their way; after which we arrayed for battle, and formed three orders, to whit: the advanced-guard, composed of d'Espenan's carabins, the chevau légers of Roches Baritaut and of the guard, with the 5 battalions of

Israel excud. cum Priu

Quelques rudes que soient les atteintes de
Et les coups que son bras porte de toutes

the regiment of the guards; the main body, composed of the king's gendarmes, and the Swiss; and the rear guard of the 5 battalions of Navarre and Normandie with the three last cavalry corps."
The precision of such orders of battle can be seen by referring to Cardinal Richelieu's description of the battle of the Pas de Suse in the appendix of this book.

This "rhombus" arrangement appears to be standard practice as we find it in the *Mémoires* of the Duc de Rohan ; he describes the arrangement of the army of the Duc de Montmorency at the beginning of November 1627 near Revel: *"The aforesaid Duc, his army composed of four thousand infantry and fifteen hundred highly capable maîtres, formed four battalions of his infantry, that he arranged in rhombus, leaving large spaces between them for the cavalry which he put at the opposite side of the enemy army, and which he changed according to whether he marched at the front, on the side or behind, and all with great order; and the baggage train he put in the middle*

of these four battalions, being resolved, in this order, either to pass or to fight..."

Once the army was arranged for battle, it could be required to salute a personality, as reports Bassompierre in his memoirs in 1629: *"On Wednesday 21 (March), we arranged our infantry for battle on the plain above Boussolengue. There I received Madame and Monsieur the Prince of Piedmont (who had come to see the king), halfway from Veillane; then below Saint Jory I presented the gendarmes and chevau légers of the king's Guard, who marched in front and behind as they did for the king. Mr. De Luxembourg came to pay his respects, whom she kissed as she had done for me. From there I led her past the front of the infantry, who saluted her waving pikes and flags."*

The army was arranged in two or three lines on the battle field as explained in Richelieu's memoirs in the description of the positions of Schomberg at Casale on the 26 October 1630: *"After having reached the open plain, the army was arranged*

The battle, plate 3 from The Miseries and Misfortunes of War (1633), engraved by Israel Henriet (c.1590-1661), Jacques Callot (after 1592-1635). Grosjean collection, Paris, France.

P. 72-73 :
At the Red Inn, George Derville Rowlandson (1861-1930), private collection.

Cela n'estonne point l'invincible courage
De ceux dont la valeur sçait combatre l'orage,

Et qui pour s'acquerir le tiltre de Guerriers,
Du sang des ennemis arrousent leurs Lauriers.

for battle in full view of the entrenchments and the Spanish army, and without further ado, went straight to the enemy in the best order and the greatest determination imaginable. As the army was a thousand paces from the enemy entrenchment, and as the plain was wide enough to permit the use of any order of battle, the army was halted to arrange the troops according to the order that had been decided upon for the attack, and this was as follows: seven battalions were placed in a straight line, facing the enemy, at such a distance from each other that there was space between them for the squadrons which were destined to lead the cavalry. Of the first seven battalions, there were two on the right wing from the corps of Maréchal La Force, who had the advanced guard that day; two on the left wing from the corps of Maréchal de Marillac, who had the rear guard; three in the middle from the corps of Maréchal Schomberg, who, having command of the main body that day, consequently commanded all the army; and on the wings of the infantry two cavalry squadrons and five carabin companies, a little ahead of all the others. Around a hundred paces behind these first seven battalions, which made the actual vanguard of the entire army, there were seven others to defend them, and eight squadrons arranged in such a way that there was nothing directly in front of them that could prevent the enemy from seeing them, and this corps, on another straight line further back, made up the main body. Around one hundred and fifty or two hundred paces behind this second corps, there was another of six battalions and twelve squadrons, also arranged in a straight line, which were the rear guard of the main body, and fifty or sixty paces behind them, there were three reserve squadrons, and all this in such order that all were defended like a fortification. Between the main body and the rear guard was a squadron of one hundred and thirty gendarmes, commanded by Maréchal de la Ferté Imbault, who was to be at the place of Maréchal de Schomberg; a little further forward on the right was Maréchal de la Force, leading the gendarmes and chevau légers of the king's Guards, and at the same distance from the enemy on the left hand side was Maréchal de Marillac, leading a squadron which included his company of chevau légers. This was the arrangement of the whole army, in number around eighteen thousand infantry, two thousand three hundred horses under cornettes and four hundred and fifty noblemen

of the Dauphiné, without counting the officers of the cavalry or infantry; the seven battalions that were to attack first detached their enfants perdus, around two hundred in number, with as many pikes as musketeers in each battalion, which advanced a few hundred paces before the rest. It was then marched straight on the enemy, up to the old entrenchments that had been made at the time of the first siege, and distanced from the new entrenchments only by the range of a musket: there it was halted to kneel and pray. After the soldiers had risen, they were given a short speech to incite them to do well; but there was not much need of this because of the good humour that the presence of the enemy gave them. The four cannons that had been brought were advanced to the rear of the first battalions, and three carts loaded with picks and shovels to force open the

Ce Metal que Pluton dans ses veines enserre,
Qui faict en mesme temps, et la paix, et la guerre,

enemy entrenchments, and render them accessible to the cavalry. (...) This was the situation of the two armies when signal was given to the king's army to advance on the enemy, which may have been around four o'clock in the afternoon; so the cavalry took sword and pistol in hand, and all the officers of the infantry dismounted, and the entire army marched at the same time and at the same pace straight towards the enemy, with as much determination as gaiety; even the cannon fire from the enemy (which they did somewhat poorly) could not sow the slightest confusion among the soldiers, nor whiten a single face, although this was on passing the old entrenchments mentioned above, which was somewhat inconvenient; on the contrary, they seemed to march more resolutely and more closely, in a silence that is rare on such occasions. Until this point, the maréchals de France were still marching at the head of the first battalions, although they were close enough to the enemy to be wounded by their musketry." But that day battle would not take place; Mazarin ran between the two armies, announcing the peace negotiated by the pope. "After embraces and compliments were exchanged on both sides, and it had been agreed what should happen next, each man withdrew to his army, without having taken any other assurance from each other than word of honour, and the faith of the generals." This beautiful and precise description by Cardinal Richelieu gives us a perfect representation of an army in battle – in three lines, with the cavalry on the wings.

Jacques Callot provides us a graphic representation of the royal army at La Rochelle in 1628. His engraving shows three lines of infantry,

The raising of an army, plate 2 from *The Miseries and Misfortunes of War* (1633), engraved by Israel Henriet (c.1590-1661), Jacques Callot (1592-1635). Grosjean collection, Paris, France.

Israel ex. Cum Priuilegio Regis.

Attire le soldat, sans creinte des dangers,
Du lieu de sa naißance, aux Pais estrangers

Ou seſtant embarqué pour suiure la Milice
Il faut que sa vertu sarme contre le vice

nearly forming a rhombus; the first is made up of two groups of two battalions, the second of three groups of two battalions and the third of two groups of two battalions. On each wing were 4 cavalry *cornettes*: one in the first line, two in the second line and one in the third line.

As in the previous century, each regiment could detach *enfants perdus*. Bassompierre relates in his memoirs that for the attack of Suse on the 6 March 1629, *"the order was that each corps should cast before it fifty enfants perdus, supported by one hundred men, who would be supported by five hundred. (...)The king arrived at the same time with the comte and the cardinal: he wished his musketeers to be joined with the enfants perdus of the guards."*

On the 6 June 1630 at Bourg-Saint-Maurice, the *Gardes Françaises* detached 50 *enfants perdus* to take Séez. Two months later, on the 6 August 1630, the *enfants perdus* of the *Picardie* and *La Meilleraye* regiments were the first to arrive at the fortifications of Carignan, and held a bridgehead. Most often these were small groups of musketeers detached from a regiment to carry out a particular mission, or to be deployed at the front of a regiment. On the plain between Lovera and Mazzo on the 3 July 1635, the Duc de Rohan arrayed his army for battle, dividing it in two corps and "detaching" the *enfants perdus*. At Morbegno on the 10 November 1635, the *enfants perdus* who marched at the head of the battalions *"gave battle so furiously on all sides that the Spanish were repelled to their last entrenchments"* as told by the Duc de Rohan in his memoirs. There is a somewhat surprising description of the composition of the units of *enfants perdus* by Richelieu, when he details his battle array at Casale on the 26 October 1630: *"The seven battalions (...) detached their enfants perdus, around two hundred in number, as many pikemen as musketeers from each battalion, who advanced a few hundred paces before all the others."* This is indeed the only example, to my knowledge, where the *enfants perdus* include pikemen.

However, most of the time, a military campaign was a series of sieges. To be able to hope for a degree of success, these operations had to be prepared with a great many resources, especially cannons and mines. The *Memoirs of Richelieu* provides a clear image of this, when he describes

the siege of Montauban in September 1621: *"On the first of September, the battering of the town began with fifty five cannons, which were divided into 9 batteries, three for each attack. On the 4th, the Duc du Maine, who had too much ardour and courage to be armed with the prudence and consideration required of a captain, decided to launch the assault after two days of battery against a demilune that was before the gate of Ville-Bourbon, without having sufficiently investigated whether the breach was reasonable and the defences truly beaten, considering only that it must be so given the quantity of cannon shots that he had fired (...) On the sally of the trenches, the Marquis de Thémines had hardly taken ten paces when he was killed by a musket shot; this so surprised the musketeers that followed him that it was impossible to make them advance; only the nobility, who had dismounted, gave battle and with so much courage that, although the curtains were all on fire, they managed to enter the moat, where, finding the places from which the enemy were firing, they chased them, mounted the demilune and took possession of it, and also the bastion which was next to it, where they put ladders; but after a little time, because the infantry were not following to defend them, the enemy regrouped and attacked them in such large numbers that they were obliged to withdraw in much disorder and with many losses."* Also in his account of the siege of Saint Jean d'Angély at the beginning of June 1621: *"On the last day of May, Monsieur de Créqui immediately seized the suburb of Taillebourg, surrounded by the Boutonne river, the only bastion they had kept, before burning all the others; the Comte de Montrevel was killed here. This done, Soubise was ordered to surrender the town to the king. He answered that he was there on behalf of the assembly and that the execution of the king's commands was not in his power. The opening of the trenches began, and the batteries were installed; the king had sent for the Liégeois, who began to mine the ravelin of the Canlot tower on the 13 June; the mine having been detonated on the 17, it was not possible to prevent the nobility from launching the assault, where the Barons Desery and Lavardin were killed, and a few others injured."*

A siege that was poorly prepared, or conducted with few resources, was doomed to swift failure. In his *Memoirs*, the Duc de Rohan, relates his bitter experience of this at the siege of Cresseil, during the 1628 revolt: *"Once all the troops had arrived, the siege was laid and the battery began with two cannon, which had not fired six rounds before the carriage of one fell to pieces, and when it had been repaired, that of the other followed suit; in this way we spent nearly all our time in remaking the carriages, and of such poor wood that, when all had been restored, it was hardly better than before: so much so that the breach was not made in one day, but it was necessary to recommence the following morning, which gave time to repair it at leisure, and stronger than it had ever been."*

In his memoirs, Maréchal de Bassompierre relates the attack of the forts of Saint-André and Tournon on the 26 May 1629, during the Protestant rebellion: *"Pfalsbourg opened the dance, attacked and forced entry into another house against the gate of the town, which had been fortified by the enemy. A little while after, Picardie attacked the 'corne' which was first won, then retaken by the enemy, and then again won by the gentlemen volunteers; at this same time, I positioned myself with the regiment of Normandie below the counterscarp, having arranged on the corner of this counterscarp two positions of eight musketeers each, we defended it for three hours(...) The same evening and at the same time, Mr de Portes, with the regiments of Champagne and Piedmont, attacked the Boutières area and took the forts of Saint André and Tournon by assault, killing all who were found inside. (...) We held our position and at two o'clock in the morning of Monday the 28, as we had pierced the moat, we discovered a hole in the fortifications through which the enemy had access to their moat, and there was no more fire from the town. I spent some time before finding a volunteer to try this hole; having finally sent a sergeant with a roundel, he entered the town and found no-one, as the enemy had abandoned it to withdraw to the fort of Thoulon on*
the mountain; we entered the town, and found it already occupied by the Pfalsbourg regiment, who had entered it after having been told by a poor woman that the enemy had abandoned Privas; and shortly after all the regiments were sent to pillage all the districts of the town, and most had slackened in such a way that if I had not taken Swiss arms to invade Thoulon, the enemy would have been able to withdraw without hindrance. I took Thoulon with 1,200 Swiss while Privas was being pillaged, and shortly after set fire to it."* This account illustrates that when a town was taken, the inhabitants had to pay the price – especially when the conqueror had few scruples. In 1628, the Duc de Rohan was witness to such behaviour by his adversary, the Duc de Montmorency, as he recounts in his memoirs: *"At the beginning of this journey, the Prince de Condé and the Duc de Montmorency began their campaign, and went to the region of Foix to attack Pamiers, a large yet weak town. By misfortune, Beaufort decided to defend it, gathering together all the forces of the region, including his own; but once the breach was made, each man was surprised to meet little resistance, and the traitors even helped to intimidate the others. Beaufort, seeing this disorder, wished to flee to Anros; they were captured, taken to Toulouse and executed. The town was pillaged, with the cruelties and liberties that can be imagined under a leader such as he."*

CHAPTER III

The french army in battle, by Jacques Callot

 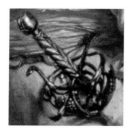 

THE FRENCH ARMY IN THE THIRTY YEARS' WAR   [1635-1648]

According to Grimoard, the forces of Louis XIII in 1635 were composed of 5 armies totalling 100,000 men and 18,000 horses. Before the end of 1635, Richelieu himself states that he had increased the army to 150,000 infantry and more than 30,000 horses – theoretically more than 100 infantry regiments and more than 300 cavalry *cornettes*. In 1636, this total was 164,000 infantry and 22,000 horses, not counting the troops of the Duke of Saxe-Weimar and in 1648 reached a theoretical total of 273,000 infantry and 50,000 horses. In December 1648, numbers fell to the 1635 level; the accounts of the king list no more than 40,000 infantry and 4,000 light-cavalry in service, plus a reserve of 18,000 gendarmes in 100 companies and 25 infantry regiments plus 50,000 men from the provincial legions.

In 1635, the king still called on the *arrière-ban* and this was notably the case in 1636, the year of Corbie. Paris that year provided what was needed to raise and maintain an infantry of 12,000 and 3,000 horses.

Le Tellier was now in charge at the War Office, but he kept on a large part of the personnel, including the brilliant Timoléon Le Roy. Military administration continued to be more and more professional, and in his *Histoire militaire de la France*, André Corvisier lists 25,000 letters written between 1635 and 1642 with an average increasing from 830 per year at the time of Servien (1631-1635) to 1,100 letters per year under Sublet de Noyers (1635-1643) and 2,400 under Le Tellier (from 1643 to 1666). As for the pre-war period, the recruitment

and upkeep of the soldiers, the numbers of which increased considerably, remained the main preoccupations of the military administration.

After the theoretical developments of the preceding period that only the Maréchals d'Estrées, de Créqui, de Montmorency and de Schomberg were able to put into practice during operations in the Valtelline, Saintonge and Piedmont, the art of warfare underwent a genuine evolution from the 1630's; little by little, the teachings of the Swedish King and Captain Gustavus Adolphus replaced those of the Nassaus. Technological innovation complemented these new practical methods: the first flintlock rifles combining a steel hammer and a flint appeared around 1630, and the bayonet appeared around 1640, in the archaic form of a knife that was pushed into the mouth of the musket barrel. The rifle was not really used by French troops until 1650, despite its light weight and ease of use.

Battles were costly in human life, and generals preferred to ruin the country rather than risk their "capital". The siege therefore remained the favoured type of operation during this period, and ranged battles were in many cases direct or indirect consequences of this siege war. While the besieging infantry dug trenches and built protections, the cavalry foraged and brought supplies for the army. The siege then continued with a progression of trenches towards the town, followed by a war of sapping and counter-sapping, mining and counter-mining.

Musketeer, (1870), Jean-Louis Ernest Meissonier (1815-91). Saint-Petersburg, Russia, Hermitage museum.

79

The French infantry from 1635 to 1648

In addition to the *Gardes Françaises, Gardes Suisses* and *Gardes Ecossaises,* at the beginning of 1635 the French army had 6 *vieux corps* (*Picardie, Champagne, Piémont, Navarre, Normandie* and *La Marine* – formerly *Cardinal duc*) and 6 *petits vieux*: *Nerestang* (which became Bourbonnais in 1673 after being Silly and Castelnau*), Rambures* (which became Béarn in 1762, after being called Feuquières, Leuville, Richelieu, Rohan, La Tour du Pin and Boisgetin), *Auvergne, Sault* (which became Flandres in 1762 after being Tessé, Tallard, Monaco, Belsunce and Rougé), *Vaubecourt* (which became Guyenne in 1762 after being called Mailly, Bueil Racan, La Brosse, Boufflers, Pons, Marsan, Bouzols, Talarn) and *Beaumont*.

Before the end of 1635, the *drapeau blanc* had been given to the following 8 regiments: *Bellenave, Plessis-Praslin* (formerly Hostel, which became Poitou in 1682), *Lyonnais, Montausier* (which became Aunis in 1762 after being Angoumois, Crussol, Autin, Montboissier and Vaubecourt), *Nettancourt* (which became Dauphiné after being Dampierre, Humières, Charost, Saillant, Noailles, Custine and Saint-Chamond), *Turenne, Hepburn* (Scots) and *Chamblai* (Swiss). Seventeen infantry regiments had the *drapeau blanc* in December 1635 and were permanent. The others were disbanded at the end of the campaign or when the army to which they belonged was dissolved.

Before entering the war, the number of regiments increased rapidly – from 72 regiments in 1633 to 135 regiments in 1635, then 174 in 1636, with a peak of 202 regiments in 1647, and returning to 170 just after the war, in 1649.

1635 was the year Richelieu reformed the infantry: regiments were to be composed of 20 companies of 53 men (a captain, a lieutenant, an ensign, two sergeants, three corporals, five anspessades and 40 soldiers – 40% pikemen and 60% musketeers); 1,060 men per regiment. The *drapeau blanc* regiments, the *vieux corps* and *petits vieux* (*Rambures, Nerestang, Vaubecourt, La Roue, Villandry, Persan, Sault, Couvonges,*

and *La Meilleraye*) were to be organised in 30 companies. However, in practice, the number of soldiers per company or the number of companies per regiment rarely followed theory: in a letter dated 15 August 1648, the Prince de Condé, asks Le Tellier for the muster pay for the garrison of Ypres which had *"10 companies of infantry regiments from Rambures, 30 from Harcourt, 20 from Mazarin, 30 from Jonzac, 20 from Palluau, and 28 companies from the Bournonville regiments, besides the Swiss."*

Theoretical numbers established 53 men per company from 1635 to 1637, 75 men in 1638 and 1639, then 56 to 60 men from 1640 to 1642 and 70 men per company in 1643 and 1644. But the real numbers were something like 42 men between 1635 and 1640 (820 men per regiment) and 22 men between 1641 and 1648 (440 men per regiment). The army of Maréchal Châtillon, in Flanders in 1641, had an average 500 men per regiment, or 20 men per company, with a differential ranging from 140 men for 20 companies to 960 men for 26 companies.

These estimated figures allow us to extrapolate the real number of infantry from the number of regiments: around 125,000 to 130,000 men in 1635 including the guard, 150 to 155,000 men in 1636 and less than 100,000 infantry in 1647.

The number of foreign regiments increased sharply during the period from 1635 to 1648, from 25 regiments in 1635 to more than 50 in 1648. Foreign regiments mainly included Weimarian regiments (from 1636) which totalled 12,000 men in 6 regiments, theoretically making a total of 2,000 men per regiment. The Swiss regiments were still a major part of the foreign regiments, but saw the strength of their companies fall to 200 men for 8 to 20 companies (with an average of 10 or 12 companies). The Swiss regiment of Roll had 20 companies while the Schmidt and Greder regiments had only 8. The Hebron regiment, formed in 1633 by Sir John Hepburn, veteran of Gustavus Adolphus' green brigade, was the largest of the Scottish regiments. In 1643, there were also four Scottish regiments in the French army in addition to the *Gardes Ecossaises: Douglas, Gray, Lundy* and *Fullerton.*

At the inn, a reiter and Sloughy, the artist's greyhound (1853). Jean-Louis Meissonier (1815-1891). Paris, Orsay museum.

Bandoleer with gunpowder charges. First half of 17ᵗʰ century. Paris, Musée de l'Armée

Although the battalion already existed before 1635, as we have seen, the paternity of this tactical unit is officially accredited to Richelieu, who institutionalised it as a regiment subdivision in 1635. The size of the battalions at this time remained highly variable, shrinking as the campaign advanced, reaching 800 to 900 men for the 18 battalions of the Duc d'Enghien at Rocroi but more usually 500 to 600 men as at Allerheim in 1645. The battalion remained at this time a tactical formation and therefore temporary, the opposite of the regiment or the company, which were administrative formations. Within the line of battle, the battalion was frequently formed in 6 rows, even if in certain cases it could be up to 8 rows deep, such as for inexperienced units. Tactically, the French infantry was more and more influenced by Swedish practices, even if it did not adopt the army formations of Gustavus Adolphus, such as the complex Swedish brigades of 3 or 4 battalions; the battalions were grouped in brigades of 2 to 4 battalions, a more flexible organisation than the heavy battle corps of 6 battalions before 1629. At the Battle of Thionville in 1639, the *brigade* was made up of 3 battalions: 2 from the *Navarre* regiment, and the third from the *Beauce* regiment. In Turin on the 11 July 1640, *Villandry* appears to form a brigade with *Mothe-Houdencourt*, while *Turenne*, *Alincourt* and *Plessis-Praslin* as the reserve, also apparently constituting a brigade. At the battle of Honnecourt in May 1642, *Piémont* and *Rambures* formed the Rantzau brigade within Guiche's army.

The French infantry did not have to adopt the Swedish practice of musketeer detachments, as this already existed long before, either in the detachment of *enfants perdus* or through the constitution of parties of a few hundred musketeers to carry out particular missions (defence of a strategic point, attack of a barricade, protection

The Guard always included the *Gardes Françaises* which theoretically counted 30 companies of 200 men. But Bassompierre relates that in April 1638, the royal troops had been denied their rations when they left their winter quarters, and *"forced the towns where they found themselves to provide for their upkeep, and then came with impunity to plunder the region and create much disorder (...), and then the soldiers, loaded with loot and plunder, and believing that they would be made to pass the summer without pay because of the subsistence they had had during the winter, preferred to spend the entire summer in peace in their houses or those of their friends, where they could live on that which they had collected, instead of going to war during the summer were they would suffer fatigue and worse, and receive no pay; with the result that, with most soldiers having abandoned their companies, these companies were so weak when it was time to leave on campaign that there was hardly a third of the intended soldiers; he (the king) proceeded to break up Chandenier's company of the regiment of the Gardes, which was supposed to be of 200 men and was only of 50, and to reduce most of the other companies of the said regiment to 150 men. These examples, and the care taken to fill the companies of other regiments, reinforced them a little; nevertheless the infantry troops were not as handsome or as complete as they had been in previous years."*

The *Gardes Suisses* had 12 companies of 200 men (2,400 men) and the newly-created Gardes *Ecossaises* had 30 companies of 150 men (4,500 men).

Arquebus drill. Plate 8 from *Les Exercices militaires* (1635). Jacques Callot (1592-1635). Paris, Musée de l'Armée

82

of a wing etc.). Some regiments, like Cardinal La Valette's fusiliers in 1639, were formed solely of musketeers. The name of these detachments of musketeers evolved towards that used by Turenne (or Ramsay) and Gramont: *"commanded musketeers"*, a term possibly borrowed from the Weimarians. At the surrender of Philippsburg in 1644, *"... the day after the town was seized, Turenne crossed the Rhine with all the German cavalry and five hundred commanded musketeers ..."* and at Nördlingen in 1645, *"...the infantry (of the emperor) stretched in battle array behind the village (of Allerheim), and nearly all the infantry fought to defend the village; but at the beginning it was occupied only by a few commanded musketeers in the church and the bell tower."* In the memoirs of the Comte de Guiche (or Duc de Gramont) we read: *"...The night that had been decided upon for us to march, the Comte de Guiche left with five hundred horses and five hundred commanded musketeers, as many Gardes as other regiments that were in the army"* (1644), and a little further on: *"... the captain still led with the intention of reaching General Mercy, unaware that he had been killed by the first commanded musketeers on the attack of the village ..."* (Allerheim 1645).

In 1642, the *drapeau blanc* regiments, the *vieux corps* and *petits vieux* (*Rambures, Nerestang, Vaubecourt, La Roue, Villandry, Persan, Sault, Couvonges* and *La Meilleraye*) were probably 30 companies 60 men strong. The companies formed battalions of 700 to 900 men, a third of whom were pikemen who were positioned in the centre, and the other two thirds musketeers, positioned on the wings (*les manches*). The *enfants perdus* occupied the threatened flanks. The company's staff was: a captain, a lieutenant, an ensign or sub-lieutenant, all three armed with 10-foot pikes, 2 sergeants armed with halberds, 3 corporals,

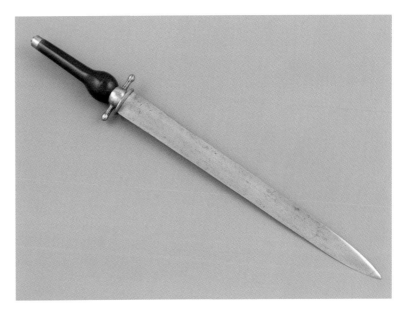

3 anspessades and 1 drummer. The pike measured 14 feet, and the musket, which was lighter, was used more and more without a musket fork. The corporals and anspessades had the armament of the soldiers they commanded. Officers and sergeants were at the front and behind the battalion, the ensigns behind the pikes and the drums on either side of the last row.

In December 1642, Louis XIII created the royal companies, the 30 soldiers of which were called the *Royaux*. These companies were present at the battle of Rocroi.

The *Règlement* of 1633 stipulated fire by rank for the battalion when marching and fire by file when at a standstill. For the latter, the file advanced and passed to the front of the battalion with their wick ignited, then lined up opposite the enemy, fired by file and returned to their point of origin to reload. Fire by rank was simpler: the first row fired then passed behind the other rows to reload. Proportions in 1636 were one pikeman to one musketeer, as we are

Cap bayonnet, 17th century.
Paris, musée de l'Armée

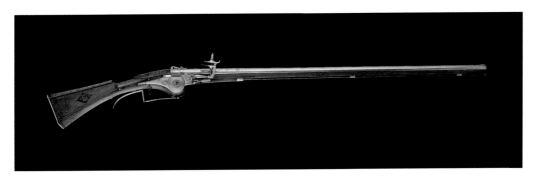

Wheel-lock arquebus, hand crafted by François Poumerol (circa 1580 - circa 1640).
Paris, Musée de l'Armée

told by the Duc de Rohan in his observations of the war in 1636: *"There is no diversity between the companies as there is with the cavalry; they are all the same, with half pikemen and half musketeers."* But in some cases, notably in the newly raised regiments, the proportion of musketeers in a battalion could exceed this figure by up to as much as 60%. It was only in 1653 that a royal *ordonnance* fixed each company at 1/3 pikemen and 2/3 musketeers.

In battle – and this was to be the case for a long time afterwards – fire at point blank range was favoured, followed by a pike charge. Isaac de la Peyrère gives us this description in his account of the Battle of Lens on the 20 August 1648: *"The Gardes Françaises are at the centre in two battalions, supported on the right by the Gardes Suisses, and on the left by the Gardes Ecossaises. The order to hold and endure enemy fire is formal; the musketeers rest their weapon on the fork and wait. All of a sudden, the officers of the Gardes, impatient, raise their hats and cry: "Fire!" A terrible point blank volley fells the first files of the three opposite regiments: one Spanish and two German. The pikemen charge those remaining; the Swiss follow by generous emulation, and a wide opening is made in the middle of the first French line."*

The offensive was also a recurrent characteristic of French behaviour during the Thirty Years' War, as for many periods that followed. Mercy recounts to the Baron Sirot the attack of Enghien's brigades in 1644 (*Persan, Enghien, Conti, Mazarin* regiments) on his solidly entrenched infantry: *"We were entrenched in places that I believed approachable only by the birds; we had covered the entire mountain with tree trunks that we had pushed down the slope; we were fortified in different places and covered by a number of forts. These difficulties did not hinder Enghien*

from ousting us and neither blood nor carnage could stop his impetuosity. He fought like a lion, and the grandeur of the peril only increased his courage. In truth, there is only the French that are able to undertake such things; other nations are not capable, and it requires more than human virtue to succeed in such undertakings." In the same vein, Maréchal de Gramont said of the French soldiers at Philippsburg at the end of 1644: *"The first day the trench was opened, the enemy made a sally on Persan's regiment, somewhat sluggish and with little effect, but nonetheless with a few officers and soldiers killed: which happens often in these situations, especially with the French whose ardour pushes them ever further."*

84

English pikemen officer's armour. Paris, Musée de l'Armée.

Flintlock musket, circa 1630 and 1640. Paris, Musée de l'Armée.

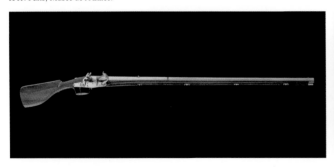

Flintlock musket, between 1615 and 1620. Paris, Musée de l'Armée.

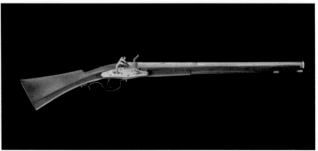

A musketeer, time of Louis XIII,
Ernest Meissonier. By kind
permission of the trustees of The
Wallace Collection, London.

85

The French cavalry from 1635 to 1648

On the 16 May 1635, Richelieu had the king sign an *ordonnance* organising the cavalry into 12 regiments of French cavalry (created from 84 companies), 3 regiments of foreign cavalry and 2 *carabin* regiments (one regiment grouping together the French companies, commanded by *Arnauld de Corbeville* and one regiment grouping

A cavalier, time of Louis XIII, Ernest Meissonier. By kind permission of the trustees of The Wallace Collection, London.

86

together the foreign companies). These seventeen regiments ~ *Canillac, Chaulnes, Cardinal Duc, Enghien, Le Ferron, Guiche, Matignon, La Meilleraye, Nanteuil, Sauveboeuf, Sourdis* and *Treillis* for the French cavalry, *Souvre* (Piedmontais), *Castellan* (Savoyard) and *Gassion* (German) for the foreign cavalry, plus two *carabin* regiments ~ were the first attempt at the creation of a regimented organisation. These regiments were made up of 2 or 3 squadrons of 2 companies. In his writings on the war of 1636 which appears to refer to this period, the Duc de Rohan tells us: *"To form regiments (of cavalry), four or five companies are combined with one carabin regiment, and the eldest captain commands this corps."* In July, 5 new regiments were raised (*Harcourt* and *La Moussaye* ~ both Lotharingian ~ *La Meilleraye, Sirot* and *Espenan* ~ all 3 Hungarian), followed by 3 Liège regiments in September (*Moullard, La Brocquerie* and *Leschelle*).

On the 15 September 1635, non-regimented French companies of less than 25 men were dissolved, and on the 26 October, Bernard of Saxe-Weimar's 16 German regiments passed to the employ of the King of France (*Streef, Eggenfeld, Batilly, Lee, Zillard, Muller, Schack, Tupalden, Rosen, Forbus, Watronville, Vaubecourt* ~ Lorrain -*Nassau* ~ Dutch ~ *Humes* ~Scots ~ *Bouillon* ~ Lorrain ~ *Trefski* ~ Polish). Before this, the cardinal had used the *ordonnance* of 27 May 1635 to add 6 dragoon regiments, made up of *carabin* companies, for reconnoitring and aid; these were *Cardinal, Alègre, Brûlon, Bernieules, Mahé* and *Saint-Rémy*.

However, through opposition from the captains, this first attempt at regimentation failed, and on the 30 July 1636 Richelieu broke the regiments of French cavalry, returning to an organisation in *esquadrons* ("squadrons", which replaced the term *escadres*). In consequence, the *ordonnance* of 31 July 1636 reviewed the recruitment of the French cavalry by replacing the armed service of the nobility (*arrière-ban*) with a tax which allowed the recruitment of paid horsemen, even if they continued to be called *maîtres*. The regiments were replaced by 3-company squadrons: the company comprised a captain, a lieutenant, a *cornette*, a quartermaster, two brigadiers, one trumpet and 48 horsemen ~ a total of 55 men. The light cavalry squadron or the dragoons were

87

Horse musketeer, Jean-Louis
Ernest Meissonier. Faure
museum, Aix les Bains, France.

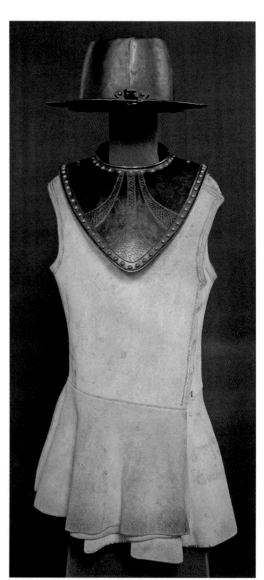

Buff coat, "chapeau d'arme" and throat defence of Chevau-léger, circa 1630-1640. Paris, Musée de l'Armée

88

Armour of a gendarme
of the king's guard.
Paris, Musée de l'Armée.

commanded by the eldest captain and therefore had 12 officers, 6 brigadiers, 3 trumpets and 144 *maîtres*.

The gendarmerie was organized exclusively in companies. The remaining 16 gendarmerie companies in 1643 were recruited from the lower nobility; the king, princes of the royal bloodline and the grand lords were captains. The first four companies, called *Grande Gendarmerie*, each had 1 captain, 1 lieutenant, 1 sub-lieutenant, 1 ensign, 1 guidon, 4 quartermasters, 2 brigadiers, 2 sub-brigadiers, 1 drummer, 2 trumpets and 160 gendarmes, totalling 175 cavaliers. The 12 other companies had the same staff, but the number of *maîtres* depended on the fortune of their captain.

The cardinal did not abandon his first idea and, on the 24 January 1638, ordered the creation of 36 French cavalry regiments, each composed of 8 companies of light cavalry and 1 company of musketeers (*Alais Colonel Général, Aumont, Aubais, Beauregard, Boissac, Canillac, Cardinal Duc, Castellan, Coislin, Crussol, Du Roure, Du Terrail, Des Roches Baritaut, Enghien, Fusiliers à cheval du cardinal, Gesvres, Guiche, Harambures,*

La Chapelle-Baloue, La Ferté-Imbaut, La Ferté-Senneterre, La Luzerne, La Meilleraye, La Valette, Lenoncourt, Lignon, Linars, Merinville, Montbrun Saint-André, Praslin Mestre de camp, Saint-Aignan, Saint-Preuil, Saint-Simon, Treillis, Vatimont, Villeneuve) in addition to the 25 mainly Weimarian foreign cavalry regiments still in service. These 61 cavalry regiments rapidly increased to 70 units, to which were added the non-regimented gendarmerie companies (*La Reine, Monsieur, Monsieur le Prince,* and companies of other princes and maréchals) and the king's Household (the 4 companies of *gardes du corps, gendarmes* and *chevau-légers de la garde,* and the king's musketeers). The *ordonnance* of the 15 May

1638 states that *gendarmerie* companies remained *franches* (non-regimented) and had to serve as the guard to the army general.

In January 1638, the *cardinal* dragoon regiment became the regiment of *Fusiliers à cheval de son Eminence*. The unit was renamed *Fusiliers à cheval du Roy* in the *ordonnance* of 1 August 1643, and became a permanent cavalry regiment on the 16 February 1646, the regiment *du Roy*.

In 1646, Mazarin, who tried unsuccessfully to force the resignation of Treville, captain lieutenant of the king's musketeers (the king himself was the captain), broke up the company of musketeers under the pretext of *"an unnecessary expense"*. It was not until January 1657 that the king re-established this company, which then had 150 musketeers. The second company of musketeers, the former infantry company of the cardinal's *Gardes*, was only mounted on horseback in 1663.

Theoretical numbers (including officers) of cavalry companies varied from 100 men between 1635 and 1637, to 60 men between 1639 and 1642,

70 men in 1643-44, 50 men in 1645-46 and 44 men in 1647-48; however, actual numbers were rarely more than half of this theoretical total. André Corvisier in his *Histoire militaire de la France* estimates that the actual numbers would have been 35 to 38 men between 1636 and 1638, 41 men in 1639-40, 49 men in 1641, 30 men in 1642 and 41 men in 1643. These figures are of course averages, and the reality is even more complex, as shown by this passage from the *Gazette extraordinaire de Picardie no. 58* (1636): Villequier *"promptly called his cavalry and advanced into enemy land with three hundred horses, made up of his own company of one hundred maîtres, commanded by d'Ivran, and those of Barons de Busca, de Painleu, Alincthun, Godinctun and Brunieaubois."* His regiment, *Aumont*, was therefore composed of a company of 100 maîtres and 5 companies of 40 maîtres each. In Flanders, 1641, Maréchal Châtillon's army had 3 regiments of 6 companies and 3 regiments of 4 companies; all these companies had on average 50 horses each. As we can see, few regiments managed to gather together the theoretical 9 companies.

The many reorganisations complicated the

Louis XIII's armour, between 1620 and 1630. Paris, Musée de l'Armée

Spanish spurs, hand crafted circa 1601-1651. Paris, Musée de l'Armée.

of the strength of a company at the end of a campaign! At the battle of Rocroi, the *Cardinal duc* cavalry regiment, whose first captain was François Barton, vicomte de Montbas, had *"400 horses in all, because the remaining equipage and the large distances that we had travelled had exhausted part of my horses, which I divided into two squadrons: 5 companies in mine ~ Hocquincourt, Flavacourt, of which the captain was absent, Freigneville and Esclinvilliers; the other six with d'Estournelle, which I left with de Gassion, who gave the order to charge on the left, which was the side of the Italians and the Walloons."* (François Barton, Vicomte de Montbas, in a letter dated 20 May 1643 which recounts the battle of Rocroi). We can deduce from this that a regiment was formed by two squadrons divided into 11 companies of 36-37 horses each.

situation, and sources sometimes mention squadrons, even after the aborted reorganisation of July 1636 to December 1637; in theory, these squadrons were to have 165 horses. But this appellation was still used by some authors, perhaps in error, into the 40's: in Turenne's memoirs, Ramsay tells us that Rosen's cavalry in 1644 had 8 squadrons for 600 horses, or 75 horsemen per squadron. This figure is in reality close to the theoretical strength of the company and nearly double the actual average numbers. However, in Turin in 1640, Maréchal du Plessis *"keeps only three small squadrons of 20 maîtres each"*, a number reminiscent

The French squadron was 3 to 6 rows deep, while the depth was 6 to 12 rows for the Germans, 5 rows for the Dutch and 3 rows for the Swedes. Light cavalry and gendarmes fought with a sword and pistol.

In combat, many generals favoured the sabre charge, after a preliminary pistol discharge. Gustavus Adolphus' horsemen abandoned the caracole, and Bernard of Saxe-Weimar generalised the full-gallop cavalry charge. Isaac de la Peyrère describes a cavalry action taking place during the battle of Lens, on the 20 August 1648:

Wheel-lock pistols, circa 1635. Paris, Musée de l'Armée.

Chevau léger "capeline". Paris, Musée de l'Armée.

"The prince of Salm advanced at a trot with his first line of Walloon and Lorraine soldiers against Condé's first line, who advanced at a walk to receive them. The two lines met horse to horse, pistol to pistol, and remained in this position for a fairly long time, awaiting who would fire first, with neither side wavering.

The enemy was more impatient and opened fire; it was as though the gates of Hell had opened! All our front line officers were killed, injured or dismounted. Condé gave the signal to fire, then, with his sword held high at the head of the Gassion regiment, he crushed the squadron facing him. His other six squadrons followed him, and, on his example, charged the first enemy line so violently that it was overwhelmed."

However, once the battle was underway, a charge without preliminary fire was preferred. Isaac de la Peyrère describes another episode of the battle of Lens: "One of our squadrons, ascending by the most precipitous part of the hill, was fought off by an enemy squadron, which in return attacked Persan's battalion next to it. La Ferté-Senneterre, who had just beaten a Spanish cavalry regiment, charged this squadron with so much vigour that he forced them to flee, and pushed it into the main part of the enemy troop, where it added chaos to disorder." Then a little further: "Gramont was so valiant and so happy throughout the battle that his wing was not even weakened. He defeated all he charged ..."

The cavalry could transport infantry in "commando" operations. After the battle of Lens in 1648, a hundred horsemen from the *Chappes* regiment went ahead, with a hundred musketeers riding behind them to *"work the bridges"*.

The light cavalry protected themselves with a cuirasse worn on the buff jerkin, or a buff

Chevau léger or carabin "bourguignotte", circa 1620-1630. Paris, Musée de l'Armée.

Wheel-lock carbine, circa 1640.
Jean Launoy (1582?-1652)
French arquebus maker.
Paris, Musée de l'Armée

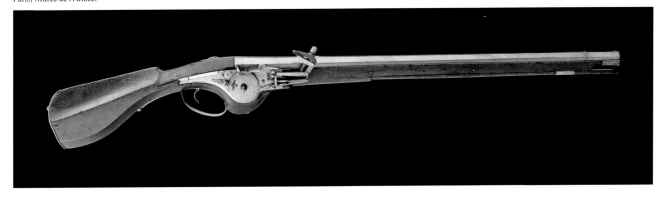

jerkin only, leather boots, and a helmet, now mainly of the capeline type, although the wide-brimmed hat often replaced the capeline. The army museum has an *"iron hat"* in the shape of a musketeer hat, which appears to have been particularly appreciated by the French cavalry. In his letter of 20 May 1643 recounting the battle of Rocroi, François Barton, Vicomte de Montbas and first captain of the *Cardinal duc* cavalry regiment, says that some officers had the habit of covering their armour with a cassock: *"They did not think I was armoured, although I was indeed fully so, because of a small cassock that covered my armour with my scarf on top."* And of course, this captain wore an "iron hat": *"The Liégeois gave me such a stroke of the sword that he made my helmet fall."*

The gendarmerie still appears to have been heavily equipped in some representations (in particular a contemporary engraving representing the battle of Rocroi), but in reality their equipment had lightened over time. The army museum has armour from the end of the reign of Louis XIII, which comprises a "salade" helmet, a cuirasse, doublet, and "brassats", while the legs were protected by boots alone. Another suit of armour from the army museum which belonged to a horseman from the king's Household is fuller: it comprises an iron hat, doublet, leg armour, a neck piece, brassats, and gauntlets, to use the terms of Jean de Billon. An anonymous embossment of Louis XIII at the storming of Corbie in 1636 (National Library) shows us a company of gendarmes from the king's Household wearing cuirasse, doublet and "brassats", but sporting a superb feathered hat rather than a visored helmet.

Chevau léger dummy,
circa 1640-1650.
Paris, Musée de l'Armée

P. 93 :
French chevau léger
circa 1635-1645.
Painting by Suzanne Dana.

92

Artillery from 1635 to 1648

Plate with various artillery equipment. TAB. IX von der Artillerie, 17th century. Paris, Musée de l'Armée

There were 17 types of cannon, from the basilisk with a cannonball weighing 48 pounds, to the *émerillon,* which shot a 1/4 pound ball (see the main types in the previous chapter). Heavy or campaign cannons were divided into brigades under the command of an artillery commissioner, seconded by the ordinary and extraordinary com-

missioners and firing officers. The *light brigades* were equipped with campaign weapons that could fire 25 or 30 shots. The *heavy brigades,* equipped with battery cannons, were used for sieges, and the attack and defence of entrenched positions. This brigade had the ammunition, siege equipment, gunpowder, cannonballs and infantry wicks; this was the *reserve equipment* and an infantry escort was given to each brigade. The Swiss had had the privilege of guarding the artillery since the time of François 1st, but this was less and less the case under Louis XIII.

From 1635, the French artillery followed closely the developments of its European cousins. In emulation of the infantry, which adopted a few

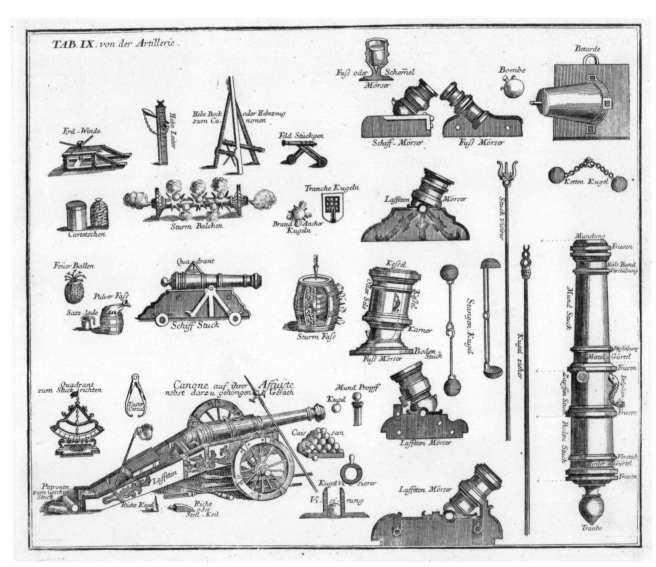

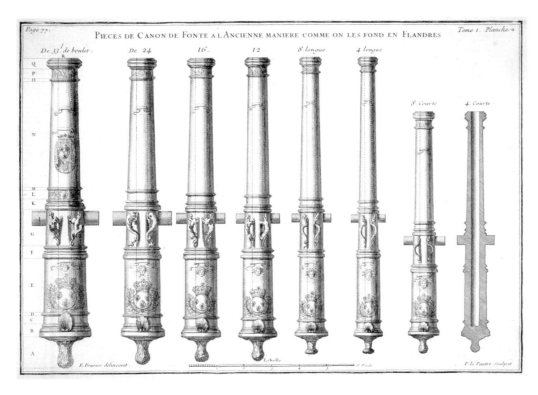

Cast-iron cannon cast in Flanders. Engraved by Pierre Lepautre (1660-1744) from a drawing by Edme Fourier, 1697. Paris, Musée de l'Armée. Author: Fourier Edme (17th century) (after) Architect, draughtsman, Lepautre Pierre (1660-1744) Sculptor, draughtsman, engraver. 1697.

light cannons following the Swedish example, the artillery adopted the exploding shell projected by a *Hauwitzer*, a German term which became *obusier* in French. This technique was probably first used by the English at the siege of La Mothe in 1634.

The French used less artillery on the battlefield than the Swedish and the imperialists. Range was generally 1,500 paces for the "ball" (cannonball), and 300 to 400 paces for the "rounds" (for volley fire). French cannoneers were less skilled than their Spanish, imperial or Swedish counterparts, as noted by the Baron de Sirot at the beginning of the Battle of Rocroi: *"The town was behind them within range of cannon fire, and the two armies were only at a distance of two musket ranges from each other, and they remained thus for the entire day; but this was not without large skirmishes, and the cannon made much noise on all sides. Nevertheless, that of the enemy caused much more damage to our army than they received from us; for, besides the fact that it was better placed, it was also much better used, and their cannoneers were more expert and more skilful than ours (...)"* This was the reason why foreign cannoneers were used wherever possible, especially soldiers from Liège.

Cannon drill: preparation. Plate 10 from *Les Exercices militaires* (1635), Jacques Callot (1592-1635). Paris, Musée de l'Armée.

Cannon drill: the shot. Plate 12 from *Les Exercices militaires* (1635), Jacques Callot (1592-1635). Paris, Musée de l'Armée.

Command

From 1636, experience improved the efficiency of high command, in particular via the limited nomination of army commanders. But jealousies and dissensions between maréchals remained a necessary evil. Maréchal du Plessis Praslin recounts this anecdote, which took place in 1639: *"At the time the Comte d'Harcourt was chosen to command the army of Italy; and as he passed through Grenoble to reach there, Cardinal Richelieu told him that he should do nothing of importance without the counsel of Comte de Plessis beforehand, to whom this honour gave much disquiet: he told Cardinal Richelieu that this favour would attract much jealousy from the other field marshals of the army, Maréchal de Turenne and Maréchal de La Mothe-Houdencourt who, having much merit, would not tolerate Comte de Plessis appearing to have more credit than themselves in the army. To which Richelieu replied that they were too honest to be jealous and that this should not cause him difficulties."*

Rapid army growth also allowed the accelerated promotion of talented officers, and resulted in the creation of a military academy in 1636. In 1642 there were 12 maréchals: Bassompierre, Brézé, Châtillon, La Force, Guébriant, Guiche (who became Gramont at the end of 1644), du Hallier-L'Hôpital, Harcourt, La Meilleraye, La Mothe-Houdencourt, Schomberg and Vitry. However, at the time, the maréchals still fought most often in the front line, at the head of their corps; in order to be recognised, the French maréchals always wore a white scarf, as in the times of Henri IV. This is confirmed by Maréchal de Gramont in his memoirs: *"During the siege (the siege of Arras in 1640), which was one of the best of the entire war, the Comte de Guiche was extremely favoured by fortune; it was he who took the demilune, so valiantly defended by the reformed Spanish officers against the attack of Maréchal de Châtillon, and who broke the large and formidable squadron of the Comte Bucquoy in the battle of Bapaume, which most of our troops did not dare attack; he charged with his regiment, and broke it, but without defeating it. There were many men killed in this first charge, in which the Comte de Guiche himself was hit 3 times, and as they were embroiled with each other for a long period of time, he found himself enveloped and swept up into the enemy squadron when he performed his caracole to regroup and charge. It is at this point that the Comte de Guiche was saved by his presence of mind, discreetly allowing his white scarf to fall so as not to be recognised; he put himself on the first row and charged towards his own regiment, which had reformed at the same time as the enemy; and Rouville, who was in command and recognized him, distinguished him from the enemy and then fought them so well that all were killed or taken".*

It was during this period that a new generation of great leaders appeared, following in the footsteps of the Duc de Rohan who died in 1638: Harcourt, Guébriant, Condé and Turenne distinguished themselves most particularly. For Henri de la Tour d'Auvergne, Vicomte de Turenne, the Thirty Years' War would only be the beginning of a long and successful military career.

P. 96 :
Portrait of a man, rear view.
From a 17th century Dutch master.
Pierre Poterlet (1804-1881). Paris,
Eugène Delacroix museum.

P. 97 :
Cavalier twirling moustache
(1880). Jean-Louis Ernest
Meissonier (1815-1891). Paris,
Orsay museum.

Louis II de Bourbon ("le Grand Condé" 1621-1686), in front of a scene from the Rocroi battle. From Justus Van Egmont (1601-1674). Versailles, châteaux de Versailles and Trianon

98

Louis II de Bourbon, Duc d'Enghien, who became Prince de Condé on the death of his father on the 26 December 1646, was one of the rare French generals who remained unbeaten. Even if his role in the Rocroi victory is today questioned (see the excellent analysis by Gerrer, Petit and Sanchez Martin in *Rocroy 1643, vérités et controverses sur une bataille de légende*), the fact remains that the "Grand Condé" was an excellent tactician, and above all a charismatic, courageous, even impetuous general. Maréchal Gramont paints these two last traits for us in his memoirs, with this anecdote which took place near Llerida in 1646: *"(The enemies) realising that most of the troops had hastily stationed themselves on the high ground, and that only five squadrons remained with Maréchal Gramont on the plain, the Marquis d'Aytonne, at the head of twenty two squadrons, charged him at a canter. Maréchal Gramont, having no other choice than to fight with the few men he had, sounded the charge and marched straight towards them; for withdrawing on a flat and open plain with the enemy so close would mean certain defeat; a quarter turn to rejoin the Prince de Condé was not a safer option; and when they were one hundred paces from each other, the Marquis d'Aytonne stopped dead; which gave extreme joy to Maréchal de Gramont, who also stopped, and*

he immediately fired four small cannon that he had just received against the Marquis d'Aytonne; which blocked him all the more. The Prince de Condé, seeing great danger in which Maréchal de Gramont found himself from the high ground where he was positioned, did something worthy of his stout heart and his great courage: he left his troops, alone and accompanied by a page, and went at full gallop to rejoin Maréchal de Gramont, embraced him warmly and told him that he wished to fight alongside him, and to share the imminent danger". But this anecdote should not let us forget the other great qualities of the Prince: he was an exceptional leader of men, who knew instinctively how to make necessary decisions. None is more convinced of this than Maréchal de Gramont who, speaking of the 19 August 1648, the day before the Battle of Lens, exclaims: *"And it was indeed his presence of mind and this perfect knowledge he had of men which put him always above the others in the most perilous and the greatest occasions; for everything he had to do came to him in an instant. Such men are a rare genius of warfare, a species of which there are only one in a hundred thousand."*

Through his four great battles – Rocroi, Freiburg, Allerheim and Lens (accounts of these four battles are included in the appendix) – we are able to perceive a relatively standard system of battle: a frontal attack of the main body at the centre to fix the enemy line, defended by the two wings of the cavalry; it was the stronger of these two wings, led by the great Condé himself, that was to break through. The objective was to decide the articulation of this wing and the infantry.

Henri de la Tour d'Auvergne, Comte de Turenne, became one of the greatest generals of his time through his qualities of leadership and strategy. He knew perfectly how to apply the principles of war: well-trained and well-maintained troops; a detailed analysis of the conditions and the environment; caution before action but promptitude once the decision had been made. And as a grand general should, he also knew how to recognize his errors, especially that of Marienthal in 1645.

In his memoirs, the Baron de Sirot relates this scene that precedes the battle of Freiburg (on the 3 August 1644) and which highlights the differences of character between Condé and Turenne:

"We held a council of war to discuss what should be our course of action on this occasion. There were many opinions; but after long discussion, we followed only two. The Duc d'Enghien wished to attack the enemy head on; it was the strongest place and the most dangerous and, despite the remonstrations made on this point, he refused to change his mind. Turenne tried hard to make him realise the peril of the attack he wished to undertake, and that he ran the risk of losing all his troops:

'Very well', he said, 'Keep yours, I shall fight with mine; I did not come here to be a spectator of imperial conquests!'

'Because you so wish', said Turenne, 'I shall fight in the mountains; but allow me to attempt to win the enemy rear, to divert their forces and so that they do not all fall on us at the same time."

But who better placed than Napoleon to praise the qualities and demonstrate the weaknesses of these two grand generals? In his *Précis des guerres du maréchal de Turenne*, Napoleon reproaches Condé for his impetuosity at Freiburg: *"The Prince de Condé violated one of the principles of mountain warfare: never attack troops occupying good positions in the mountains, but flush them out by occupying camps on their flanks or their rear,"* and in his *Mémorial de Sainte-Hélène* he also reproaches him for *"having behaved as a soldier rather than as a general, by attacking the front of well positioned troops in mountainous country ...."* Napoleon also condemns Condé's choice at Nördlingen in 1645: *"The Prince de Condé was wrong to attack Mercy in his camp, with an army nearly completely composed of cavalry and having so little artillery; the attack of the village of Allerheim was a grand affair."* But further on he concedes that *"Condé deserved victory by this obstinacy, this rare intrepidity that distinguished him for, even if this trait did not serve him well in the attack of Allerheim, it is this that advised him, after having lost the centre and the right, to recommence the battle with the left, the only troop left to him; for it is he who directed all movements of this wing, and it is he to whom glory should be given."*

On the other hand, he approved of Turenne's manœuvre after Freiburg: *"The conduct of Turenne, after the departure of the prince de Condé, was skilful; it is true that he was much aided by the terrain. The armies of Bavaria and Lorraine were separated by the Rhine and mountains; their junction was difficult."* Then, evoking the campaign of 1645, he writes: *"Turenne, with his army, was cornered below Philippsburg by a very large army; he found no bridge over the Rhine, but made use of the terrain between the river and the town to establish his camp. This should be a lesson for engineers, not only for the construction of strongholds, but also for the construction of bridgeheads ..."* Napoleon becomes even more admiring when he talks about the campaign of 1646: *"Turenne's march along the left bank of the Rhine is worthy of him. His march along the Danube and the Lech to take war to Bavaria, thus making use of the ruses of the Archduke was full of audacity and wisdom (...) The manœuvres to remove the archduke from his camp between Memmingen and Landsberg were full of audacity, wisdom and genius, producing excellent results. The military should study them."* That same year, Turenne and Wrangel put a screen of 2,000 horsemen in front of the army of the Archduke to mask their march to Landsberg. Concluding with the campaign of 1648, Napoleon could not speak more highly of Turenne: *"Turenne is the first French general to have planted the national colours on the banks of the Inn. In this campaign, and in that of 1646, he travelled Germany in all directions, with a mobility and hardiness that contrast with the way in which war has been conducted since. This stems from his skilfulness, and the sound principles of warfare of this school ..."*

Equestrian portrait of Henri de la Tour d'Auvergne (1611-75) Marshal Turenne. Adam Frans van der Meulen (1632-1690). Pushkin museum, Moscow.

The Swedish influence

In 1636, with the integration of the regiments of Bernard of Saxe-Weimar, Rantzau and Gassion, Swedish tactical influence transformed the French army.

King Gustavus Adolphus reorganised the Swedish army at the beginning of the seventeenth century. Not only did he set up a modern organisation based on conscription and the creation of regional regiments, but he was also at the origin of many tactical and technical developments. In 1634, the Swedes had 12 regional infantry regiments and 5 cavalry regiments.

The Swedish infantry was recruited on the basis of compulsory conscription for a 3-year period, an early "military service" affecting a portion of men aged 18 to 20. The Swedish infantry regiment had 8 companies of 142 men: 16 officers and sub-officers (1 captain, 1 lieutenant, 1 ensign, 3 sergeants, 1 standard bearer, 1 harbinger, 1 clerk, 3 drummers and 4 valets) and 126 soldiers (54 pikemen and 72 musketeers) divided into 6 squads (sections), 2 pike and 4 musket, arranged in 6 rows with the pikemen in the centre under the command of the captain and the ensign, and the musketeers on the wings, commanded by the lieutenant on the right and the sergeant-major on the left. A regiment was therefore made up of approximately 1,200 men (theoretically 1,160 men including the general staff). The regiment was the administrative and command unit but, on campaign, the companies were organised into two "squadrons" (battalions) of 4 companies or more totalling 568 men (504 soldiers and 64 officers/sub-officers). Although in theory these battalions had 4 companies, in reality the companies had less than 100 men, and an average of 6 companies was needed to make up a unit of this size. In September 1631, just before the battle of Breitenfeld, the Swedish army had 212 companies in 27 regiments. The number of companies per regiment varied from 4 to 12, with an average a little under 8 companies per regiment. These 212 companies totalled 18,346 men, i.e. 87 men per company, with 3,670 officers and sub-officers (20%), 4,578 pikemen (25%) and 10,098 musketeers (55%). The colonel was at the centre with his company and the *colonelle* company led the regiment. On campaign, squadrons were regrouped into permanent brigades, commanded by a brigadier; a brigade such as this had two squadrons up until Breitenfeld, but three at Lützen. The brigades were identified by the colour of their flag; the yellow and blue brigades particularly excelled themselves at Lützen in 1632. The Swedish infantry used *feu de chaussée* ~ salvo fire ~ by squad, section or company; the average range of fire was 200 feet (65 metres). When marching, the infantry was arranged in squads of 4 men abreast, or sections of two squads with 8 men abreast and the musketeers in front of the pikemen. The Swedish infantry also had Gustavus Adolphus to thank for the reduction in weight of the musket, the suppression of the fork, the *chenapan* (snaphaunce) lockplate (with a flint replacing the wick), rounds of shot which replaced the powder charges, and ready-loaded weapons, increasing firepower by up to three or four times; this was also true of the shot-pouch.

Ever since it replaced the lance by the pistol, the German cavalry formed in 8-row deep masses which supported the infantry with firepower, without drawing swords. Gustav Adolphus used the Swedish cavalry for impact: it charged at a trot from 50 or 60 metres from the enemy formation, then, when within a dozen metres, increased speed to charge at a gallop; the first rows fired their pistols at very short range (less than 5 metres). A regiment was made up of 8 companies, 1,000 horses, and theoretically 125 men including 13 officers and sub-officers. On campaign, the tactical formation was the cavalry squadron, which grouped together 2 or 3 companies arrayed 3 rows deep. At the beginning of the action, the Swedish cavalry was protected by platoons of 50 to 200 musketeers who were interspersed between the squadrons.

Above all else, Gustavus Adolphus changed the art of war by developing inter-arm tactics, in which the campaign artillery, the infantry and the cavalry provided each other with mutual support and defence. His army adopted a small iron cannon, 4 feet long and weighing only 625 pounds including the carriage, which fired 3-pound cannonballs. This cannon, which was loaded rapidly with a round like the musket, followed the brigade and was pulled using cords attached to the axles. Gustavus Adolphus focused on simplifying his artillery and retained just 3 calibres: the 24-pound, 12-pound and 3-pound cannons, operated by 2 men. The artillery was organised in a regimental structure made up of a number of companies: 1 company grouping together the regimental 3-pound cannons (in theory 2 per regiment); 3 companies including the 24- and 12-pound heavy artillery, 1 company of sappers and 1 company of workers. In 1630, this artillery "regiment" had around 1,200 men; Wallenstein's artillery never had more than 80 cannon, and Tilly's never more than 30, but Gustavus Adolphus' artillery regularly exceeded 100 cannon, distributed mainly between the infantry brigades.

Portrait of Jean, Comte de Gassion (1609-1647), Maréchal de France. Jean Alaux, ("Le Romain", 1786-1864). Versailles, châteaux de Versailles and Trianon

On campaign

From 1635, a French army on campaign was hardly larger than at the beginning of the century ~ rarely exceeding 30,000 men ~ but the cavalry rapidly accounted for a larger share. Rarely exceeding 20% until 1638 ~ except for the army of Condé in 1636 which had a total of 20,000 infantry and 8,000 horses ~ the cavalry frequently represented 20 to 30% between 1639 and 1643, in some cases reaching 45 to 50% in 1644 and 1645, then returning to around 28% in 1646. Army numbers diminished rapidly as the campaign progressed, with losses, illness and desertions all taking their toll, but also because garrisons had to be left in towns. This represented a few hundred men each time, as occurred during Turenne's campaign of 1644, where 200 to 300 men were left in Worms and nearly 400 men in Mentz, while the Bavarians had nearly 700 men in Philippsburg. Sieges immobilised many thousands of men; Turenne left a corps of 2,000 in Philippsburg in 1644. At the beginning of the 1644 campaign, Turenne's army had 6,000 infantry and 3 or 4,000 horses; there remained a little under 1,500 infantry and less than 4,000 horses at the beginning of 1645 before the arrival of the 6,000-strong Hessian reinforcements. Regiment numbers dwindled rapidly, as Turenne illustrates in his memoirs before the battle of Freiburg in 1644: *"(Turenne) ordered the regiments of Montausier and Mezieres, which made a Battalion of a thousand men..."*

As for the previous period, *ordonnances* show the difficulties encountered in recruiting soldiers. Compliance with the specifications and instructions of the 1629 *ordonnance*, extensively covered in previous chapters, became much more difficult with the war. Volunteers stayed only the minimum 3 months, and desertions remained a blight on the armies beyond the Rhine and the mountains, especially as the number of musters decreased from 8 musters of 45 days in 1634, to 6 musters of 45 days in 1636 ~ another reason for the increase in devas-

tations and other miseries of the war. The soldiers continued to live off the land and to extort money from the towns, when they did not simply destroy it totally. Turenne's Weimarians even mutinied in 1647, as he recounts in his memoirs: *"(...) Mr de Turenne had orders to march into Flanders; he had plainly foreseen that the German cavalry would hardly be persuaded to follow him, because there was five or six months pay due to them. This he had represented to the court, which not being in a condition to give any considerable sum, promised only one month's pay, and even this, because of the difficulty the merchants made of accepting the bills of exchange, was not ready at the time the army was to march. In order to remedy this evil, Mr de Turenne sent the cavalry into good quarters, divided the whole country among them, treated them in the best manner he could, and marched with the French infantry to take Hoeft and Stanheim, and other small places, which secured his conquests along the Rhine. (...) None of the German horse passed but the regiment of Turenne: the old regiment of Rosen having presently sent to the other German regiments, they all joined it in two hours. The next day, the chief officers of the army came to Mr de Turenne and demanded all the pay that was due. He gave them to understand that it was impossible for them to have any money before the opening of the campaign; but if they would march, he promised them to get full assurance from the court for their complete payment. They returned with this answer. (...) When Mr Rosen and Mr Tracy came to the cavalry, those of the officers who had been the most intimate with Mr Rosen remonstrated to him that the affair was come to that pass that there was no accommodation to be hoped; and that if he did not resolve to put himself at their head, they would choose another, and so he would remain amongst the French without being in any consideration. Mr Rosen determined to stay with them, alleging that the troops kept him by force (...)"* In the end, Turenne charged the mutinied regiments with his cavalry.

One of the ways to increase the number of soldiers was to increase the recruitment of foreign mercenaries ~ German, Swiss, Italian, Scottish, Irish, Swedish, Hungarian and Croatian. But at their side, who were these Frenchmen who enlisted into the armies of the king, either willingly or under duress?

P. 103 :
The great Condé, battle of Lens,
August 20th, 1648, victory over
the Spanish commanded by
Archduke Leopold circa 1835
(detail). Jean-Pierre Franque
(1744-1860). Versailles, châteaux
de Versailles and Trianon

P. 104-105 :
Inn scene, Henry Graves
(1846-1881), private collection.

According to a study carried out by R. Caboche on a sample of 1,429 invalid soldiers in 1648, most soldiers came from the northern half of France. One out of 10 was from Normandy, and another tenth were from Champagne. Picardy represented a little over 9%, as did the inhabitants of the Ile de France. These were followed by Burgundy and Aquitaine, with 7.5 to 8%. The Languedoc and Cévennes represented a little under 6% of the numbers, and Limousin and Charente a little over 5%, followed by Touraine, Anjou Maine, Lorraine, the Dioceses, Auvergne, and the Dauphiné, each representing between 3 and 4% of enlistments. Brittany and Quercy came next, with a little over 2.5% each, then the Forez Lyonnais, Provence and the Centre with 2 to 2.5% per region. Finally, Alsace and Franche-Comté each accounted for less than 1% of the total. Foreigners represented 20% of soldiers in the study, among which recruits from the empire – nearly 40% of foreigners – were the majority. For the rest, a little over a quarter of foreigners were Swiss, a little less than 1/10th were Irish and a little under 1/20th were Italian.

City dwellers were over-represented at more than 50%, at a time when 85% of the population lived in the country. 24% of enlistments were under 20 years old, 61% were between 21 and 30, and 15% were older than 30. The cavalry was mostly represented by tall men, mainly from the East or the countryside.

These recruits were not better trained than before the war. The main preoccupation of many captains at the time (happily not all!) was to obtain the bonus for reaching a target number of recruits, no matter where or how these soldiers had been recruited, and regardless of their aptitude. Until they attained this bonus the recruits would be taken care of, but then the captain would lose interest, leading to the abovementioned conduct. And yet, although these French soldiers had a poor reputation, it was they who were to be the artisans of the many victories of this war. Thus lived and died the soldier of Rocroi and Lens.

On campaign, the troops had of course to be fed, and the musters rarely provided for this. At the beginning of the campaign all went well, as for the army of Turenne at the beginning of the campaign of 1644: *"Alsace being too much ruined, in the month of January he entered the mountains of Lorraine, where he put the Army into quarters: he enlarged them afterwards, by the taking of two small places, called Luxuel and Vesoul in Franche-Comté, where he left three or four regiments. At the same time some money was received from the court, with which, and the help of the quarters, the army, that is to say the cavalry, was put in a good condition; but as for the infantry, it was a very hard matter to complete them again during the winter."* A little further on he gives a few more details: *"The king's army lay that night in the hills without advancing as all that were left of the infantry were accustomed to receive their*

L'Arquebusade, plate 12 from *The Miseries and Misfortunes of War* (1633), engraved by Israel Henriet (c.1590-1661), Jacques Callot (1592-1635). Grosjean collection, Paris, France.

Ceux qui pour obeir a leur mauuais Genie
Manquent a leur deuoir, vsent de tyrannie ,

Ne se plaisent qu'au mal violent la raison ;
Et sont les actions pleines de trahison

Produisent dans le Camp mil sanglans vacarmes
Sont ainsi chastiez, et passez par les armes   12.

bread, and not to shift for it, like the old troops that have served long in Germany, it was not possible to follow the enemy into the country of Wurtemberg." We see the same situation at the beginning of the 1645 campaign, with the troops ready to march: "Mr de Turenne thought fit not to go to court during the winter, that he might be in a condition to take the field the sooner; and the cardinal having approved of it, he staid at Spires: from thence he sent to desire Mr de la Ferté, governor of Lorraine, to pay the troops with all expedition their winter quarters. Mr de la Ferté did it most punctually in all the places of his government, and ordered three months pay to be given them. Thus the cavalry, amounting to five thousand, and the infantry to five or six thousand, with twelve or sixteen pieces of cannon, about the end of the month of March were ready to repass the Rhine, upon a bridge of boats that was made at Spire."

However, after a few weeks, they had to forage for food, as illustrated by this event that occurred in 1648 just before the Peace of Westphalia: "The corn being ripe, the infantry fell to threshing it, while the cavalry went foraging; so that there was no want among the troops. We remained four weeks in the camp, the enemy being very near, and the guards in fight of each other all the while; so that there were frequent actions on occasion of the convoys of the forage, and by the excursions of parties." (Ramsay, Histoire de Henri de la Tour d'Auvergne vicomte de Turenne). Naturally, these resources were inexistent in a ravaged area, as Ramsay tells us when describing Mercy's army at the end of 1644: "The Bavarian army were always afraid of passing the Rhine, and of being undone for want of forage and provisions, which was so great, that from Philipsburg to Mentz on this side of the Rhine, there was nothing sowed, and nothing for horses to eat but in the towns." Turenne therefore takes the following measures for his own army: "Mr de Turenne finding that there was no danger of the Bavarian army's passing the Rhine, and that all his cavalry was perishing for want of forage, kept only three or four regiments of cavalry, without baggage, which he put into the towns, and furnished them with straw, but very little oats, and sent away all the rest of his cavalry into the hills of Lorraine, having written to court that directions might be given to provide them with winter-quarters in that country, and in the Bishopricks of Metz, Toul,

and Verdun, keeping all the infantry with him in Germany, and leaving a body of two thousand men under Philippsburg, until he should know that the Bavarian Army was separated, which was not till the month of December." In winter, not only did food and animal fodder have to be provided, but also equipment; Turenne did so in February 1648, which required "(...) ten days for repairing the artillery, sent into Switzerland for horses, in the month of February returned to Mentz, where he repassed the Rhine, and marched into Franconia to join the Swedes, although he was eight days during this march, scarce finding in this way straw for the horses. As for the infantry, because the winter was very severe, he ordered cloaks to be made for them. When he got on the other side of the Rhine, he found his strength consisted of four thousand infantry, four thousand horses, and twenty pieces of cannon, with twelve or fifteen conquered towns in very good condition." This need for supplies could put the army in a delicate situation, as Turenne learnt to his expense when he lost a part of his army at Mergentheim at the beginning of May 1645: "To speak the truth, Mr de Turenne's too easy compliance that the cavalry might not suffer for want of forage, his great desire that they might quickly put themselves in a good condition, several of the officers promising to buy horses in their quarters for their dismounted men, and likewise the distance from the enemy, who were near ten leagues from thence, the parties reporting that they were separated, made him unadvisedly resolve to send them into little close places."

A marching army was divided into three corps: the advanced guard, the main body, and the rear guard. In principle, marching troops maintained 40 paces between the squadrons and 25 paces between the battalions. In battle, the arrangement of a vast army on the battlefield and its first engagement were critical phases. The units took their positions. In his Histoire des Princes de Condé, the Duc d'Aumale gives us the Battle Array of the Infantry at Rocroi: "The right wing of the main body: Picardie, on the right wing. La Marine, after, shall double on its left, on the same line, at 170 paces. Persan, after, and shall double as above. The first battalion of Molondin shall march after and shall double as above. The second battalion of Molondin shall march after and shall double as above. Vervins and La Prée shall march after, and shall remain under Picardie and La Marine, at 300 paces in the second line. Vidame shall march at the rear of Vervins and shall double on the left at 170 paces. The first battalion of Watteville shall march after Vidame and shall double on the left at 170 paces. The Gardes Ecossais shall array for battle to the left of Watteville.

The left wing: Piémont shall march on the left wing. Rambures shall follow after and shall double on the right at 170 paces on the same front. Bourdonné and Biscaras shall march after and shall double as above. Bussy and Guiche shall remain in battle array at 300 paces below the interval of Piémont and Rambures, in the second line. Brézé and Langerons shall double on the right of Bussy and Guiche, at 170 paces. Roll shall march after Brézé and shall double on the right at 170 paces.

Reserve corps: Harcourt, Aubeterre and Gesvres shall march at the head of the reserve corps and shall remain in battle array at 400 paces below the interval of Vidame and the first battalion of Watteville. Second battalion of Watteville shall march after, and shall double on their left at 300 paces to support the first battalion. The Royaux shall march after and shall double on the left at a same distance."

To complete the picture, the cavalry of the Duc d'Enghien was arranged as thus: on the right wing under Gassion, 15 squadrons in 2 lines, 10 in the first line and 5 in the second line, with musketeer *manches* in the intervals; on the left wing, 13 squadrons on two lines, 8 in the first line and 5 in the second line, commanded by La Ferté-Senneterre, and also with musketeer *manches* in the intervals.

The battle marshal, an office that appeared just before the battle of Rocroi, was in charge of the battle array and the combat formation of the army during the battle. He was aided in this task by battle sergeants. Just before the battle of Lens, on the 20 August 1648, they had to keep a scrupulous eye on the alignments, while reminding the deployed units of their orders, as illustrated by the Duc de Gramont's instructions in his memoirs: "In the evening, we halted the battle array, and we gave three most important recommendations to all the troops: the first, to watch each other as they marched, so that the cavalry and the infantry would remain on the same line, and so that they could keep their distances and intervals; the second, to charge only at a walking pace; the third, to allow the enemy to fire

first". Then the generals galvanised their troops, as did Maréchal de Gramont at the battle of Lens in epic style: "Maréchal de Gramont left the Prince de Condé and returned to his wing; and passing to the head of the troops, he told them that battle had just been decided; he asked them to remember their valour and what they owed the king, and also to observe well the orders they had been given; he said that this action was of such importance given the current state of affairs, that it was either victory or death, and that he was going to show them the example by entering first into the enemy squadron that would be opposite his own. This short and moving speech was infinitely pleasing to the soldiers; all the infantry shouted for joy and threw their hats in the air; the cavalry took their sword in hand and all the trumpets sounded fanfares with an inexpressible joy. The Prince de Condé and Maréchal de Gramont embraced warmly, and each thought of their own business."

The battle itself progressed in a succession of charges and counter charges, the battalions and squadrons supporting each other. La Peyrère, in his account of the battle of Lens, describes such an engagement: "It was around eight o'clock in the morning when the army began to march in excellent array to the sound of trumpets, drums and cannons. The prince called a halt from time to time to redress the lines and to maintain distances and, the cannon of the Comte de Cossé was so well and so diligently used that it fired while marching, which is a significant feat; they had the advantage that, by firing from the plain onto the hillock of the enemy position, all shots reached either the squadrons, or the battalions, and created great confusion for them to array themselves for battle. Their cannon, which fired from the top of the hill to the foot, did not have the same effect as ours, although the numbers were unequal, with the Archduke having 38 and the Prince 18.

The enemy was impatient to fight; they looked brave and marched resolutely towards us. However they were attempting two things at the same time, marching and arraying for combat, which is a hindrance when marching to a decisive battle (...)

The two armies were at 30 paces from each other when three shots were fired from the left wing of the enemy into our right wing. Condé, who feared the precipitation of his soldiers, halted them and forbade the musketeers from opening fire before the enemy had fired; fire should not begin until at point-blank range. This halt had three good effects; it tempered the ardour of our troops, readjusted the battle array and confirmed the soldier in the resolution to withstand the enemy discharge.

The prince of Salm advanced at a trot with his first line of Walloon and Lorraine soldiers against Condé's first line, who advanced at a walk to receive them. The two lines met horse to horse, pistol to pistol, and remained in this position for a fairly long time, awaiting who would fire first, with neither side wavering.

The enemy was more impatient and opened fire; it was as though the gates of Hell had opened! All our front line officers were killed, injured or unseated. Condé gave the signal to fire, then, leading the Gassion regiment with his sword held high, he crushed the squadron facing him.

His six other squadrons followed him, and, on his example, charged the first enemy line so violently that it was overwhelmed."

The Duc d'Enghien attempted to hold the fire of his regiments until the last moment, well below 30 paces. It would appear from various accounts that 50 paces was the "security" distance for the two enemy armies. An army wishing to put itself out of range withdrew to more than 40 paces, as Mercy's Bavarians did in 1644: *"The Bavarian lost a great many men, and retired about forty or fifty paces from our infantry, having all their cavalry, and a body of infantry of the second line, to sustain them. The two armies continued thus facing one another, the Bavarians not daring to come to a close engagement again with those regiments that were ready to receive them with their pikes, and the French not daring to enter further into the plain, having no*

Horsemen in a military camp.
Philips Wouverman (1619-1668).
Paris, Louvre Museum.

109

Riders watering their horses.
Philips Wouverman (1619-1668).
Paris, Louvre Museum.

110

cavalry to sustain them." And a little later that day: "The night did not put an end to the fight, but the troops on both sides remained for seven hours continually firing at the distance of forty paces till it was day." (Attributed to La Moussaye, in Turenne's Memoirs).

However, sometimes the battleground was not as clear and flat as at Rocroi or Lens, and the generals had to adapt to the situation, as was the case of the Duc d'Enghien at Nördlingen (or Allerheim) in 1645: *"About twelve a clock the army advanced into the great plain, and about four a clock the two armies came in fight of one another. It took up a good deal of time to extend and put ourselves in a posture of fighting. That village, which was before the enemy's army, justly made it doubtful, whether it were better to attack it, or march towards the two wings with the horse only: but as it is not very safe to attack wings, without at the same time charging the foot posted in the centre, it was not judged proper, whatever difficulty there might be in attacking the village, to charge with the horse, without the infantry marching in the same front ; and as the village was above four hundred paces more advanced than the place where the enemy's army was, it was thought best to halt with the two wings, while the infantry should attack and make*

themselves masters of the nearest houses of that village, or at least of some of them. For that end, our cannon were brought up, that we might not be annoyed by those of the enemy, without annoying them with ours: but as cannon that are planted have a great advantage over those that march, because the horses must always be put to the carriages in order to advance, whereby a great deal of time is lost, those of the enemy did a great deal more damage than ours. In this disposition the infantry of the king's army marched straight to the village; the right wing being opposite to the enemy's left wing in the plain, and the left wing to the enemy's right, which was upon that hill, from which there was an insensible descent to the village." (Ramsay, Memoirs of the vicomte de Turenne).

When the terrain did not permit the constitution of large cavalry wings, the cavalry's role was to defend the infantry. On many occasions we find the following arrangements, as set out in La Moussaye's account of the Battle of Freiburg: *"Then the prince thought fit that Mr de Turenne should march with his infantry, the Maréchal de Gramont was to have charged the enemy in the flank, or to have sustained with the horse, if the attack had succeeded. We marched straight to the fall of trees which was in the middle of the hill, and opposite to the left of the prince's army. The cavalry regiments of Mr de*

Turenne and Tracy, sustained the prince's infantry, who were repulsed after a very obstinate fight, where this cavalry performed wonders, in bearing the fire without moving." And again in this description a little after Freiburg: "The enemy's cavalry dare not pursue them briskly, for fear going too far from their foot; or else, because being as yet stunned with the battles of the preceding days, their main design was to retire without fighting. Rosen's foremost squadrons being sustained by those of the second line, and the whole body of the enemy's cavalry and infantry continuing to march against them, and being between forty and fifty paces from one another, they retired five or six hundred paces, mixed with the enemy, who made more use of the fire of their infantry than of their cavalry." This defensive role was the most delicate to put into practice. Here is an illustration, once again from the same account: "Mr de Mercy (...) faced about upon Mr de Rosen with the whole body of his troops; but some of the enemy's squadrons advan-cing before their infantry, Mr de Rosen beat them back, and following them in order, three or four battalions fired upon him, which stopped his detach-ment, however, without putting them into confusion; seeing himself very near the enemy's main body, and their front very much larger than his own, he began to retire. Two or three squadrons of the second line sustained those of the first, that were very little moved by so great a fire, and after having lost four or five standards, they retired very slowly in good order."

In open country, the cavalry was used on the wings, and was a decisive element to fight and defeat the enemy. In his account of the Battle of Rocroi, the Marquis de la Moussaye, aide-de-camp of the Duc d'Enghien, relates the effect of a cavalry charge: "But nothing is as dange-rous as making wide movements in front of a powerful enemy when about to come to hand-to-hand combat. These squadrons, already wea-kened, were broken at the first charge, and all

Horsemen resting. Philips Wouverman (1619-1668). Paris, Louvre Museum.

the troops of Albuquerque were knocked down on top of each other. Enghien, seeing them take flight, ordered Gassion to pursue them and turned instantly against the infantry." Between charges, the cavalry rallied and reformed behind the infantry, as recounts this Condé officer present at the battle of Lens in 1648: "Our cavalry suffered greatly for the enemy had always three squadrons against one, but when they were broken, they always came to rally behind Picardie; (many officers) after having charged twenty times and breaking the corps that they fought, came here to refresh themselves, and Streif came here to die."

However, when circumstances required, the cavalry could also simply skirmish, as relates the Marquis de La Moussaye during the battle of Freiburg on the 5 August 1644: "The French gendarmerie performed excellently; La Boulaye, who was in command, took it to the edge of this entrenchment of trees, and, in spite of the enemy fire, he skirmished for a very long time with pistol shots."

Infantry fire could be terrible at close range. In his memoirs, Gramont relates this episode from the battle of Allerheim on the 3 August 1645: "All I could do was to put myself at the head of the two infantry regiments. They did not move from their positions in the slightest, and muzzle to muzzle they fired such a furious discharge into the charging Bavarian squadrons that charged, that they were forced open. I made use of this to enter inside with what remained of the cavalry behind me; which was not particularly useful, as I found myself surrounded on all sides and taken prisoner." The Marquis de La Moussaye gives a graphic account of the effects of continuous infantry fire in his account of the battle of Freiburg: "The two parties fired with such fury that the noise and the smoke confused everything, and they could only make each other out by the light of cannon and musket fire. All the woods around echoed with a terrible booming which further added to the horror of the battle. The soldiers were so fierce and unrelenting, both those trying to force the entrenchments, and those trying to defend them, that, if night had not fallen, both sides would have seen the greatest carnage ever seen in our times."

As in the previous period, during the Thirty Years' War the French armies used skirmishers, or enfants perdus, who were generally detached from their regiment. The Relation de Rocroy cites in the list of losses: "Pédamont, captain in Picardie and commander of the enfants perdus of the same, injured by a musket shot to the shoulder...." However, the generals of the German army such as Turenne and Gramont, used the term commanded musketeers, which could equally designate a musketeer unit, or musketeers detached from a regiment.

When battles did not go to their advantage, the maréchals had to take steps to maintain the cohesion of their troops. In his memoirs, Sirot describes this episode from the battle of Rocroi: "The battle marshal, the Chevalier de La Vallière, gave the order to retreat to the discouraged troops from the left wing, whom I had rallied, for the battle was lost. These were Picardie, Piémont, La Marine, the Swiss of Monlondin, and Persan. They had suffered greatly and obeyed willingly; but upon seeing that they abandoned me, I went to them and told them to hold fast.

As they withdrew in spite of my remonstrance, I blamed them for their lack of heart and I had a grave dispute with the Chevalier de la Vallière, to whom I said that it was not for him to command my troops. Prayers and threats had such effect on the spirits of the officers that I hardened them; but as I led the charge, La Vallière halted them a second time and I was followed only by what remained of my reserve corps, Harcourt, Bretagne, the Royaux, and, for the cavalry, my own regiment, which had suffered greatly. I charged the Spanish troops, but I was not able to crush them because our men were too weak in numbers. I therefore ran to these 5 withdrawing regiments which were at more than 100 paces from me, and I shouted:

Are you cowards, men of little honour and little heart, to withdraw without seeing the enemy? I shall proclaim it throughout France; I shall complain to the king and the Duc d'Enghien. Stay and we shall win the battle! Do not abandon me for a man who shall lose you your reputation forever; rally my troops, I promise to give you victory!

Officers and soldiers replied: 'To the Baron de Sirot!' I led them to join my troops that were waiting for me."

When there was not a brave captain or maréchal to rally the troops, sanctions were immediate, as relates Ramsay in his Histoire de Turenne, in his account of the Battle of Mergentheim, on the 5 May 1645: "When he was about a hundred paces *from the wood, and before the infantry had made any discharge, Mr de Turenne marched with his cavalry to encounter the enemy's right wing, all the squadrons whereof were broken, and the second line was shaken. At the same time, the enemy's infantry advancing towards the little wood, those of the king's army gave only one fire, and ran confusedly into the wood. Thus the enemy's left wing found means to advance by the favour of the wood which their infantry had gained."*

When the battle finally ended, losses had to be counted; losses prove the essential role of officers in a victory, as illustrated in the *Relation de Rocroy: "We have had 1,200 or 1,500 killed or injured, including Baron d'Ernault, captain of the cavalry of the Harcourt regiment who was killed, and Boislapierre, captain of the same regiment, who was injured ten times; d'Esclainvillers and Regnéville, captains of the king's regiment, each injured by four or five shots; the Baron d'Ecquancourt, captain of the regiment de la Ferté and Monsieur de La Roche, his lieutenant, gravely injured; de Bougy, cornette of Gassion, injured; de Choisy, cornette of the company of the Marquis de Lenoncourt, killed; de Verigny and d'Avanne, lieutenants in the Coislin regiment, injured by many shots; de Vivans, captain of the Sully regiment, killed; d'Arrènes, captain of the same, injured; the Comte d'Ayen, commander of the cavalry regiment of Maréchal Guiche, killed; and La Motte-Maressal, captain of the same regiment, gravely injured; d'Hédouville, captain of la Clavière, de Mongneux, captain of the Marolles regiment, and du Sens, captain of the Sirot regiment, injured by many shots; de Beauvau, colonel, injured by a musket shot to the hand, and d'Altenove, lieutenant-colonel of Leschelle, killed; Pédamont, captain of Picardie and commander of the enfants perdus of the same, injured by a musket shot to the shoulder; the Marquis de la Trousse, mestre de camp of La Marine, and the Chevalier de la Trousse, his brother, after having done all they could, injured; Clément, captain of Piémont; du Mesnil, Froyelles, Birgues and Villers, captains of the Rambures regiment, and the lieutenant-colonel of the Biscaras regiment, killed; du Mesnil, first captain of the Harcourt regiment, injured."*

Siege warfare remained the main form of action during the various campaigns that took place between 1635 and 1648 even if many generals, such as Rohan and Turenne, tried to avoid it. The siege of Llerida, led by the Prince de Condé in 1647 and recounted by the Duc de Gramont, illustrates this type of warfare:

"The beginnings of the siege gave hope for a happy success; for we found all the old circumvallation of the Comte d'Harcourt, which the negligence of the Spaniards had left nearly whole and in defensive condition: this won us much time, and meant the troops were not fatigued through work. What is more, the town had been well reconnoitred, and appeared neither easy, nor difficult to take.

The Spanish army, always slow in its operation, was not yet ready to begin their campaign, which gave us all the time necessary to bring into the camp the cannon, victuals and munitions required to realise the siege at our leisure. Besides

Battle of Rocroi: the Duc d'Enghien reviewing his troops on the eve of the battle, 1898 (coloured engraving) by Alphonse Lalauze (1872-1930). Condé museum, Chantilly, France.

113

114

this, the Chevalier de La Vallière, who had led our attacks in the grand sieges of Flanders, had been governor of the town, and gave mathematical assurance that the town was worth nothing at all; which strengthened further our hopes, because with knowledge of the fortifications, and because he had commanded in the town, he had a perfect knowledge of the enemies' strengths and weaknesses. (...)

There were three thousand natural Spanish in the town, and the governor was the Portuguese Don Antonio Brit, a man of honour and valour, and with perfect manners, sending every morning ices and lemonade to the Prince de Condé for his refreshment; he was proud and intrepid in his manner of defending his town, of which we were not able to take an inch without the sword, and without being constantly fought off.

We made two attacks, one on the side of the Prince de Condé, and the other on the side of Maréchal de Gramont: these attacks pushed fairly energetically to the foot of the battlements that Brit had made halfway up. But when we wished to attach the mine to explode it, we found the rock so hard that we were not able to do so; and despite all our efforts, the nights passed by without any headway being made: which distressed the generals, the officers and the soldiers. Also the fire was terrible, continuous, and the mortality very great. The governor made two significant sallies, both on the trench of the Prince de Condé. At the first, the Swiss who were guarding it were so severely attacked that they abandoned it entirely, and were never able to rally; in such a way that it was necessary for the Prince de Condé and the Maréchal de Gramont to come to the camp to regain it and to retake all the positions that had been abandoned, which was done at extreme peril; for because the enemy had retaken possession a sufficiently long time ago to repair and improve them, it was necessary to regain the lost positions in full daylight and without cover, under the tremendous fire of the entire town, and put back the guard where they had been in the first place: this made the pill even more difficult to swallow.

The other sally was also to attack the prince. The regiment that had the guard did not abandon him completely, for he was supported by Persan, who was in Maréchal de Gramont's trench. However, the enemy killed a great number of officers and soldiers, and generally all

the miners, whose work they ruined totally: after which the governor was not remiss in sending his two little mutes to the Prince de Condé, laden with ice and cinnamon water for refreshment after the fatigues of the day.

To this poor success was added the desertion of the troops, in number more than four thousand, who surrendered to the enemy: which so weakened the army that the trench guards, ordinarily of twelve hundred men, were no more than three hundred, and nearly all the circumvallation abandoned."

The siege of Ypres in 1648, once again told by Maréchal de Gramont, was more positive for his side; he gives a thorough description of the system of trenches, moats, counterscarps, and the way to reduce enemy defences: "The same

evening, we opened the trench in two places in fair proximity to each other: the front that we attacked was large, the moat very wide, deep and full of water, and a most handsome counterscarp, with excellent palisades. The Gardes Françaises defended against both attacks and pushed up to a hundred paces from the corner of the counterscarp. The ninth day after the trench was opened, the Poles, leading the attack of Maréchal Gramont, swam across the moat of the demilune; and after hacking through the palisades of the moat, they entered within; and having killed all those who were inside, they constructed a superb position on the point. This was done in daylight, and was one of the most hardy ever seen: the mine was attached to the demilune on the side of the attack of the Prince de Condé;

after which the enemy beat a retreat, with the advantage of being very poorly defended. The man they sent to surrender was a Walloon lieutenant colonel, one of the most ridiculous personages ever seen (...)" A fort could be composed of *bastions*, fortifications with two corners and two sides; *curtains*, battlements separating the bastions; *scarps*, slopes inside the moats and ditches; and *counterscarps*, which were the outer slopes of these moats and ditches. A *demilune* was an advance bastion outside the fort. The assailants used *fascines* ~ faggots of branches ~ to fill moats and ditches, and dug *saps*, or approach trenches, while the assieged party attempted to prevent them by digging *countermines*, or mine tunnels.

After the battle. Jacques Courtois ("Le Bouguignon", 1621-1676). Italy, Rome, Galleria Doria-Pamphili.

Laughing cavalier, 17th century
(1865). Jean-Louis Ernest
Meissonier (1815-1891).
Château de Compiègne, France.

CHAPTER IV

UNIFORMS AND COLOURS

The infantry was dressed in a short jacket, most often with button sleeves, but which could be left unbuttoned. Ribbons or laces could be used for decoration. Officers often wore a cloak over this jacket, and were recognisable on the battlefield by their white scarf. Breeches were worn half-length, and were tied just below the knee by a ribbon. These could be decorated by a series of buttons on the side. Stockings covered the legs, and clogs completed the outfit, although on campaign, the infantry preferred to wear boots if they had the possibility, as recounts Captain Lieutenant d'Artagnan in his memoirs: *"He (the major of an infantry regiment) sent a captain that he had with him to the regiment to inform the lieutenant colonel of the inspection that the king wished to perform (...) Those wearing boots removed them on hearing this, and put on clogs, as was proper for an inspection of infantry."* The uniform of the drummers was usually more decorated. Horsemen and certain infantry officers were protected by a leather jacket, the "buff jerkin".

Swords were generally worn on the right, and held by a belt. Musketeers were also equipped with a bandolier, which held twelve powder charges, the so-called "twelve apostles". Officers were equipped with a halberd or partisan.

In this first half of the seventeenth century, units generally did not yet wear uniforms, as the would from 1660; only a few guard units did so, such as the four companies of the king's *Gardes du corps* and the king's musketeers. The latter wore a blue cassock with white edging, and a white cross embroidered in the middle.

It is however highly probable that many regiments had certain "uniformity" at the beginning of a campaign. Equipment and clothing were mainly provided by the government, or the mestre de camp of the regiment, and this would be more and more the case under Richelieu's administration. It is therefore most likely that clothing was tailored out of one same sheet and one same cut for a unit. Dull colours, especially grey and brown, appear to have been dominant. Of course, as the campaign advanced, wear of the equipment and plunder added more and more to the variety of this general appearance.

Each regiment had its own colours. Those of the guards and the *vieux corps* are best known as they did not change when a new colonel was appointed. This was also the case for the regiments which bore the name of a province; it is much more difficult to find the colours of the temporary regiments. Each cavalry company displayed its own colours, even when grouped together in regiments. A series of flags are shown on the following pages.

The colours carried by the infantry regiments were large, and usually square in shape. Those of the *Gardes Suisses* measured 3x3 metres, while the colours of other regiments measured 2.80 m or a little less. They were carried on a pole which measured up to 3.60 m in length. The cavalry *guidons* were of a more modest size, but were all edged with gold or silver fringes.

GARDES FRANÇAISES, 1563

GUIDON
DES GENDARMES
D'ORLÉANS, 1647

CHAMPAGNE, 1559

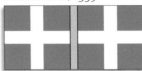

PIÉMONT, 1569

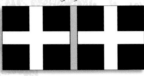

NORMANDIE, 1616

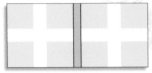

PICARDIE, 1569

NAVARRE, 1589

CARDINAL-DUC, 1635 -
LA MARINE, 1636

AUBETERRE, 1635

AUVERGNE, 1635

MONTLUC, 1597 -
RAMBURES

LYONNAIS, 1635

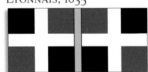

MONTFERRAT, 1584 -
CHAPPES - NERESTANG

GUIDON DU RÉGIMENT
DE SULLY, 1643

GUIDON DU RÉGIMENT
DE CHAROST, 1644

GUIDON DE LA COMPAGNIE
DES MOUSQUETAIRES
DU ROI, 1657

VAUBECOURT, 1610 -
ENTRAGUES - GUYENNE

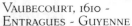

LESDIGUIÈRES, 1609

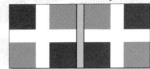

TOURAINE, 1636

LA HOCQUERIE
(LIÉGEOIS), 1629 - GUICHE
OU GRAMONT LIÉGEOIS

SIROT, 1635

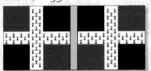

GRANCEY, 1630

TURENNE, 1625

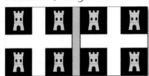

VON ROLL (SUISSE),
1642-1649

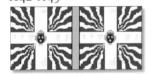

DRAPEAU BLANC DE
LA COMPAGNIE COLONELLE

GARDES ÉCOSSAISES, 1635

HEBRON OU HEPBURN
(ÉCOSSAIS), 1633-1636

HEBRON OU HEPBURN -
DRAPEAU DE
LA COMPAGNIE COLONELLE

GUIDON DU RÉGIMENT
CARDINAL-DUC, 1635

GUIDON DU RÉGIMENT DE
L'ÉCHELLE (LIÉGEOIS), 1635

CHAPTER V

OPERATIONS OF THE FRENCH ARMY ~ *main actions* [1620-1648]

P. 120-121 :
The Battle of Rocroi: the army emerging before Rocroi, c.1898 by Alphonse Lalauze (1872-1930). Condé museum, Chantilly, France.

P. 122 :
Stirrup cup, by Jean-Louis Ernest Meissonier. Reproduced with permission from the Thomas Ross Collection, UK

The French army fought intensively during the first half of the seventeenth century, both to repress internal revolts and to combat its secular enemy, Spain. Let us look at the service record of the *Gardes Françaises*, and the four oldest of these *vieux corps*: *Piémont*, *Picardie*, *Champagne* and *Navarre*. These five regiments are present during the internal campaigns against the Huguenots: in 1620 at the battle of Les Ponts-de-Cé in Normandy; in 1621 at the sieges of Saint-Jean d'Angély and Montauban; and in 1622 in Nègrepelisse and the siege of Montpellier. As part of the Italian army, they were not present in the Valtelline between 1624 and 1625, but we find the *Gardes Françaises*, *Champagne* and *Piémont* at the siege of La Rochelle in 1627, then the *Gardes Françaises*, *Navarre* and *Piémont* with the King's army in the Piedmont at the beginning of 1629. The charge of the *Gardes Françaises* at the Pas de Suse gave a magnificent and memorable example of France's offensive spirit, the famous *furia francese*. The *Gardes Françaises*, *Champagne* and *Piémont* were again present in the spring of 1629 for the repression of a Huguenot revolt in the Languedoc. On this occasion, the brigade of *Champagne* and *Piémont* launched an assault on the fort Saint-André. The regiments of the *Gardes Françaises*, *Picardie* and *Champagne* were also in the army that went to conquer the Savoy in 1630, and the five regiments were in the king's army in the Piedmont in 1630.

After a few years' rest, we find the *Gardes Françaises*, *Picardie*, and *Navarre* in the army of La Sarre in 1635, and then in 1636, the *Gardes Françaises*, *Piémont*, and *Champagne* were brought together in the army of Champagne. Note that during the French period of the Thirty Years' War, the *Gardes Françaises* and the *vieux corps* rarely formed a brigade together; the king had to divide his experienced troops among a number of armies: Champagne, Germany, Lorraine, Franche-Comté, Italy and the Pyrénées. *Picardie* and *Navarre* were exterminated at the Battle of Thionville, while the *Gardes Françaises*, *Piémont* and *Champagne* contributed to the storming of Hesdin in 1639. The *Gardes Françaises*, *Picardie*, *Piémont* and *Navarre* were present at the siege of Thionville in 1643 while at Rocroi the same year, the army of the Duc d'Enghien had only the *Picardie and Piémont* regiments. It was *Picardie* that massacred the 1,000 Spanish musketeers in a dawn ambush. *Piémont* was attacked by the entire cavalry of Alsace, bur resisted, although it suffered heavy losses. However, that day *Picardie* and *Piémont* had to be rallied with the rest of the French infantry, which was done with difficulty. In April 1646, *Champagne* was decimated at the siege of Llerida. In Lens, 1648, the *Gardes Françaises* and the *Gardes Suisses* crushed three enemy battalions, one Spanish and two German, but then, drunk on success, they allowed themselves to be surrounded by the Spanish *tercios viejos*. *Picardie*, the only *vieux corps* present at Lens alongside the three guard regiments, was one of the regiments that rushed to the aid of the *Gardes Françaises*, breaking the *tercios*.

The service actions of these regiments did not of course stop there – *Picardie*, for example, retook Saumur from insurgents in April 1650 – but this is where our story ends, interrupting a list of military actions that would only end with the French Revolution.

To conclude, here is the composition of the main French armies during the 1620 to 1648 period.

At the *"drôlerie des Ponts-de-Cé"*, on the **7 August 1620**, the French army had 8,000 infantry and 600 cavalry, commanded by the Prince de Condé; the Maréchal de Praslin was the *lieutenant general* and the *field marshals* were Tresnel, Créquy, Nerestang and Bassompierre. Present were: the *Gardes Françaises, Piémont, Picardie, Champagne* (in 2 battalions), *Navarre* and companies of *chevau légers* and *carabins*. The *Gardes Françaises* were at the centre, *Picardie* on their right and the two battalions of *Champagne* on their left. Each infantry regiment had *enfants perdus*.

The French army at the siege of Saint Jean d'Angély in June 1621 included the *Gardes Françaises* and the *Gardes Suisses*, the *Picardie, Piémont, Champagne, Navarre, Normandie, Rambures, Chappes* and *Lauzières* regiments. The cavalry was made up of 7 *cornettes*: the *chevau légers de la Garde*, the *gendarmerie*, the *chevau légers de la Reine, Guise, Châteaubriant*, and the *Carabins d'Esplans*.

Siege of Montauban, August-November 1621: three corps were formed to attack at different points of the town; the first was the *Gardes Françaises* and *Suisses* reinforced by *Piémont, Normandie, Chappes* and *Estissac*. The second included *Picardie, Champagne, Navarre, Villeroy* and *Vaillac*. The third grouped together *Languedoc, Rambures, Saint-Étienne* and *Lauzières*. **In October 1621, the Duc de Montmorency** reinforced the royal army in Montauban with 500 horses and 5 Languedoc regiments, totalling 6,000 infantry (1,200 men per regiment): *Rieux, Réaux, Moussoulens, Fabrègues* and *La Roquette*.

The army of the Duc d'Elbeuf that fought the Marquis de la Force in February 1622 included the *Piémont* regiment, 9 companies of which had been left to garrison Duras, the *Riberac* and *Grignaux* regiments and 5 companies of *chevau légers*.

This small army was joined by the regiments of *Bordeilles, Curson, Loson, Ramburges* and the cavalry.

For the assault of Nègrepelisse on the 6 June 1622, *Picardie* was on the left, the *Gardes Françaises* at the centre and *Navarre* on the right.

The army of Louis XIII in 1622, from Saintonge to the siege of Montpellier (April-October), included: the king's Household (the *Cent-suisses*, the *cent gentilshommes à bec-de-corbin*, the *Gardes de la porte*, the *Gardes de la manche*, the *Gardes de la prévôté* and the 4 companies of mounted *Gardes du corps*, one French and three Scottish, of 336 guards each), the *Guard (gendarmes and chevau légers)*, the *Gardes Françaises (5 battalions)*, the *Gardes Suisses (2 large battalions)*, *Navarre (3 battalions)*, *Normandie (2 battalions)*, *Picardie, Piémont, Champagne* (left at La Rochelle), many other regiments *(Nerestang, Berry, Estissac, Saint-Chamond, Fontenay Mareuil etc.)*, a few companies of *gendarmes (including the Gendarmes de Condé)*, *chevau-légers (including those of La Reine, Chateaubriand, Condé, Guise, Praslin, Vitry)* and *carabins (Carabins d'Esplans)* plus 7 *couleuvrines*.

In July 1622, Maréchal de Praslin went to take Bédarieux with *Picardie, Navarre* and 9 cannon. On the 2 August, he laid siege to Lunel and the Duc de Montmorency took Massillargues with *Normandie*, 5 regiments from the Languedoc (*Rieux, Réaux, Moussoulens, Fabrègues* and *La Roquette*), 6 cannon and a *couleuvrine*. At the siege of Montpellier in September 1622, two attacks were made: the attack on the left, with the *Gardes Françaises, Gardes Suisses, Navarre, Piémont, Picardie, Estissac* and *Saint-Chamond*; and the attack on the right with *Normandie, Nerestang* and the 5 regiments from the Languedoc (*Rieux, Réaux, Moussoulens, Fabrègues* and *La Roquette*); for the siege of Montpellier on 7 October, 6 infantry regiments of the Dauphiné arrived as reinforcements: *Tournon, Sault, Trémond, Calard, Labaume* and *Montchamp*. On 20 October, the king entered Montpellier and left there *Picardie, Navarre* and *Normandie. Champagne* was still at La Rochelle. The newly raised infantry regiments were disbanded.

The army of Annibal d'Estrées, Marquis de Coeuvres, in Italy in 1624, included 10 companies of the *Normandy* regiment, *Vaubecourt* (regiment from the Lorraine), 6 companies of the *d'Estrées* regiment and 3 Swiss regiments (*Diesbach, Schmidt* and *Siders*) of 1,000 men each.

The army of Genoa commanded by Constable Lesdiguières on the 4 March 1625 had 23,000 men, including the *gendarmes* and *chevau légers dauphinois*, the *Sault, Chappes, Trémond, Bonnes, Blacon, Sancy, Tallard, Beaufort, La Grange*, and *Uxelles* regiments. The artillery had only 2 small cannon.

There were two armies of the king at the siege of La Rochelle in 1627: the first, commanded by Bassompierre, had 3 companies of *Gardes Suisses*, the Fort Louis detachment of *Champagne, Navarre, Vaubecourt, Beaumont, Plessis-Praslin, Riberac, Chastelier-Barlot, Monsieur's gendarmes* and 6 companies of *chevau légers*. The second army, that of the king, with the Duc d'Angoulême and Maréchal Schomberg, was composed of *gendarmes* of the king's Household, the *Gardes Françaises, Gardes Suisses, Piémont, Rambures, Chappes, Estissac, La Meilleraye, gendarmes* (including the *gendarmes* of the queen mother) and the *chevau légers de la Garde*.

For the Piedmont campaign in February 1629 to liberate Casale and for the attack of the Pass de Suse (6 March 1629): Richelieu reinforced the permanent corps and raised 6 new regiments in the Dauphiné, the Lyonnais and Provence. Three armies were to invade the Piedmont: the king's army, the army of Provence (on the right) commanded by the Duc de Guise and Maréchal d'Estrées, and the army of Lyons (on the left) which was to be commanded by Schomberg. But only the king's army, at the centre, would be drawn up in time; it had 23,000 infantry and 3,000 horses: *Gardes Françaises, Gardes Suisses,*

Navarre, Piémont, Sault, Estissac, Vaubecourt, La Grange and *Riberac*, the *Chasseurs des Alpes*, the cavalry of the king's Household, 12 companies of *chevau légers* (including *Toiras, Canillac, Boissat, Cournon, Maugiron, Meigneux)* and *Arnaud de Corbeville's carabins*. **The army of Lyons**, drawn up at the beginning of April, had 8 regiments (it was planned that it would have 10,000 men): *Picardie, Normandie, Phalsbourg, Lestrange, Pérault, Montréal, Logères* and *Annibal*.

On the 28 April 1629, the king left the army of *au delà les monts* to repress a new uprising of Rohan in the Cévennes, with his *gardes du corps, gendarmes, chevau légers,* musketeers and 6 companies of *Gardes françaises*. He joined with the **Languedoc army** commanded by the Duc de Guise and the Duc de Montmorency which included *Picardie* and 4 Languedoc regiments. The Prince de Condé and the Duc d'Epernon were at the head of the **army of Guyenne** which was watching over Montauban. **The army of Provence** was commanded by Maréchal d'Estrées: it included 6,000 infantry (including the *Montréal* and *Lestrange* regiments) and 400 horses before the arrival of the reinforcement of 1,500 voluntary *chevau légers*. **On the 19 May 1629, Richelieu and Bassompierre** arrived to reinforce the armies of the Languedoc and Provence with the *Gardes Françaises, Gardes Suisses, Champagne, Piémont, Rambures, Languedoc, Vaillac* and *Annonay*.

The rest of the infantry of the **army of Au delà les monts** left behind in Suse under the command of de Créqui included: *Navarre, Estissac, Sault, Pompadour, La Bergerie, Vaubecourt* and one company of *Gardes Suisses*.

At the end of May 1629, the army of *Au delà les monts* (totalling 10,000 men), which had stayed in Suse against Charles-Emmanuel of Savoy and was commanded by Créqui, was to be reinforced by the Languedoc army. On the 29 December 1629, Richelieu left for Suse with the Duc de Montmorency, the Cardinal de la Valette, Maréchals d'Estrées, Schomberg and Bassompierre and 10 companies of *Gardes Françaises* of 300 men each. Richelieu sent Bassompierre to raise 6,000 men in Switzerland. In addition to the 6 detached regiments at Casale, and 2 regiments guarding the Pas de Suse, Richelieu had 21,000 combatants. Richelieu's lieutenant generals were Maréchals Charles de Créqui, Jacques de Caumont, La Force and Henri de Schomberg. The field marshals were

Etienne d'Auriac, Jean de Toiras and the Marquis de Feuquières. Bassompierre tells us in his memoirs: *"Our troops passed, that is 7 companies of Gardes, 6 Swiss, 19 Navarre, 14 Estissac, 15 Sault and the king's mounted musketeers (...) We carried also six six-pound cannon (...) On Thursday 8 March we left Suse with what we had of the guards, Suisses, Navarre and Sault, with the gendarmes and chevau légers of the king's guards, Bussy Lauriéres, Boissac and Arnault, with Mr de Créqui's guards and my own..."*

Conquest of Savoy, 1630: the army of Savoy with which Richelieu joined on the 2 May 1630, had 8 companies of Gardes Françaises, and was commanded by the Maréchals de Créqui, de Bassompierre and de Châtillon. Field marshals were de Chastellet and du Hallier and the intendants were de Chastellet and d'Emery. The army had 8,000 infantry and 2,000 cavalry before being joined by the 6,000 Swiss of Bassompierre. It included the Gardes Suisses, Picardie, Champagne, Normandie, Rambures, Chastelier-Barlot, La Meilleraye, Plessis Besançon, Juigné, Autremont, Maillard, Montausier, Pizieux, Jauson, Verdun, Langeron, Chouain, the garrisons of the Dauphiné, and 18 cavalry cornettes. At the battle of Séez *on the 6 july were present 8 compagnies from Gardes Françaises,* Picardie, La Meilleraye, Plessis Besançon, Juigné, 1,500 Swiss and cavalry cornettes under Châtillon. On Saint Ambrosius' Day, on the 10 July 1630: the infantry was on the right and the cavalry on the left; the rearguard of the army, which was to be engaged, was composed of 4,000 infantry (4 companies from *Gardes Françaises, Picardie, Normandie, Rambures*) and 320 horses (80 *gendarmes* and 80 *chevau légers* of the king's Household, the *gendarme* companies of *Monsieur* and the *Comte de Noailles). Picardie* was on the right and the *Gardes Françaises* on the left, with *Normandie* and *Rambures* in second line. On the left of the guards were 4 cavalry companies, each forming a squadron of 80 horsemen (including the *gendarmes* of the king and Noailles).

The army of the king in the Piedmont under the Duc de Montmorency in 1630 (battle of Carignan, on the 6 August 1630) was commanded by Maréchal de La Force whose field marshals were Feuquières and Villeroy:

The cavalry included half of the king's *gendarmes,* 6 *gendarmerie* companies (*Monsieur, Montmorency, Alaincourt, Ventadour, Créqui, Noailles*), the king's *chevau légers,* 34 *chevau légers* companies (*Monsieur, Mestre de Camp, Condé, Montmorency, Monceaux, Hocquincourt, Roches, Saint-Trivier, Montgon, Marcillac, La Borde, Lignières, Busay, Laurière, Arbourse, la Roque-Massebaut, Canillac, Morconnay, Créqui, Dizimieux, Gerboulle, Roche-Baritaut, Lesche, Montastruc, la Flocellière, Cluis, Aubais, Bandol, Saint-Julien, Beauregard, du Hallier, Luserna* and *Philippes*), 12 *carabin* companies (*Arnault, de Corbeville, Maubuisson, Autichamp, Saint-Angolin, Bellot, Saint-Fargeau, Conflans, Cendre, Cavois, Biderau, Saint-Martin,* and *Evreux*).

The infantry had 29 regiments: the *Gardes Françaises, Champagne, Piémont, Picardie, Navarre, Normandie, Phalsbourg, La Meilleraye, Rambures, La Rochefoucault, Sault, Plessis-Praslin, La Bergerie, Vaillac, La Tour, Longjumeau, Bussy, Blacons, Goudrin, Vaubecourt, Languedoc, Annibal, Perrault, Jeanson, Saint-Forgeux, Mirepoix, Naves,* the Swiss of *Ariac* and the Liégeois of *La Hocquerie.* The army of Toiras in Casale had 3 infantry regiments (*Ribérac, Pompadour, La Grange*) and 6 companies of *chevau légers* (*Toiras, Canillac, Brissac, Courvoux, Maugiron, Migneux*).

The army of Maréchal de Schomberg in the Piedmont, 1630 (from 17 August 1630) included:

Cavalry: a detachment of the king's Household (*gendarmes* and *chevau légers*), the Duc de Bellegarde's *gendarmes* and 7 companies of *chevau légers* (*Bligny, La Palice, Schomberg, Chambray, Mollinet, La Chapelle-Baloue* and *Faucon*).

Infantry: 6 companies of *Gardes Françaises,* 8 companies of *Gardes Suisses* and 20 infantry regiments: *Aiguebonne, Saint-Paul, Plessis Joigny, Grancey, Lecques, Longueval, Maugiron, Conches, du Pallais, Chabrilles, Urfé, Sautour, Turenne, Croisille, Montréal, Thoré, Vercoiran, Soyécourt, Crussol* and *Danti.* Most of these regiments were new levies.

The army of Maréchal de Marillac, sent as reinforcements for Schomberg in the Piedmont in October 1630 comprised:

◇ Cavalry: 3 companies of *gendarmes* (*de Chaulnes, Effiat, Tavannes*), 450 nobles of the *ban* and *arrière-ban* of the Dauphiné, 22 companies of *chevau légers* (*Effiat, Bonneval, Linars, La Ferté-Senneterre, du Terrail, du Mascheix, Feugly, Chaulnes, Sesseval, Lignières, Allamont, Beaucourt, Boufflers, Verneuil, Thouars, Marillac, Marinville, Boury, Lignon, du Jeu, Quinçay, Commarin*).

❖ Infantry: 4 companies from *Champagne* and 14 regiments (*Chappes, Bonnivet, Brazey, Houdancourt, Espagny, Hocquincourt, Piles, Beaulieu, Persac, Peslières, Tonneins, Nicey, Magland, Fiémarcon*).

On the 17 October, the regiments were divided into battalions of 1,000 men (3 brigades of 6 battalions of 1,000 men) and the cavalry companies were grouped together in squadrons of 100 to 150 men. The army of Schomberg and Marillac (18,000 infantry and 3,750 horses) was divided into 3 brigades (the advanced guard commanded by Schomberg, the main body by Marillac and the rear guard commanded by La Force) of 6 battalions and 6 squadrons. One of the 3 brigades was reinforced by the battalions of the *Gardes Françaises* and the *Gardes Suisses,* and also by the 450 nobles of the Dauphiné. The army had 4 cannon.

At Casale (26 October 1630): the 3 brigades were placed side by side; on the right, La Force's advanced guard, the main body in the middle, led by Schomberg, and the rear guard under Merillac. In the first line were 7 battalions, each detaching 200 *enfants perdus* 100 paces from the front, sufficiently spaced to allow the cavalry of the second line to pass through the intervals. On the wings were 2 squadrons covered in front and on the flanks by 5 *carabin* companies. 100 paces behind, in the second line, were 7 battalions between which were placed 8 squadrons. At 200 paces was the third line, with 6 battalions in the centre and 12 squadrons on the wings. At 50 paces behind was a reserve of 3 squadrons. Between the second and third lines was a squadron of 130 *gendarmes* with Maréchal de Schomberg. A little in front, in the right-hand brigade, Maréchal de La Force led the king's Household. At the same distance in the left-hand brigade, Maréchal de Marillac led his company of *chevau légers*. Toiras, in the citadel, was ready to intervene with 600 men and 250 horses.

The army left in France by Marillac had 11 infantry regiments (*Menillet, Castel Bayart, Sy, Nubécourt, Cignolles, Nettancourt, Atichy, Bettancourt, Renel, Dauphin, Hostel*) and 6 regiments, 5 companies of *gendarmerie* (*Reine Mère, Reine Anne, Elbeuf,*

Longueville, Matignon), 9 companies of *chevau légers* (*Rouville, Mèche, Vandy, du Hamel, Grandpré, Vaubecourt, la Valette, Crespy, la Bescherelle*), 3 companies of *carabins* (*Pré, Salles, Fontenay*), 6 companies of Liégeois (60 men in each) and the garrisoned regiments (*Marillac* in Verdun, *du Kergrist* in Calais, *Nevoy* in Boulogne and Ardres, *Cerny* in La Fère and Saint-Quentin).

Condition of the king's army in 1633 under Maréchal de La Force, Field Marshals de La Force, Arpajou and Hebron, and Battle Sergeant d'Espenan:

❖ 34 companies of *chevau-légers*: *du Roi* (200 men), *de la Reine, du Prince, du Cardinal Duc, de Mouy, Colonelle, Maître de Camp, Ecossaise, de Blagny, de Lortières, de La Force, des Roches Bariteaux, de la Frezelière, de la Cressonnière, de la Ferté-Senneterre, de Praslin, de Vatimont, de Vientel, du Terrail, de Pouillé, de Beauveau, de la Bloquerie (Liége), de Miches (Liége), de la Guiche, de Villeroy, de Feuquières, du Premier, de la Porte, de la Maillerais, de Saint-Chaumont, de la Valette, de Brassac, de Dapierre, de Fourille.*

❖ 7 companies of *carabins*: *Mestre de Camp, d'Arancourt, du Pré, de Corval, de Villars, de Bideram, de la Motte.*

❖ 27 infantry regiments: *Picardie, Navarre, Piémont, Champagne, Normandie, Varenne, Vaubecourt, Rambures, Alincourt, Villeroy, Bettancourt, Castel-Moron, Tonneins, Noailles, Auquincourt, Effiat, la Maillerais, Saint-Aunay, Nettancourt, Plessis Joigny, Hebron (Scots), Chastelliers-Barlot, Saint-Étienne, Montozier, la Boullez, Saint-Hilaire, Turenne.*

Reinforcements: 18 cavalry companies and 6 infantry regiments for a total of 34 infantry regiments and 58 cavalry companies.

Artillery: 16 large calibre cannons, 22 medium-calibre cannon and 600 munitions chariots.

At the battle of Avins on the 20 May 1635, the army commanded by Maréchals Châtillon and Brézé totalled 25,000 infantry and 5,000 horses at the beginning of the campaign.

The artillery, commanded by La Meilleraye, was covered by the *Genlis* and *Lusignan* regiments and the *carabins* of *Alexis* and *Moulinet*. The Brézé corps was on the right, Châtillon on the left (along with *Champagne and Longueval* among others). The infantry was in the middle and the cavalry on the wings. A reserve of 4,000 infantry and 1,000 horses remained under the orders of Chastelier-Barlot.

The army of Maréchal Henri de Rohan in the Valtelline, June to October 1635, comprised:

❖ Infantry (8,000 at the beginning of the campaign): 11 French regiments (*Lèques, Montausier, du Landé, Roquelaure, Serres, Cerny, Vandy, la Frezelière, Canisy, Biès, Neuville le Grand*), 2 Swiss regiments (*Schmidt, Greder*), and 7 Grisons regiments (*Schawenstein, Molina, Salis, Brugger, Jenatsch, Guler, Florin*);

❖ Cavalry (400 horses): 6 *cornettes* including Rohan's mounted musketeer company and the *Canillac* light cavalry regiment (*Canillac, Montbrun, Miche, Saint-André, Amanty,* and *Villette* companies*)*. After this, the Duc de Rohan only mentions 3 squadrons (*Canillac, Saint-André* and *Villeneuve*).

The rest guarded the passages of the Valtelline. In 1637, the Grisons regiments – unpaid – were handed over to the emperor, although the Swiss regiments remained in the pay of Louis XIII.

Army of La Sarre in October 1635 under Maréchal de La Valette (with two field marshals, Henri de la Tour d'Auvergne, Vicomte de Turenne and Antoine de Gramont, Comte de Guiche):

❖ Infantry: 12 companies of the *Gardes Françaises, Gardes Suisses, Picardie, Navarre, Normandie, Vaubecourt (Petit Vieux), Turenne, Nettancourt* and 3 German regiments;

❖ Cavalry: 1,700 horses in 11 regiments (*Cardinal Duc, Enghien, Sourdis, la Meilleraye, Matignon, Guiche, Sauveboeuf, le Ferron, Nanteuil, Chaulnes, Treillis*) plus the cavalry reserve (4 companies of *gendarmes* and *chevau-légers* of the king and Cardinal Richelieu).

The army of La Sarre joined the Swedes of Bernard of Saxe-Weimar in Mentz in September 1635. On the 23 September 1635 (in Saverne), the army of La Sarre totalled 6,000 infantry and 5,000 cavalry.

The army of the Prince de Condé in Burgundy

and Franche-Comté in 1636 (20,000 infantry and 8,000 horses) included among others the *Picardie* and *Navarre* regiments. The cavalry included among others the Hungarian regiments of *Rantzau* and *La Meilleraye*, the Swedish regiment of *Gassion*, and the French regiments *Rostignac, la Motte, and Batilly*. **The armies of the Cardinal de la Valette and Bernard of Saxe-Weimar were in Alsace.** The army of La Valette included among others the *Normandie* and *Conti* regiments. **The army of the Duc d'Angoulême and Maréchal de la Force was in Lorraine.**

The army of Louis de Bourbon, Comte de Soissons, was in Champagne. This army was reinforced at the beginning of June by the army of Urbain de Maillé and Maréchal de Brézé, who had returned from Holland (8,000 infantry including the regiment of *Champagne* and 500 cavalry), then in August by the army of the Duc de Chaulnes from Picardy (which included a part of the *Gardes Françaises*). In August, this army comprised the *Gardes Françaises*, the *Garde Suisses, La Marine, Piémont, Champagne, Vaubecourt, Saintonge, la Roche-Giffart, Charost* and *Bellefonds*. And in reserve at Senlis: the regiments of *La Trémoille, de Brézé, de Poitou, d'Anjou, d'Avenoux, du Mesnil* and *de Landieu*.

The army of *Au delà des monts* (Piedmont), commanded by Maréchal de Créqui (16,000 infantry and 1,300 cavalry): the infantry included the regiments *Sault, Auvergne, Lyonnais, de Pierregourde, de Florinville, de Roquefeuille, d'Henrichemont*; the cavalry was composed of the *chevau légers* regiments of *Nerestang, Cauvisson, Lorraine, Marolles, Bois David, le Tour, la Ferté, Chamblai, chevau légers* squadrons of *Moissac* and *Palluau Clérambault*, *carabins* companies of *Corvoux, Venterol* and *Saint-Benoît*, dragoons of *Bouillac* and the *gendarmes d'Alincourt*.

The army of Field Marshal d'Aurine in Italy (6,000 men) included 5 infantry regiments (*Vernatel, Féron, Puy Saint-Martin, Castreville, Urfé*) and 10 cavalry companies (*Féron, Saint-Bouages, la Bruyère, Saint-Benoît, Scoli, Auriac, Sauveboeuf, Lignidy, Saint-Aulaire, Montcara*).

The army of Maréchal Brézé at the battle of Cerisy on the 2 August 1636:

The infantry included the *Gardes Françaises, Gardes Suisses, Piémont, Champagne, La Marine, Saintonge, Vaubecourt, la Roche-Giffart* plus 400 horses. The *Charost and Bellefonds* regiments were in Bray.

The army of the Prince de Condé in Languedoc, bringing relief to Leucate on the 24 September 1637:

- ◇ Infantry (10,000 footsoldiers) : 7 regiments (*Languedoc, la Tour, Castellan, Serignan, Saint-André, Saint-Aunès, Vitry*), battalions of milices of *Montpellier, Nîmes, Carcassonne, Narbonne, Béziers* and *Castres*; battalions of *Mirepoix, la Jonquière, Merville* and *Vaillac.*

- ◇ Cavalry (900 nobles): mounted guards of the Duc d'Halluin (100 gentlemen), *Gendarmes d'Halluin,* 50 *Gendarmes de Cramail, chevau légers* companies of *Boissac, Espondeilhan, Mirepoix, Montsoulins, Mauléon* (50 *maîtres* each), 200 gentlemen from the Languedoc, the dragoons of *Toulouse* and the mounted musketeers of *Saussan, Sainte-Croix* and *Malves.*

The army of Maréchal de Châtillon in 1639 at the battle of Thionville, on the 7 June 1639 included 7 infantry regiments (8 to 9,000 footsoldiers): *Picardie, Navarre* (in 2 large battalions), *Rambures, Beauce, la Perche, Canisy, Bussy-Rabutin* and 2,600 cavalry.

Army of Maréchal de la Meilleraye in Champagne, 1639 (Storming of Hesdin, 29 June 1639):

- ◇ Infantry: half of the *Gardes Françaises* and *Gardes Suisses,* the regiments of *Piémont, Champagne, La Marine, la Ferté, Calstelmoron* and *Langeron.*

- ◇ Cavalry: many *gendarmerie* and *chevau légers* companies (companies *du Roi, de la Reine, de Monsieur, des Princes,* and *des Maréchaux*), commanded by Gassion.

Army of Henri de Lorraine, Comte d'Armagnac, Brienne and Harcourt (replacing Cardinal de la Valette), in the Piedmont, 1639 and 1640 (October 1639 to July 1640): 9,500 men (6,000 infantry and 3,500 horses); Plessis-Praslin commanded the infantry, and Turenne the cavalry:

- ◇ Infantry: regiments of *Gardes Françaises* (two battalions), *Gardes Suisses* (one battalion), *Auvergne, Lyonnais, Nerestang, Alincourt, Florinville, Villandry, Turenne, Plessis-Praslin, Roussillon, Tavannes, Villandry, la Mothe-Houdencourt, La Valette* and the *Couvonges* regiment (in the citadel of Turin).

- ◇ Cavalry: *gendarme* squadrons of *Beauregard Champoux, Arzillières, Condé, chevau légers Enghien, Marsin, du Terrail, Beauregard, la Luzerne, la Valette, Souvré, Montpezat, la Rochette, Lesdiguières, Villeneuve, Tavannes, Saint-André,* squadrons of *Ligondès* and *Dizimieux,* the non-regimented company of *Sarroty, carabins* of Savoie and dragoons.

Reinforcements expected in July 1640: 4,000 highlanders of the *Dauphiné* commanded by the Marquis de Villeroy.

Army of Guébriant in 1641 and 1642: Guébriant took command of the Weimarian army on the death of Baner, on the 20 May 1641. In addition to German troops, this corps included two French infantry regiments (*Montausier* and *Nettancourt)* and 6,000 Hessians. Weimarian regiments: Rosen's *chevau légers* and dragoons; *Streef, Eggenfeld, Batilly, Humes, Lee, Zillard, Boillon, Watronville, Nassau, Muller, Schack, Vaubecourt, Tupalden, Forbus* and *Trefski chevau legers.* The artillery had twelve cannon.

The army of Rocroi, 16 May 1643, commanded by Louis de Bourbon, Duc d' Enghien with Maréchal de l'Hôpital as lieutenant general and three field marshals (Jean de Gassion, *mestre de camp* general of the light cavalry, the Marquis de la Ferté-Senneterre and the Baron de Sirot).

- ◇ Infantry: 16,000 infantry in 21 regiments (3 *vieux corps*: *Picardie, Piémont, La Marine*; 2 *petits vieux*: *Rambures* and *Persan*; 3 Swiss regiments: *Molondin, Watteville* and *Roll*; the *Gardes Ecossaises*; 12 temporary regiments: *Bourdonné, Biscara, Vervins, La Prée, Vidame d'Amiens, Langeron, Brézé, Bussy, Guiche, Harcourt, Aubeterre, Gesvres*; and 8 royal companies);

◆ Cavalry: 7,000 horsemen in 24 regiments and 7 companies forming 32 squadrons (6 *gendarme* companies, 1 company of the *gardes d'Enghien*, 1 dragoon regiment – the *Fusiliers du Roi* – 16 regiments of *chevau légers*: *Cardinal Duc, Mestre de camp général, Lenoncourt, Coislin, Sully, Roquelaure, Menneville, La Clavière, La Ferté, Guiche, Marolles, Heudicourt, Gesvres, Aubeterre, Harcourt, Charost*; the Hungarian regiment of *Sirot*, the Liège regiment of *Beauveau*, the German regiments *Zillard, Leschelle* and *Von Bergh*, and the Croat regiments *Raab* and *Schack*).

◆ Artillery: 12 cannon.

The infantry was formed at the centre in 15 battalions in a chequered pattern on two lines, the Swiss regiment *Molondin* forming two battalions. The 12 pieces of artillery covered the front. The Cavalry was formed on the wings, 15 squadrons on two lines on the right, with intercalated musketeer *manches*, and 13 squadrons on two lines on the left, also with intercalated of musketeer *manches*. Behind them was a reserve comprising the Hungarian cavalry regiment, 6 *gendarmerie* companies, 3 infantry regiments and the royal companies.

The army of the Duc d'Enghien at the Siege of Thionville, August 1643:

The infantry comprised the *Gardes Françaises, the Gardes Suisses, Picardie, Piémont, Navarre, La Marine, Rambures* and the Swiss *Molondin*.

The army of Germany of Maréchal Guébriant on the Rhine on the 2 September 1643 (12,000 men):

7,000 infantry in 12 brigades, 15 cavalry regiments making up 27 squadrons, 2 dragoon squadrons, 4 half-cannon, two 12-pound pieces, small cannon of 6 and 3 pounds and a howitzer.

The Weimarian army of Rosen in Tuttlingen on the 24 November 1643:

7 cavalry regiments (4 Weimarian: *Wittgenstein, Betz, Flechstein* and *Rusworms*; 3 French: *du Tot, Roncherolles* and *Batilly*), one *Rosen* dragoon regiment and 3 infantry regiments.

The army of Picardy, commanded by Gaston d'Orléans, lieutenant general of the kingdom, 1644: Maréchals de France La Meilleraye and Gassion, Lieutenant Generals Rantzau and Charles de Lorraine, Duc d'Elbeuf, with 30,000 men.

The larger corps of La Meilleraye included the *Gardes Suisses* and the *Gardes Ecossaises*.

The Gassion corps included the infantry regiments *Navarre* and *Langeron*.

The army of France commanded by the Duc d'Enghien, including the army of Turenne, at the battle of Friburg on the 3 and 5 August 1644:

The army was formed in 3 lines, Turenne on the right with the Weimarians, the infantry of the French army in the centre, and the cavalry of Maréchal Gramont on the left wing. The infantry regiments of the Duc d'Enghien (*Persan, Enghien, Conti, Mazarin français, Mazarin italien, Le Havre, Guiche, Desmarets, Fabert*) were formed in 3 brigades. Turenne's infantry was made up of the French regiments *Montausin, Mézières, de la Couronne* and the Weimarian regiments of *Tot, Aubeterre, Hatstein, Bernhold* and *Schmidtberg*.

The cavalry comprised the *Gardes d'Enghien* and *Guiche*, the *gendarmerie* companies of *Enghien, Condé, Conti* and *Guiche*, the cavalry regiments *Enghien, Guiche, Cardinal Mazarin, Mazarin français, L'Eschelle* and *Beauveau* (both from Liège), *Turenne*, and the Weimarian regiments *Alt Rosen, Fleckenstein, Berg, Baden, Wittgenstein, Russwurm, Neu Rosen, Scharfenstein, Erlach, Tracy, Guébriant, Taupadel* and *Kanoffsky*.

Turenne drew up a detachment of 1,000 musketeers and 4 pieces of artillery from all the infantry regiments of both armies. Rosen defended the infantry with the Weimarian cavalry, and Gramont was in reserve with the French cavalry (*chevau légers* and *gendarmes*).

Turenne's German army, March 1645:

On the 31 March 1645, the army had 11,000 men: 6,000 infantry, 5,000 horses and 11 cannon.

At the battle of Marienthal, or Mergentheim, on the 5 May 1645, the infantry had a total of 3,000 men: *Turenne, Mazarin Italien* and *Oysonville* regiments for the French, *Schmidtberg* and *Truchsess*

131

Battle of Rocroi:
Gassion on a reconnaissance
of the surrounding woods,
1898 by Alphonse Lalauze
(1872-1930). Condé museum,
Chantilly, France.

regiments for the Weimarians. The cavalry comprised the French regiments *Oysonville, Duras* and *Turenne*, the Liège regiment *Beauveau* and the Weimarian regiments *Betz, Alt Rosen, Öhm, Wittgenstein, Fleckenstein, Taupadel, Baden* and *Tracy*.

The battle of Allerheim (or Nördlingen) on the 3 August 1645:

On the right wing: Maréchal de Gramont and 16 French cavalry squadrons (*Gardes de Gramont, Gardes d'Enghien, Carabins,* and *Mazarin, Enghien, Gramont, Chambre, Boury, La Clavière, Marchin, Neu Rosen* regiments) and 2 infantry regiments, *Wall* (Irish) and *Fabert*.

At the centre: 10 infantry battalions from France, Germany and Liège under the Comte de Marsin: *Mazarin Français, Mazarin Italien, Oysonville, Conti, Enghien, Persan, Gramont, Montausier, Le Havre* and *Truchsess* (Weimarian), plus the queen mother's *gendarmes* and *chevau légers*. 27 pieces of artillery were spread out along the front.

On the left wing: Turenne with 12 French and Weimarian regiments: *Cardinal Mazarin, Turenne, Oysonville, Beauveau, Russwurm, Taupadel, Tracy, Neu Rosen, Alt Rosen, Fleckenstein* and *Kanoffsky*. On the second line were 6 Hessian regiments (*Betz, Rauchaupt, Schwert, Groote, Geiss, Beaucourt*) and two Weimarian regiments *Öhm* and *Betz*, plus 6 Hessian battalions (*Franc, Lopetz, Uffel, Vrede, Staufer, Kotz*).

The Catalonian army of the Duc d'Enghien at the siege of Llerida in May 1646

On the 11 April 1646, the Duc d'Enghien replaced Harcourt at the head of army of Catalonia, which he reinforced with troops of his own household, totalling 4,000 men (the *Gardes d'Enghien*, a company of *gendarmes*, the regiment of *chevau légers Enghien* and 4 infantry regiments: *Condé, Conti, Enghien, Persan*) as well as 1,200 new recruits. Maréchal de Gramont, Lieutenant General de Marsin, Field Marshals La Moussaye, Arnauld, Coligny Châtillon, de la Vallière and Battle General La Brousse de Verteillac made up the general staff.

In total, on the 11 May the reconstituted army counted 10,000 footsoldiers and 4,000 cavalry, who recommenced the siege of Llerida, which finally lifted at the end of June. *Champagne* was part of the army.

The army of Condé at the battle of Lens on the 20 August 1648

In Picardy, Condé had 16,000 men and 18 cannon, of which 4,000 Weimarians remained loyal to France and were commanded by Erlach. Of the 29 infantry regiments of the army (22 French and 7 foreign), 11 were garrisoned in different towns and cities. Some infantry regiments, which counted 1,500 men at the beginning of the campaign, had no more than 300 men. In Lens, the army was composed of 12 infantry battalions and 45 cavalry squadrons.

On the right wing (Condé): 17 squadrons of which 9 in the first line (guards of *Mr le Prince, Chappes, Coudray-Montpensier, Salbrick, Vidame d'Amiens, Le Vilette* – formerly *Gassion, Ravenel*), commanded by the Lieutenant General Aumont, and 8 in the second line, under Claude de la Trémoille (*Orléans, La Meilleraye, Streef, Saint-Simon, Bussy-Almory, Beaujeu*).

In the centre (Gaspard de Coligny): a first line of 7 battalions (*Persan, Gardes Suisses, Gardes Françaises, Gardes Ecossaises, Picardie, Orléans, Erlach*) then a second line of 5 battalions (*Conti, Condé, La Reine, Dazilly, Mazarin Italien*). Between these two lines were 6 squadrons of *gendarmes* (companies of *Condé, Schomberg, La Reine, Duc d'Orléans, Enghien, Conti, Longueville* and *Marcillac*). 18 cannon were spread along the front of the infantry, under the command of Timoléon de Cossé Brissac.

On the left wing (Gramont): 16 squadrons of which 9 in the first line under La Ferté-Senneterre (2 squadrons from *Les Bains*, 2 squadrons from *La Ferté-Senneterre*, 2 squadrons from *Gramont, Mazarin*, Arnault's *carabins*, Gramont's guards and La Ferté's guards) and 7 in the second line, commanded by Du Plessis-Bellière (*Chémerault, Meille, Lillebonne, Gesvres*).

Behind the centre, the Comte d'Erlach was in reserve with 6 squadrons of Weimarian cavalry (*Fabry, Erlach, Sirot, Ruvigny*).

132

[APPENDIX]

[Appendix I : chronology]

1617 Assassination of Concini (24 April): Louis XIII takes power.

1618 Protestant revolt in Bohemia and defenestration of Prague (23 May). Archduke Ferdinand II, King of Bohemia, controls the empire (18 July).

1619 France: rebellion of the queen mother. Austria: Ferdinand II is elected emperor by the Electoral College (28 August). The states of Bohemia pronounce the deposition of Ferdinand II (19 August) and designate the Elector Palatine Frederick V King of Bohemia; coronation on the 4 November.

1620 France: rebellion of the nobility resulting in the Drôlerie des Ponts-de-Cé (7 August). Bohemia: battle of the White Mountain (8 November): the imperial army overwhelms the Protestant army of Christian d'Anhalt.

1621 France: storming of Privas by the Protestants (February). The army of Louis XIII enters the campaign: siege of Saint Jean d'Angély (June).

1622 Campaign of Saintonge and Languedoc, storming of Nègrepelisse by the royal armies (10 June), siege and Treaty of Montpellier (18 October).

1623 Victory of Tilly over Christian of Brunswick at Stadtlohn (6 August).

1624 Richelieu enters the conseil. French expedition under François d'Estrées in the Valtelline (October).

1625 France: second Protestant revolt (January). Intervention of Christian IV, king of Denmark in the Thirty Years' War.

1626 English landing on the Isle of Rhé (26 July). Defeat of Christian IV of Denmark by Tilly on the 26 August at Lutter-am-Barenberg.

1627 Beginning of the siege of La Rochelle (15 August). Beginning of the succession of Mantua.

1628 Surrender of La Rochelle (28 October). Siege of Stralsund by the Danish navy. The Danes are defeated by Wallenstein at Wolgast (September).

1629 Code Michau (ordonnance of January 1629). Edict of Grace of Nimes (28 June). Mantua campaign (1629-30)

1630 Landing of Gustavus Adolphus in Pomerania (6 July). Battle of Carignan (6 August); the "Day of Dupes" (11 November) reinforces Richelieu's powers while Louis XIII sends the queen mother into exile.

1631 Italy: treaty of Cherasco (26 April). Storming and massacre of Magdeburg by Tilly's imperialists (20 May). Battle of Breitenfeld (17 September): victory of the Swedes under Gustavus Adolphus over Tilly's imperialists.

1632 France: revolt of the Duc de Montmorency. In May, La Force and Effiat fight a Hispano-Lotharingian army in Mars la Tour. Saxony: battle of Lützen (16 November); victory of the Swedes under Gustavus Adolphus over Wallenstein's imperialists.

1633 Louis XIII enters Nancy (25 September). The Swedes defeat the Lotharingians at Pfaffenhofen.

1634 Abdication of the Duc de Lorraine Charles IV (19 January) who joins the imperial army. Battle of Nordlingen (6 September): the Swedes (Bernard of Saxe-Weimar) are defeated by the imperialists.

1635 Declaration of war by Louis XIII against Philip IV. Battle of Avins (22 May): victory of Brézé and Châtillon over the Spanish army of Prince Thomas François de Carignan. Campaign of Henri de Rohan in the Valtelline (battles of Livigno on the 27 June, Mazo on the 29 June and Morbegon on the 10 November).

1636 The Cardinal Infante attacks in Picardy (2 July): storming of Corbie (15 August) and siege of Saint-Jean-de-Losne which is lifted on the 4 November. Battle of Tornavento (22 June): victory of the Franco-Savoyards under Charles de Créqui and Amedeo of Savoy over the Spanish of Leganez. Battle of Wittstock (4 October): victory for Baner's Swedes against the imperialists.

1637 Death of Emperor Ferdinand II (15 February); succession of Ferdinand III. Campaign of Bernard of Saxe-Weimar on the Rhine. 30 July: victory of Bernard over the imperialists at Breisach. Flanders campaign (1637-38). In Languedoc: battle of Leucate (24 September 1637): victory of the French under the Duc d'Halluin against the Spanish under Cerbelloni. Death of Duke Victor Amedeo of Savoy (8 September).

1638 Winter campaign of Bernard of Saxe-Weimar. Death of the Duc de Rohan at Rheinfelden (February). Storming of Brisach by Bernard of Saxe-Weimar and Turenne (18 December).

1639 Death of Bernard of Saxe-Weimar (8 July). Battle of Chenmitz (14 April): victory of Baner's Swedes against the Saxons. Battle of Thionville (7 June 1639): defeat of Châtillon against Piccolomini's imperialists. In the Piedmont: battle of La Rota (20 November 1639): victory of Harcourt over the Spanish of Leganez.

1640 Siege and storming of Arras by the French (8 August). Battle of Casale in the Piedmont (29 April): victory of Harcourt over the Spanish of Leganez. Battle of Turin (11 July): victory of Harcourt over the Spanish of Leganez.

1641 Battle of Ziegenhaun (25 November): victory of a Weimarian detachment under Rosen against an imperial force. Battle of Wolfenbüttel (29 June): victory of the Weimarians and Swedes under Königsmark and Guébriant against the imperialists. Battle of Sedan (6 July 1641): defeat of Châtillon by the imperialists under Lamboy allied with the Comte de Soissons and the Duc de Bouillon, both in rebellion.

1642 Battle of Kempen (17 January): victory of Guébriant at the head of 10,000 Weimarians over Lamboy's imperialists. Battle of Honnecourt (25 May): defeat of the French under de Guiche against the Spanish of de Melo. Battle of Llerida (7 October): victory of the French of La Mothe-Houdencourt over the Spanish of Leganez. Second battle of Breitenfeld (2 November): victory of the Swedes under Torstensson against the imperialists of Archduke Leopold. Death of Richelieu on the 4 December. He is replaced at the council by Mazarin. Léopold.

1643 Spain: on the 16 January, Olivarès is distanced from power. France: death of Louis XIII on the 14 May. Battle of Rocroi (19 May): victory of the Duc d'Enghien (16,000 infantry, 7,000 horses) over the Spanish of Don Francisco de Melo (18,000 infantry, 9,000 horses and 18 cannon). Battle of Tuttlingen (24 November): Rantzau's Weimarians are decimated.

1644 Battle of Freiburg in Brisgau (3-9 August); victory of the Duc d'Enghien over Mercy's Bavarians.

1645 Battle of Jankau (6 March): victory of the Swedes under Torstensson against Hatzfeld's imperialists. Battle of Mergentheim (5 May): victory of Mercy's Bavarians against the French under Turenne. Battle of Alerheim or Nordlingen (3 August): victory of the Duc d'Enghien over Mercy's Bavarians. Gaston d'Orléans (with Gassion and Rantzau) completes the conquest of Flanders (July-August). Catalonia: battle of Lhorens (20 October): victory of Harcourt over the Spanish.

1646 Storming of Courtrai (15 June) and Dunkirk (10 October) by the Duc d'Enghien. Franco-Swedish expedition (Turenne and Wrangel) in Bavaria. Storming of the Isle of Elbe and Piombino in Italy (16 October) by La Meilleraye. Failure of the Comte d'Harcourt against Llerida (5 October).

1647 Plessis Praslin victorious over the Marquis of Caracena on the Oglio in Italy (4 July). Failure of the Duc d'Enghien against Llerida (May to August). Mutiny of Turenne's Weimarians (June-July).

1648 Battle of Zusmarchausen (17 May): the Franco-Swedes (as well as the Weimarians and the Hessians) of Turenne and Wrangel defeat the imperialists of Melander, Montecuccoli and Holzupfel. Battle of Lens: on the 20 August, the French under the Duc d'Enghien defeat the Spanish under Archduke Leopold. Treaty of Westphalia (24 October)

135

P. 136-137 :
The favourite, by Auguste César Detti (1847-1914). Private collection.

[Appendix II : eyewitness accounts]

1 The Battle of the pas de Suse, on the 6 march 1629

1 ◈ ... *eyewitness accounts*

THE BATTLE OF THE PAS DE SUSE, AS RECOUNTED BY CARDINAL RICHELIEU

"That day, the 6th, at eight o'clock in the morning, with the king on horseback and all the troops in battle array, Comminges was sent to those commanding the barricades in order to inform them that the king was present in person and that he wished to know if they would open a passage for him and if Mr de Savoie would treat him as a friend or foe in his domain. The Comte de Vérue replied that since we had come so far the affair would have to be settled by force and that we were not dealing with the English. Immediately afterwards, the barricades were attacked; the advanced guard of the king, consisting of the guards, the Swiss, the regiment of Navarre and those of Sault and d'Estissac had been placed in battle array between Chaumont and the place which was to be attacked three hours after midnight. The guards, the Swiss, Navarre and Estissac were deployed to attack the barricades from the front. Sault's regiment, whose officers knew the country better than anyone since most of them came from there, were, with the assistance of good guides, to take a certain path by means of which they could reach the area behind the barricades, in order to attack simultaneously from all sides. The enfants perdus were placed in three troops so as to take the said barricades from the middle and the two sides. The troops in the middle were made up of one hundred musketeers, fifty of them guards and the same number of the king's musketeers. Those on the right flank consisted of fifty guards, and those on the left flank, fifty men from the regiment of Navarre. These three corps were supported by three others of one hundred men each from the same regiments as above. There followed a battalion of volunteers commanded by Mr de Longueville with nearly three hundred gentlemen, many of whom were of good quality. After, came five hundred of Navarre's men. While Sault's regiment was ordered to advance on the right in an attempt to take the barricades from behind, that commanded by d'Estissac was ordered to climb a hill on the left which dominated the enemy barricades. The enemy, with this in mind, had lined the hill with musketeers, and the five hundred men mentioned above, half pikes, half muskets, were under orders to clear them so as then to be able to fire on those who were defending behind the barricades, which fortunately, is what took place. Then came a culverin and two moyennes along with fifty pioneers to break through the barricade. These were followed by two corps, guards and Swiss, each consisting of five hundred men. The rest of the troops, four thousand men, were in battle array, ready to receive their orders, whether to reinforce the attacks, according to need, or advance further when the passage had been opened.

The attack began at eight o'clock and was soon over, as much because of the violence of the French as because of the enemy, seeing that they were under attack from all sides, took to their heels after their first volley. It can be said in truth that all did well on this occasion; however all the order that had been desirable, and that had been decided upon, was not able to be maintained, as much through the difficulties of the terrain which was harsh and narrow, separated every hundred paces by low dry stone walls, which broke up the battalions, as through the nature of the French, which has always been considered more courageous than wise, and which led each man to march as he wished, which could greatly prejudice the service of the king. In consideration of this, Maréchals de Créqui, de Bassompierre and Schomberg, and the field marshals were all together at the head of the volunteers, contrary to reason which would have placed them separately in diverse locations, to give orders in all places. Maréchal de Schomberg received a musket ball in the side, but in fifteen days he was well again; commander de Valençay received another in the thigh, which did not stop him being active throughout the attack, showing courage and bravery, having ordered the Swiss to climb the hill by means of a difficult passage, which was very useful for driving off the enemy.

Before turning to other things, I must mention the perverse effects provoked by the jealousy between the Maréchal de Créqui and Maréchal de Bassompierre; this unfortunate situation did not prevent the king being victorious and the fighting so intense that Mr de Savoie and the Prince de Piémont, who were present on the barricades, were almost captured (...)

While the front of the pas de Suse was under attack, the Comte de Sault wasted no time since having encountered Belon's regiment of Milanese, it was cut to pieces to such an extent that he brought to the king nine flags along with ten captains, lieutenants and ensigns. The Marquis de Ville, the duke's general of cavalry, and one of his best men, was wounded by a musket volley that broke his arm and his shoulder. We lost very few men, five or six officers were wounded and there were no more than thirty dead. Many of our troops entered the town of Suse in pursuit of the enemy, but we ordered them out of the town, because the place was not safe, being difficult to defend and we preferred to accept its surrender twenty four hours later, peacefully, rather than take it immediately; which could not be done without the risk of pillaging and disorder, inevitable when towns are taken by force. His Majesty strongly recommended this course of action so that his armies should not be denigrated in Italy, where the French were seen as being brave but undisciplined. The town's castle surrendered the following day, but this was not the case with the citadel nor with a fort called Talasse."

THE BATTLE OF THE PAS DE SUSE, AS RECOUNTED BY MARÉCHAL DE BESOMPIERRE

"However, Mr de Créqui and I, along with the field marshals held a meeting to determine the order to be established. The regiments of the French and Swiss guards would take the lead; the regiment of Navarre would take the right flank and Estissac the left flank; the two flanks would send two hundred musketeers each up the hills so that they were in a position to dominate and outflank the guards defending the barricades; once that was achieved, at our signal, they would fire a volley from behind the barricade while we attacked it frontally with the two guards regiments; the Comte de Sault with his regiment would proceed below Jalasse, by a roundabout route with local peasants as guides and would then descend on Suse and take the enemy from behind if they were still resisting; at the same time Jallon would be attacked by another regiment, commanded by Mr d'Auriac. The orders being given, at eleven o'clock in the evening, we began to move the troops through Chaumont. The weather was very bad and there was two feet of snow under foot.

On Tuesday, March 6th, the king arrived in Chaumont at two o'clock in the morning, with the Comtes de Soissons, de Longueville and de Moret, Maréchals de Schomberg, d'Halluin, de la Villette and others. Our troops followed – seven companies of guards, six Swiss, 19 of Navarre, 14 of Estissac, 15 of Sault, and the king's mounted musketeers. The Comte de Sault and his regiment left at three o'clock to take up their positions as ordered: the rest remained in battle array five hundred paces from the village of Jalasse. We advanced also six pieces of six-pound cannon, pulled along using a hook, to force the barricades. Estissac was ordered to leave one hundred men to guard the ordinance. The order was that each corps would send forward fifty enfants perdus, supported by one hundred men, who would be supported by five hundred more. We placed the princes and the noblemen at the head of five hundred guards.

At six o'clock in the morning, Mr de Créqui and I with de la Vallette, Valençay, Toiras,

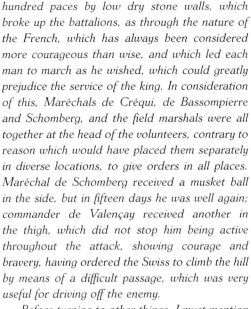

139

140

Canaples and Tavannes placed our troops in the battle array outlined above. The king arrived at the same time with the comte and the cardinal: he wanted his musketeers to be mixed up with the enfants perdus of the guards.

On behalf of the king we sent Mr de Comminges with a trumpeter to request passage for the army and the king's person from the Duc de Savoie. But as he approached the barricade he was stopped, and the Comte de Verrue came out to speak to him. He said that we did not come as friends, and that, this being so, they would do their utmost to prevent our passage and that if we persisted in the undertaking, we would suffer the consequences.

After Comminges had reported this reply, I went to find the king who was one hundred paces behind our enfants perdus, further forward than most of the five hundred guards, to ask him for permission to begin the festivities and I said to him: 'Sire, Sire, the assembly is ready, the violins are in place and the masks are at the door: when it pleases your Majesty the dance can begin.' He came up to me and said angrily, 'Do you realise that we only have five pounds of lead for our ordinance?' I replied: 'This is a fine time to think of that! Just because one of the masks is not ready, should we cancel the dance? Let us proceed with it, Sire, and all will be well.' 'Will you pledge that it will be so?' he asked. 'It would be very bold of me to guarantee such a hazardous enterprise but I can say we will either be victorious or I shall be dead or captured.' 'Yes,' he said 'but if we fail, I will hold you responsible.' (...) Then, the cardinal said: 'Sire, judging from the Marshal's look all will be well: rest assured.'

Upon which, I approached Mr de Créqui and dismounted to join him, having given the signal for combat to begin. Maréchal de Schomberg, who had only just arrived having been obliged to remain behind because of his gout, had come on horseback to see the festivities. We passed the village of Jallasse which the enemy had abandoned. Leaving the village we were welcomed by numerous volleys of musket fire from the enemy who were on the mountainsides and at the great barricade, and many cannonades from the fort at Jallasse. We continued to progress and Mr de Schomberg was wounded in the back by musket fire coming from the slopes to the left. Once our men from both flanks had control of these slopes, the enemy began firing from behind the barricade and, charging headlong, we chased them off. We followed them so vigorously that they could not hold any of their positions. Then, fighting at close quarters, the Commander de Vançay took the heights on the left with the Swiss where he was wounded by a volley of musket shot in the knee, but he dispersed the Valaisans led by the Comte de Verrue: his horse was captured. I advanced below with Mr de Créqui and the French where the marquis de Ville was seriously wounded. We followed up our advance so vigorously that had it not been for the resistance offered by a Spanish captain and a few soldiers to our enfants perdus enabling the duke and the prince to retreat, they would both have been taken. Without interruption, we reached the heights above Suse where we came under heavy cannon fire from the citadel. But we were so delighted to have been victorious that we ignored the cannon fire. I saw something which pleased me concerning the French nobility present that day, as exemplified by, among others Mr de Longueville, Mr de Moret, Mr d'Halluin, the first equerry and more than sixty others. A cannonade fell at our feet and covered all of us with earth; my long familiarity with cannon fire had taught me, more than the others, that once the shot is delivered, there is no longer any danger, so I was able to look at the faces around me and to see what effect the shot had had on them: I did not see one man who gave any sign of astonishment, nor did they even seem to notice. Another cannonade killed one of Mr de Créqui's gentlemen and again they took no notice. On approaching the barricade, one of my guards who was supporting me was killed at my side; another, advancing energetically with the enfants perdus was killed on the Suse bridge: one of my gentlemen, the commander of my galiot at La Rochelle named Du Val, received a musket volley on the instep which left him crippled. None of our enfants perdus followed the enemy pell-mell into the town and none were made prisoners; and at that moment we could have taken Suse, but we ordered our men to withdraw because we wished to prevent the town from being pillaged, so that it could serve as lodgings for the King (...)

During the combat at the barricades, the Comte de Sault had gone below Jallon to take the enemy from behind. The enemy, suspecting this, had positioned colonel Belon and his Milanese regiment on the road. But the Comte de Sault surprised the Milanese with a dawn attack and defeated them, took more than 20 officers prisoner, captured nine of the ten regimental standards, and then came to join us at the Cordeliers from where, at around five o'clock in the evening we summoned the town and castle to surrender, which they did. Having given us hostages, we postponed entering the town that day, fearing that there would be disorder and pillaging by our own brave soldiers, enraged by the previous defeat, on entering the town at night."

2 The Battle of Rocroi, 1643
... eyewitness accounts

THE BATTLE OF ROCROI AS RECOUNTED BY THE BARON DE SIROT, LIEUTENANT GENERAL OF THE KING'S CAMPS AND ARMIES:

"The Duc d'Enghien summoned the council of war which consisted of the prince in person, the Maréchal de l'Hôpital, his lieutenant general; Mr d'Espenan, first field marshal; Mr de Gassion, Mr de la Ferté-Senneterre, Mr de la Vallière, battle marshal; Mr de la Barre, who commanded the artillery, and myself, first mestre de camp for the cavalry and its commander. The Duc d'Enghien asked whether it would be better to assist Rocroi with the entire army by chancing a battle or whether we could try to achieve the same end by getting men into the town itself. Maréchal d'Hôpital, d'Espenan, de la Ferté, de la Vallière, and de la Barre were of the opinion that it would be better to assist the town by trying to send in men. This would be much safer and less hazardous, in view of the present state of affairs in France, Louis XIII having died only three days before. Given the problems caused by this death, if they lost the battle and were disgraced, the State would, perhaps, be in danger. It was to be feared that quarrels would break out and that some would favour the army of the enemy, embarrassing the king's council and fostering divisions. But the Duc d'Enghien, Mr de Gassion, the Marquis de Persan, the infantry's first mestre de camp and its commander, and I were of a different opinion (...)

Maréchal de l'Hôpital and all those who agreed with him insisted. But the Duc d'Enghien stuck to his opinion and he said that we should give battle and even said that that was his wish.

Thus it was decided that we would give battle if the enemy should resist and if the siege was not lifted at the arrival of our troops. Plans were laid for the battle to come and the battle array and the role of each was determined. Mr de Gassion would command the right flank, Mr de la Ferté-Senneterre, the left. The Duc d'Enghien, Maréchal de l'Hôpital, Mr d'Espenan and Mr de la Vallière were in the centre, and I was in command of the reserve consisting of two thousand infantry and a thousand cavalry.

On May 13th, once we had decided upon all the battle arrays and each of us knew what he had to do, the Duc d'Enghien left the place where he was and dispatched all the army's baggage trains to Aubanton and Aubigny, which were only a league and a half apart, and at half past three in the afternoon he arrived within sight of Rocroi. He found it difficult to believe, for he had been told that the enemy would be there to stop him at a certain point. It should be noted that, if they had been captured, it would have prevented our army advancing. With six thousand men they could have defended this position and with the rest of their army take the town which would

142

have surrendered on the evening of our arrival. As soon as the Duc d'Enghien and our generals passed safely through this point, they placed their forces in array, as had been decided, and they marched to a certain plateau which was close to the place where the enemy was lined up for battle. The town was behind them within range of cannon fire, and the two armies were only at a distance of two musket ranges from each other, and they remained thus for the entire day; but this was not without large skirmishes, and the cannon made much noise on all sides. Nevertheless, that of the enemy caused much more damage to our army than they received from us; for, besides the fact that it was better placed, it was also much better used, and their gunners were more expert and more skilful than ours. As a result, on that day, more than two thousand of our soldiers were killed or wounded in both the infantry and the cavalry.

Night was more favourable to our army than day; it gave us some respite, and our generals reorganised and strengthened our front line; for the Marquis de la Ferté had separated the left flank, which he commanded, by more than two thousand paces from the battle corps, which could have caused the loss of the battle. If the enemy had charged our troops, as they should have done, they would have defeated them. And neither the battle corps, nor I with the reserve, would have been able to assist them.

However, on May 19th, at daybreak, the enemy's army was still in the same position as ours, and seemed to be prepared for full combat. Indeed, our soldiers having slept in battle order with their weapons, they had only to rise, blow on their fuses, place them on their cannon and fire upon the enemy. And since their intentions were the same as ours, their troops found themselves in the same position. The battle began at four o'clock in the morning, and Mr de la Ferté committed the same error that he had made the day before, since he once again, separated the left flank under his command, from the main battle. The enemy charged them, breaking them and putting them to flight. The troops took to their heels without offering any resistance, and only a few officers and the marquis who held firm. They were made prisoner and the latter was wounded in two places. Thus, the entire right flank of the enemy fell upon the reserve under my command. But I was content to resist their

assault, and even to beat them back so vigorously that they threw down their weapons and fled back to their reserve, in great confusion, during which time I recaptured seven cannons that they had previously captured. But seeing that their reserve did not budge, I ordered my troops to halt having ensured that they were once more in condition to fight. Hardly had I halted the small corps under my command that the enemy's reserve cavalry charged us. However, seeing that they were not supported and that I had fought off their left flank, that Gassion and the Duc d'Enghien had put their battle corps to flight and that their right flank had folded, they attacked me with apprehension, and they thought more about fleeing than defending themselves when they were charged. So much so, that after defending for a certain time, I pushed them back so vigorously that finally they were forced to yield and to abandon their infantry, consisting of four thousand five hundred Spanish naturals in four regiments, the most experienced in Flanders. One was the Burgy regiment which was the strongest; that of the Duc d'Albuquerque, who was cavalry general in the enemy army and the two others were those of Villade and de Villealbois. Although the infantry saw that they had been abandoned, they held firm, and seeing their cavalry in flight. I straightened up my squadrons and prepared them to charge the enemy infantry.

But as I was leaving, the Chevalier de la Vallière, battle marshal, arrived bringing an order for the troops that I had rallied on the flank, those commanded by the Marquis de la Ferté-Senneterre and telling them that the battle was lost. These troops were the Picardy regiment, the Piedmontese, the Marine, Molodin's Swiss and Persan's regiment. These troops, who had been very badly treated, were more than willing to obey the orders of the battle marshal. But, seeing that they were about to abandon me, I approached them. I begged them to hold firm. But, seeing that in spite of my remonstrances, they continued to withdraw, I castigated their lack of heart and had very strong words with the chevalier de la Vallière. I told him that it was not for him to command my troops and that I greatly resented it. These prayers and threats had such an effect on the feelings of the officers that they heeded me and were strengthened in their resolve. But as I led the charge, this same chevalier de la Vallière halted them a second time and I was followed only by what remained of my reserve corps, that is to say, Harcourt's regiment, and those of Bretagne and the Royals, and for the cavalry my own regiment, which had suffered greatly and were much weakened due to the great shock that they had endured and the fierce charges that they had given. Most of them had been killed or wounded and were out of action. Nonetheless, I charged the Spanish troops, but I was not able to crush them because my men were too weak. I therefore ran to these withdrawing regiments which were at more than one hundred paces from me. I called them cowards and men with little heart and honour, for withdrawing without even seeing the enemy. I told them that I would proclaim their shame all over France, and would complain of them to the king and the Duc d'Enghien. They would win the battle if they stayed, because there was only this battalion in front of them that was holding firm and if they listened to me and were prepared to act like brave and honourable men they would defeat them; that they were abandoning me for a man who would lose them their honour and reputation forever, that they should rally my troops and I promised that they would be victorious. Both officers and soldiers listened to these remonstrances and choosing the path of honour rather than follow the orders of the chevalier de la Vallière, they cried as one: 'To the Baron de Sirot, to the Baron de Sirot!' They came to me and I led them to join up with the rest of my troops that were waiting for me. But as I was placing them in battle array to attack these Spanish regiments, the Duc d'Enghien arrived and I informed him of the order that the Chevalier de la Vallière had just transmitted to me and to the troops that were with him. The prince, seeing that he was being so badly slandered in a matter of such great import, disavowed him and said that he who had said it had lied.

After this disavowal, I asked him to withdraw a little to the side, which he did, and then seeing that the Spanish battalion began to yield, I charged it so vigorously that, unable to withstand the advance of my troops, they were broken and deflated, leaving two thousand dead along with as many made prisoner. Two of their colonels were killed, de Villebois and de Villades. But before this battalion was broken, the Comte de Fontaines, who was a general

in the king of Spain's army, and who was in a chair at the head of his battalion since he could not mount his horse because he was suffering greatly from gallstones, was killed. Our troops took possession of his body and carried it to the church in Rocroi. Dom Francisco de Melo who had withdrawn to Marienbourg after the defeat of their army asked for his body back the same day. The Duc d'Enghien returned it to him, after placing it in a shroud and then in a casket. He had it transported in his carriage to Marienbourg, which is only seven leagues from Rocroi, and with it he sent all the chaplains, Jesuits and other clerics in their army whom he had made prisoner."

THE BATTLE OF ROCROI AS RECOUNTED BY THE MARQUIS DE LA MOUSSAYE
(AS DICTATED TO HENRI DE BESSÉ, SIEUR DE LA CHAPPELLE MILON, WHO WAS EMPLOYED IN THE ADMINISTRATION OF THE ROYAL BUILDINGS):

"His rank, his affairs, the interests of his house and the advice of his friends called him (Condé) back to the court. Nonetheless, on this occasion he preferred the general good to his private advantage, and his thirst for glory meant that he did not hesitate for a moment. He kept secret the news of the king's death and marched towards Rocroi the next day, persuading Maréchal de l'Hôpital that he was advancing towards Rocroi only to provide assistance in the form of men and munitions through the surrounding woods (....).

Perhaps believing that the Spanish would defend the narrow pass and that things would end in a fierce skirmish in the woods during which help could be delivered to the town, and that since the army was not engaged beyond the narrow passage it could withdraw easily without risk of a general full scale engagement (...)

De Melo was soon obliged to decide whether he would defend the pass or whether he would wait to be attacked on the plain. Nothing was easier than to defend the pass by pouring his infantry into the woods and supporting them with a large number of cavalry. He could even, by using the advantage of the woods and marshes, tie up the French army with part of his troops while finishing off the siege of the town with the other part. This seemed the best tactic and there was no one who believed that de Melo would not adopt it. But his ambitions were not limited to the capture of Rocroi. He believed that winning a battle would open the way to the heart of France and his victory at Honnecourt caused him to hope for a similar outcome in front of Rocroi. Besides, in chancing a battle, he believed he was risking at most the smallest part of his army and certain fortifications on the border. The defeat of the Duc d'Enghien, on the other hand, would bring him infinite advantage at the beginning of a regency which was hardly established.

Reasoning in this way, de Melo who, as is the Spanish temperament, sometimes neglected the present by thinking too much of the future, decided to give battle, and so as to engage the Duc d'Enghien more easily, he waited in the plain and made not the slightest effort to contest the pass; because while he was considering what he should do, there was almost no time left for reflection. The leading troops of the Duc d'Enghien were already appearing, and the French army would have finished marching through the pass before he had organised his quarters. Nonetheless, if he had wanted to do all he could to prevent our passage early enough, the Duc d'Enghien would have had difficulty in forcing a way through, for there is nothing more difficult in warfare than to emerge from a long path through the woods and marshland within sight of a powerful army posted on a plain. However this may be, it is clear that de Melo wanted a battle since he had taken pains to assemble all his forces and ordered Beck, who was in Palaizeux, to come and join him with all speed.

The Duc d'Enghien marched in two columns, from Bossu to the entrance to the pass. Gassion went ahead with a few cavalry to reconnoitre the enemy and finding the passage defended by no more than fifty horses, he pushed them back and came to report to the Duc d'Enghien the ease with which he had taken the pass.

This was the place where the prince thought he should speak more openly to Maréchal de l'Hôpital because the maréchal saw clearly that in pushing forward onto the plain, it would be impossible to avoid going to battle. Gassion

did all he could to gain his acquiescence and the maréchal continued to differ, but the Duc d'Enghien put an end to their dispute and said, in masterly tones, that he assumed full responsibility for the engagement.

The maréchal ceased arguing and placed himself at the head of the troops under his command. The Duc d'Enghien ordered his right flank to advance, placing the infantry in the most difficult places so as to protect the passage of the rest of the army. At the same time, he advanced, with some of the cavalry, as far as a small hill at half range of the Spanish cannon. If de Melo had charged the Duc d'Enghien, he would certainly have defeated him. But the Duc covered the top of the hill so well with the squadrons that he had, that the Spanish could not see what was happening behind him.

De Melo could not believe that such a large number of cavalry could advance without being supported by the infantry. This is why he was content to try by means of skirmishes to see if he could see the area behind the squadrons. But not having been able to win through, he concentrated on placing his troops in battle array.

Thus the two generals had the same ambition: the prince concentrated on the passage of his troops through the pass and de Melo was only concerned to organise his quarters. The place where the Duc d'Enghien had arranged his battlefield was big enough to deploy his entire army as he had planned. The ground was higher than the surrounding area and sloped down imperceptibly towards the plain. On the left there was a large marsh and, since the woods were not very thick they did not prevent the squadrons from assembling. The Duc d'Enghien occupied these heights and opposite there was another very similar hill where the Spanish were posted facing the French lines, and between these two positions there was a small valley.

It is easy to judge from this situation that neither of the two parties could attack without climbing above the other. Nonetheless, the Spanish had an advantage in that on the slopes of the height that they occupied and in front of their left flank, there was a dense wood which stretched quite a distance down in to the valley, and it was easy for them to position musketeers there so as to harass the Duc d'Enghien as he advanced.

The two generals worked frenziedly to get

their troops in to position as they arrived and instead of skirmishing which was the usual custom when two armies approached each other, they both took all the time necessary to arrange themselves in order of battle.

However, the Spanish cannon fire caused much more harm to the French than that of the French to the Spanish, because the latter had more guns, and they were better positioned and better employed. As the Duc d'Enghien extended the flanks of his army, the enemy fired such intense barrages of artillery fire that if it had not been for their extraordinary resistance, the French troops would not have been able to hold the ground that they had occupied. On that day, more than three hundred men were wounded by cannon fire, among them, the Marquis de Persan, mestre de camp of an infantry regiment, who received a wound in the thigh.

At six o'clock in the evening the French army had crossed the narrow pass and the reserve were coming out of the woods and taking up their position in the plain. The Duc d'Enghien was keen to begin the combat quickly in order to hinder Spanish preparations. Marching orders were given to the army when an incident occurred that almost handed victory to de Melo.

"In the absence of Maréchal de l'Hôpital, who was by the Duc d'Enghien's side, La Ferté-Senneterre was alone in commanding the left flank. On that side of the army was marshland through which the Spanish could not attack. In consequence, La Ferté had only to hold his ground and wait for the battle to commence. For his part, the Duc d'Enghien had not left the right flank and while the troops were getting ready for battle he was reconnoitring the Spanish positions and the best places to attack them. At that moment, La Ferté, perhaps following a secret order from the maréchal, or maybe in order to bring himself to Gassion's attention through some extraordinary exploit, ordered his cavalry and five battalions of infantrymen across the marsh. This detachment meant that the left flank of the army was bereft of cavalry and missing a large part of its infantry. As soon as the Duc d'Enghien was notified, he ordered the army to halt and went to the left flank where the disorder was to be found. At the same moment, the Spanish trumpeted the charge and their army began to march as if de Melo wanted to take advantage of this manoeuvre. But the prince

had filled the void in the frontline with troops of the second and the Spanish halted and gave the impression that their only goal had been to gain some terrain so as to put their second line in place. There are times at war when opportunities pass by like lightening. If the general is not sharp enough to notice them or quick enough to take advantage of them, good fortune rarely comes by again and, more often than not, turns on those who fail to grasp them. The Duc d'Enghien sent word to La Ferté to return to his initial position and before nightfall they had crossed the marsh in the other direction and were back in position. This incident only succeeded in delaying the battle and caused no more inconvenience than allowing the Spanish to better prepare their position than they would otherwise have done.

The night was dark, but due to the proximity of the forest the plain was bright with the great number of fires lit by the soldiers. Woods on all sides surrounded the armies, as if they had to fight a duel. Their guards were so close to each other that it was difficult to distinguish the French fires from those lit by the Spanish. The two camps seemed to be one. No alarm was heard. On the eve of a very bloody battle there seemed to exist a kind of peace between the two camps.

At daybreak, the Duc d'Enghien signalled his army forward. First, he led his cavalry in an attack on one thousand musketeers positioned by the Comte de Fontaines in the woods. Even though they fought on ground that was naturally entrenched and advantageous to them, the attack was so strong that they were all cast down. Fearing that his squadrons be separated from each other as they crossed the remainder of the wood, the Duc d'Enghien and the second line of cavalry turned left and he ordered Gassion to take the first line around the wood to the right. Under the cover of the wood, Gassion stretched out his squadrons and attacked the Spanish cavalry on its flank while the Duc d'Enghien attacked it head on.

Commanding the Spanish left flank was the Duc d'Albuquerque. He knew nothing yet of this first action and had not considered it possible that he could be attacked on two sides simultaneously. Counting on the musketeers posted in the woods to cover his front line, the attack therefore had seriously weakened him and he attempted to pit against Gassion some squadrons of his own.

Nothing, however, is more dangerous than to undertake important manoeuvres before a strong enemy on the point of engaging in battle. Already shaken, the squadrons were crushed by the first charge, and all of d'Albuquerque's troops fell one after the other. Seeing them take flight, the Duc d'Enghien ordered Gassion after them, and turned his attention towards the enemy infantry.

For his part, Maréchal de l'Hôpital was not as successful since having led his cavalry charge at a gallop his troops tired before reaching the enemy. The Spanish held their ground and smashed de l'Hôpital's cavalry. Having battled with great courage, Maréchal de l'Hôpital had his arm broken by a pistol shot and witnessed in an instant his whole flank take flight in confusion. The Spanish pushed them hard, cutting to shreds a number of infantry battalions and capturing the cannon. Their advance was stopped when the reserves came up against them.

While the two flanks fought with mixed fortunes the French infantry marched against the Spanish. Even though several battalions had already come together, d'Espenan, commanding the infantry, having heard of the misfortune that had just beset the left flank, and seeing before him the Spanish infantry waiting with great pride and in good order, made do with slight skirmishes in order to wait and see which cavalry would be victorious.

Meanwhile, the Duc d'Enghien had crushed the German and Walloon infantries, and the Italian infantry had taken to their heels when he realised Maréchal de l'Hôpital's rout. The duc realised that victory depended entirely on the troops he had with him. He immediately suspended his pursuit of the infantry and marched behind the Spanish battalions, against their cavalry, which was attacking the left flank of the French army. Finding their squadrons scattered, he finished them off with ease.

La Ferté-Senneterre had been caught in the rout of the left flank, having fought with great valour. He was found wounded in several places and was rescued by a charge led by the Duc d'Enghien.

In this way, the Spanish right flank which had been scattered as they chased the French, did not hold the upper hand for long. Those who were chasing took flight themselves and found Gassion in their path, who cut them to pieces.

Only de Melo's infantry was left. They were pressed together as one near their cannon. Their countenance and order indicated that they were prepared to fight to the bitter end. Their commander was the Comte de Fontaines, who, despite having to be carried in a chair because of his infirmity, was one of the best commanders of his generation.

Hearing word that Beck was marching with 6,000 men near the woods, the Duc d'Enghien attacked the Spanish infantry without hesitation, despite having only a small number of cavalrymen with him. The Comte de Fontaines stood his ground and ordered his men to hold their fire until the French were only fifty paces from them. In an instant, his battalion parted and from its ranks a blast from eighteen cannons was fired, followed by a shower of musket shots. The salvo was such that the French could not withstand it. If the Spanish had had cavalry to push forward, the French would never have been able to recover and reorganise themselves.

The Duc d'Enghien swiftly rallied his troops and attacked a second time, with as little success. He attacked a third time without defeating them. The reserves arrived where the Duc d'Enghien was and they were joined by a number of cavalry squadrons that had been engaged in battle with the Spanish cavalry. As a result, the Spanish infantry was surrounded on all sides and were obliged to surrender. The officers thought above all else of their own safety and the ones closest to the front line waved their hats in a plea for mercy.

As the Duc d'Enghien advanced towards them to exchange words, the Spanish foot soldiers thought that the prince was launching a new attack. This error led them to firing a volley at him – the greatest danger he had had to face that day. Angered by what had just occurred to their general, and believing it to be proof of Spanish dishonesty, the prince's troops charged at the Spanish from all sides without waiting for the order. The terrible carnage that ensued was vengeance for the danger the prince had been exposed to.

With their swords drawn, the French attacked the Spanish battalion to the core and despite the efforts of the Duc d'Enghien to stop the violence, the soldiers showed no mercy, especially the Swiss, who are in general more ruthless than the French in such circumstances. The prince rode to the left and to the right, shouting for mercy to be given, and the Spanish officers, and even some soldiers, sought safety by his side. Don George de Castelui, mestre de camp, was taken by the hand of the Prince himself. All those who were able to escape the soldiers' wrath massed around him to beg for their lives.

As soon as the Prince had given his orders concerning the prisoners, he rallied his troops ready to fight General Beck if ever he attacked Gassion or dared to enter the plain. It was then that Gassion returned from chasing down the runaways and told the Duc d'Enghien that Beck had not left the woods, restricting his actions to rounding up in the pass some remnants of the defeated army. He added that Beck had done so in such confusion and with such little understanding of the advantage that could be gained from the passes in the forest, that it was plain to see that the terror experienced by de Melo's soldiers had been communicated to his. Indeed, having saved some remains of the Spanish army, he retreated at an incredible pace, even leaving behind two cannon.

Seeing that victory was now assured, the Duc d'Enghien fell to his knees on the battlefield, and ordered all his men to do likewise, to give thanks to God for such a great success. Indeed, France had good reason to thank God because she had not won as important nor as glorious a battle for many centuries.

Both sides carried out great actions. The Spanish infantry's valour cannot be praised highly enough. It is almost unheard of that, following the defeat of an army, one corps of infantrymen, without the aid of a cavalry, could withstand in open field not one, but three attacks without folding. And it is true, that without the support of the reserves, and notwithstanding his victory over the rest of the Spanish army, the Duc d'Enghien would never have broken that brave infantry.

One extraordinary action by Velandia's regiment stood out. During the Duc d'Enghien's first attack, the musketeers and pikemen of this regiment, having been cut to pieces and surrounded by the French cavalry, withstood every charge that was made against them and retreated slowly until they reached the mass of the Spanish infantry.

When the left flank of the French army had been broken, Sirot was told that the battle was lost and to save his reserves. To this, he replied, 'It is not lost because Sirot and his companions have not yet fought.' And indeed, his determination played an important role in the victory. But above all else, and the Spanish concurred, nothing was more impressive than the calm and composure shown by the Duc d'Enghien at the height of the battle, and especially when the enemy's left flank was defeated. Indeed, instead of pursuing the scattered remnants of that flank, he turned instead on their infantry. Such restraint meant that he avoided scattering his own troops and retained an attacking advantage against the Spanish cavalry, who thought that victory was theirs. Gassion earned a great deal of honour and the Duc d'Enghien promised to request from the king a marshal's baton in grateful acknowledgement of his actions, a baton that the king granted soon after.

Of the eighteen thousand infantrymen that made up de Melo's army, over eight thousand were killed and seven thousand taken prisoner. The Comte de Fontaines, general mestre de camp, was found dead, by his chair, at the head of his troops. The Spanish regretted his death for a long time and the French praised his courage highly. The prince himself said that if he had not won he would have wanted to die like de Fontaines. Both Valandia and Vilalua, Spanish mestres de camp also, suffered the same fate. All the officers were either killed or taken prisoner. The Spanish lost 18 pieces of field artillery and 6 batteries. The French captured 200 flags and 60 standards. The pillage was important: added to the booty taken from the baggage train was the silver to be distributed to the Spanish army following the capture of Rocroi. The French lost approximately two thousand men, but very few officers or noblemen.

The Duc d'Enghien, having lodged his army in the enemy encampment and given his orders concerning the wounded, entered Rocroi victorious. He learned the next day that de Melo had retreated from the battle following the defeat of his army's right flank and had sought to gather the remnants of his army at Philippeville.

It was there that his cavalry rejoined him having suffered few losses. His infantry, on the other hand, was entirely destroyed. The campaigns that followed highlighted the importance of this loss, one that the Spanish have never been able to recover from. A good infantry can never be too carefully maintained, whether in time of war or in time of peace. Indeed, without a great deal of time, it is impossible, even for the greatest of Kings, to rebuild an experienced corps of officers and soldiers used to fighting together and suffering the fatigues of war."

3 The Battle of Freiburg, 3 to 9 August 1644
✦ ... eyewitness accounts

THE BATTLE OF FREIBURG AS ATTRIBUTED TO THE MARQUIS DE LA MOUSSAYE BY RAMSAY (MEMOIRS OF TURENNE):

"Mr de Turenne had advice at that time, that the Duc d'Enghien had orders to march to Brisach with his army, which consisted of six thousand infantry and three thousand cavalry: this prince having passed the Rhine, came to Mr de Turenne's camp, which was about four or five leagues from Brisach.

After the taking of Freiburg, the enemy's army had continued in their camp: parties were sent out to view it, as also all the roads both through the hills and the woods, in order to get between Freiburg and the Bavarians, and that way to march down into the plain. The Duc d'Enghien resolved to attack with his army some posts where Mr de Mercy had three or four regiments of infantry upon a rising ground at the head of his camp, and ordered Mr de Turenne to march with the army he commanded through the woods and hills, to endeavour to enter the plain where the enemy were, and attack them in the flank: It was resolved to begin the attack three hours before night.

The prince having caused the rising ground to be attacked by his infantry, they were at first beaten back, but going thither himself with great resolution, and with a body that sustained those who had been repulsed, he carried those posts, defeated the three or four regiments, consisting of over two thousand men, but lost a great many of his own men, and it growing dark, he halted in the same place.

Mr de Turenne at the head of his army entered the defile and advanced towards the plain, where the enemy were in order of battle; first he drove them from a wood, and then from a hedge, and beat them from post to post to the entrance of the plain. The Bavarians lost a great many men, and retired about forty or fifty paces from our infantry, having all their cavalry, and a body of infantry of the second line, to sustain them. The two armies continued thus facing one another, the Bavarians not daring to come to a close engagement again with those regiments that were ready to receive them with their pikes, and the French not daring to enter further into the plain, having no cavalry to sustain them.

In this posture did both armies fight above two hours before night, with great loss on both sides: the king's infantry had behind them the wood, which gave them a fair opportunity to retreat; but they never recoiled, though it was not possible to bring above one squadron of cavalry to sustain them, for want of room to draw up.

The night did not put an end to the fight, but the troops on both ſides remained for seven hours continually firing at the distance of forty paces till it was day. In this place, over fifteen hundred of the king's army were killed; and of the enemy upwards of two thousand five hundred: Mr de Roqueserviere, battle sergeant, was mortally wounded: Mr d'Aumont, lieutenant general, acted his part three exceeding well.

A little before day the enemy's fire was observed to diminish; the reason was, that they had left only some few men to fire, that their retreat might not be perceived; their army marching to a hill near Freiburg. They had reason to be afraid, that the

148

prince having been prevented by the night from advancing further, would attack them at break of day in the plain on his side. As soon as any thing could be seen at the distance of a hundred paces, we sent some soldiers into the plain, who reported that the enemy were retired; and day-light advancing, Mr de Turenne marched down into the plain, and saw the prince entering it likewise on his side. The armies being joined, the prince did not think fit to march that day to the hill, where the Bavarians had again encamped and which was not above a league from their former camp: he only went to take a view pretty near the hill, where the enemy having already planted their cannon, fired several shots at those who advanced.

It is certain, had the prince marched up to them, he would have found them in great confusion; but the infantry of the king's army were so dispirited by fighting the whole night, and by the great number of officers and soldiers killed or wounded, that they were not in a condition to undertake any considerable action. That day was spent in the camp, and it was reported, that the most part of the general officers of the enemy's army were for making use of that opportunity to retire by the hills behind Freiburg, and leave a garrison there; but Mr de Mercy carried it against them; he continued there, and caused some trees to be cut down, in order to hinder any approach, and ordered some small works to be made in the most advantageous places.

The next morning early, the army, commanded by Mr de Turenne, having the vanguard, be detached seven or eight hundred musketeers, commanded by Mr de l'Echelle, battle sergeant of the prince's army, (who did the duty of Mr de Roqueserviere, who was wounded in the last action) and eight or ten squadrons of cavalry, under the command of Mr Deubatel, lieutenant general, with four small field pieces, which marched at the head of the said detachment : as they came near the hill where the enemy was, they perceived some musketeers that were guarding some advantageous posts, and who retired to their respective bodies when they were pressed hard, while the enemy fired a great many cannon shot.

The march being very short, when Mr de Turenne's army was in this situation, it was but eight o'clock in the morning, so that they had a great deal of time, being the middle of summer. It was resolved, that by opening a great way to the right, they should make room for the prince's army

(which Maréchal de Gramont commanded under him) in order to double to the left, and then put themselves in such a disposition, that the hill might be attacked in several places at the same time. All the enemy's troops, both cavalry and infantry, having retired in close order towards the hill, after a very sharp skirmish, the king's army halted: the cannon from the hill did but little mischief, because the French were not in a defile.

In the meanwhile, an officer of Flextein, who was detached with fifty cavalry to view the disposition of the enemy from a rising ground near the king's army, came and told Mr de Turenne, that he saw a great confusion amongst the Bavarians and that their baggage was marching. Mr de Turenne told it to the prince, who thinking it would be easier to know what there was in that report, and that it might be useful for making the disposition for the attack, he went thither, taking Mr de Turenne with him, who told the troops as he passed before them, that be should return immediately, and that it was necessary before the attack, to wait the arrival of the prince's troops.   .

There were about two thousand paces from the place where the troops of the right were, to the rising ground where that officer of Flextein had been. As we were viewing the disposition of the enemy's army, which seemed to be in great confusion, we heard them make a great volley of small shot, and at the same time a noise of trumpets and kettle-drums. Mr d'Espenan, who commanded the prince's infantry, coming to the hill, and seeing small advanced work, in which the enemy had some musketeers, and by which it had not been thought necessary to begin an attack, sent some infantry to make themselves masters of it, without waiting either the prince's, or Maréchal de Gramont's orders; thinking, as I believe, that the thing would not have had so great a consequence, or, perhaps, to raise his own character in the world by some little action : this was what obliged the enemy to make for great a volley from the hill, upon those troops that were advancing at that time.

The body of Mr Doubatel's vanguard, where Mr de l' Echelle was, (to whom Mr de Turenne had spoken, in going with the prince, and told them expressly, that they must not stir from their post, and that he would return immediately) began to march towards the hill, and having passed some trees which the enemy had cut down, advanced towards a work, where Mr de Mercy was with his whole body of infantry, who, not being attacked but on that side, because the enterprise was without orders, opposed them with his whole force. This was the condition in which the prince and Mr de Turenne found their troops on their return, having galloped full speed upon hearing the noise.

There was not a man of the prince's army come, but the few musketeers Mr d'Espenan had employed to take that work, and Mr de Turenne's infantry, which in all made not three thousand men, were not engaged against that fort, but were at a great distance from it, without having orders for what they were to do. The prince staid with that first body, which was already beaten back, close to the enemy's redoubt, and so, as may easily be judged, very much exposed, there being no cavalry to sustain them but Flextein's regiment, which continued under the fire of the enemy's whole infantry with wonderful resolution, and lost the half of the men.

Mr de Turenne went to his own body of infantry that were not engaged, in order to help the retreat of those who had attacked, or in case they were not quite repulsed, and there was room for doing it, to make an attack : as he was advancing, the situation of the affair showed, that all that he had to do, was to halt a little out of musket shot, and wait for the prince's infantry.

We continued in this posture a pretty while, it requiring a long time to make the disposition for an attack, in rugged and hilly ground. Then the prince thought fit that Mr de Turenne should march with his infantry, Maréchal de Gramont was to have charged the enemy in the flank, or to have sustained with the cavalry, if the attack had succeeded. We marched straight to the fall of trees which was in the middle of the hill, and opposite to the left of the prince's army. The regiments of cavalry of Mr de Turenne and Tracy, sustained the prince's infantry, who were repulsed after a very obstinate fight, where this cavalry performed wonders, in bearing the fire without moving.

Mr de Turenne, who had Mr Tournon with him, sent word several times to the prince, that whatever his troops might suffer, he would endeavour not to retire altogether till it was night. It is certain, could the enemy have made a right judgment of the confusion of the king's troops, the whole army had been ruined, at least all the infantry. Those of Mr de Turenne were also led on to that hill at the time that those of the prince were attacking, but the soldiers were so disheartened, that they advanced very little towards the enemy.

This battle lasted two full hours, and ended with the day, the enemy not stirring from their posts. The Bavarians lost a great many men, and among the rest, Gaspard de Mecy, major general, the count's brother; but their loss was not so great as that of the king's armies, whereof the root were almost entirely ruined: nevertheless, as the enemy had lost almost the half of their infantry two days before, and had suffered pretty much on this occasion, they had but a small number of infantry left. Had it not been for that accident of Mr d'Espenan's attacking contrary to orders, which put all in confusion, and if the infantry of the king's two armies had attacked the hill abreast, according to the disposition that was going to be made, the enemy's army would have been undone, and unable to resist. In the French army there were a great many officers killed; Mr de l'Echelle and Mr de Mauvilli, battle sergeant, with almost all the commanders of the different bodies of the cavalry, and some of those who commanded the infantry.

Night having parted the two armies, which were but fifty paces from each other (the most advanced bodies, at least), that of the king returned to its former camp. A vast number of wounded were sent to Brisach, and provisions ordered from thence, and a day or two after, there came an account, that the enemy's army having decamped from that hill, and left a garrison in Freiburg, was marching into the Schwartz-Welt, which is the Black Forest, in order to get into the country of Wurtemberg. As the country, through which they were obliged to pass, is full of very narrow ways, where it is with great difficulty that baggage can follow, it was resolved to march with the whole army in order to surprise the enemy; and for that end, Mr Rosen was detached with eight squadrons, and set out three or four hours before the army. As he was an excellent officer, and of great experience, he had orders either to attack some troops which the enemy had detached to make their march easier, or to stop the body of the army by harassing it, and thereby give time for the king's army to come up.

The king's army marched at the break of day, leaving the baggage with a guard, and followed Mr de Rosen's rout, who had set out about midnight. After a march of five or six hours in a rugged country, and where the troopers were often obliged to dismount and file off; the army got upon a little rising ground. The prince was with the main body, and Mr de Turenne's army had the vanguard. We saw Mr de Rosen's troops in a valley, about a quarter of a league off; and upon the top of a hill, (which Mr de Rosen could not see, because he was in the bottom) five or six thousand men at most, which was the enemy's whole army, that were retiring. A little after, Mr de Rosen with his eight squadrons, consisting of full six hundred cavalry, began to follow the enemy, and get up that hill, which was pretty long. Mr de Turenne, by order of the prince sent immediately a gentleman, called la Berge, to tell Mr de Rosen, that it was the enemy's whole army that were marching upon the hill: before he got to Mr de Rosen, who saw only some troops of the rear-guard, Rosen was advanced so near, that Mr de Mercy perceiving he was not sustained, and that the foremost troops of the king's army were a quarter of a league from him, and were filing off one by one, to form the first squadron, (which takes up a great deal of time) faced about upon Mr de Rosen with the whole body of his troops; but some of the enemy's squadrons advancing before their infantry, Mr de Rosen beat them back and following them in order, three or four battalions fired upon him, which stopped his detachment, however, without putting them in confusion: seeing himself very near the enemy's main body, and their front very much larger than his own, he began to retire. Two or three squadrons of the second line sustained those of the first, that were very little moved by so great a fire, and after having lost four or five standards, they retired very slowly in good order.

The enemy's cavalry dare not pursue them briskly, for fear going too far from their infantry; or else, because being as yet stunned with the battles of the preceding days, their main design was to retire without fighting. Rosen's foremost squadrons being sustained by those of the second line, and the whole body of the enemy's cavalry and infantry continuing to march against them, and being between forty and fifty paces from one another, they retired five or six hundred paces, mixed with the enemy, who made more use of the fire of their infantry than of their cavalry. It was one of the most remarkable actions I ever saw, for the intrepidity of troops in the midst of so much danger; a degree of bravery to which none but those who have been in many battles, and have had both good and bad success, can arrive. The enemy who saw that there were already

two squadrons of the vanguard the king's army formed upon the rising ground, Where I said they were filing off, began to halt, and a little after, to retire.

Rosen's cavalry that had been repulsed, not being in a condition to pursue the enemy, because there was not a body of the king's army that had passed the defile strong enough to sustain them, made a halt, and Mr de Mercy retired to a wood about twelve or fifteen hundred paces from the place of action, from whence he directed his march through the hills towards the country of Wurtemberg."

THE BATTLE OF FREIBURG AS RECOUNTED BY MARÉCHAL DE GRAMONT

"We advanced without a plan for battle. Having attacked Gravelines, the king's army, commanded by the Duc d'Orléans was focused entirely on making this attack succeed. But because the Duc d'Enghien and Maréchal de Guiche (de Gramont) had entered Luxembourg where they had captured a few small castles, they were soon in a position to use His Majesty's army to glorious ends. Cardinal Mazarin sent a letter to inform them that the Bavarian army, led by Mercy, had attacked Freiburg and that it was of the utmost importance that the king's army currently in Luxembourg should join the army led by Maréchal de Turenne in Germany; and that the two armies joined together under the Duc d'Enghien's command would be strong enough to come to save Freiburg and lift the siege. But to be able to do that great speed would be needed and he promised that they would neither lack the money nor any other necessities in the pursuit of this objective. And, if the truth be told, they were amply supplied. We marched with nothing but the lightest amount of food and cannon, leaving behind the heaviest equipment. When we came to Benfeld, the Marquis d'Aumont arrived, sent by de Turenne, to bring news that Freiburg had fallen. He believed, however, that if we quickened our advance we could still engage the enemy in battle if they held their positions, or, if they abandoned them, attack the town itself. This led to the decision to cross the Rhine immediately at Brisach where Maréchal de Turenne was to be found.

The Duc d'Enghien, the two maréchals and Mr Erlach, the governor of Brisach held a war council on the spot. Erlach's opinion was not to attack the enemy where they were positioned, but instead to circle them by way of Langhenzeling and the San Peter valley, and in so doing cut off their supply lines forcing them to either die of hunger or engage a battle which would no longer be as advantageous for them as currently, entrenched and waiting as they were.

Maréchal de Guiche was of a similar opinion, but Maréchal de Turenne said that he had reconnoitred a valley which was not protected by the enemy and that his troops could attack them by that route while the Duc d'Enghien's troops attacked the entrenchments directly. His plan was accepted. The advance was very orderly and since the attack needed to be at night, the troops arrived in position at exactly the time we had decided.

The command of the Duc d'Enghien's flank was given to d'Espenan. The Duc d'Enghien wanted Maréchal de Guiche to stay at his side, but de Guiche, having advanced and seen that the enemy's fire stretched all along their position and was not fixed in one place, realised at once that d'Espenan's troops were having no effect and warned the Duc d'Enghien that things were not going well, and that since it was already engaged, there was no going back. He added that there were two regiments – Conti and Mazarin – that were good and strong, and that he would lead them in an attack of the positions in front of him. To do so he put foot to ground and marched straight towards the position. On seeing this, the Duc d'Enghien did the same. And when one of the maréchal's officers tried to dissuade him he very nearly received a sword in his stomach for his trouble. To bring the telling of this episode to a close, the Duc d'Enghien and Maréchal de Guiche marched together towards the enemy position and won a vigorous fight with such audacity that is hard to imagine. The enemy, the emperor's elite infantry, defended to the

bitter end and were spared no quarter. It is no exaggeration to say that they lost more than three thousand men in the field.

Meanwhile, Maréchal de Turenne was fighting hard on his flank and attacked vigorously, but with little success as his enemies could not be undone. Nonetheless, General Mercy, commanding the Bavarian army, seeing that the position was won, pulled back his troops and cannon with such order that cannot be overly admired and positioned them on the Black Mountain near Freiburg. Not having the time to entrench his troops he built a fortification with felled trees certain that he would be attacked a second time. He was not mistaken: at daybreak we marched against him believing, with reason, that since the night before he had been forced from a good position and having retreated to a place which he had had little time to fortify, that he would be undone with ease.

That day, Hesse's army was the vanguard of the attack. The wide area between the town and the mountain meant that the enemy could attack our rearguard with its numerous and seasoned cavalry, leading Maréchal de Guiche to position his army in the plain to rebuff such an attack. In addition, he beseeched the Duc d'Enghien (who had proved his ardour the night before) to be careful not to over commit himself to the battle.

The second attack decided, command was given to de Roqueserviere and de l'Echelle, both battle sergeants. D'Espenan, buoyed by having initially captured a tricky redoubt guarded by some dragoons below the enemy's main position, thought that he needed simply to march on them to undo them. He was, however, badly mistaken since they held their ground with peerless resolve, and d'Espenan was unable to take them. A very large number of soldiers and officers were killed there, including the two battle sergeants.

Seeing that the enemy cavalry in front of him was showing no sign of wanting to engage in battle and that the fight was raging on the crest of the hill, Maréchal de Guiche was certain that the Duc d'Enghien would not fail to enter the fray himself. And so, de Guiche decided to leave his troops under the command of the Comte de Palluau and join the battle that was being fought elsewhere.

On being told by numerous wounded officers and soldiers returning from the battle that the Duc d'Enghien was personally at the head of his infantry leading the charge under heavy fire from the enemy, de Guiche stepped up his pace to be at his side. When he arrived in the Freiburg vineyard, not twenty paces from the enemy position, his horse was killed stone dead by a musket shot to the head and he was thrown to the ground. As he was being lifted to his feet he saw the Duc d'Enghien retreating with only a small number of his men (the rest having been killed fighting by his side), having had two horses killed under him and numerous holes shot through his clothes by muskets.

The Duc d'Enghien ran to embrace Maréchal de Guiche and told him that his troops had been undone by their own fervour and that the attack had not been carried out as they had decided it should. Mr d'Espenan proposed another line of attack by which the enemy would certainly be overcome since a number of infantry regiments had not yet taken part in the battle.

It needed the bravery and boldness of the Duc d'Enghien to consider starting afresh after having endured what he had just experienced and having most of his troops either killed or demoralised. But he was of a unique breed of man: one whose courage increases proportionally to the danger he faces. There are very few like him.

Maréchal de Guiche was very pleased to hear him speak in such a manner and admired the noble-mindedness of the young prince. But since he loved him tenderly and that what he proposed did not seem feasible, de Guiche advised him with respect that what d'Espenan had done today and the night before should not strengthen His Highness' resolve in thinking that the action being proposed was wise. Maréchal de Guiche added that he was convinced that as many soldiers as took the field would be lost during the attack. The Duc d'Enghien accepted this reasoning.

At that moment, a messenger came to warn Maréchal de Guiche that, on seeing the lack of success of our infantry, the Bavarian cavalry was advancing. De Guiche quickly returned to his troops. When he arrived he saw that the Bavarian cavalry did not distance itself very far from the walls surrounding Freiburg meaning that an attack on them would require excessive boldness and complete madness in equal measure.

Then, a new infantry attack, led by Mr de Mauvilliers, was launched without Maréchal de Guiche's knowledge. Like his two predecessors, de Mauvilliers, a battle sergeant, was killed at once. This attack was as successful as the first: Maréchal de Guiche had to abandon his position for a second time and rushed to where the action was taking place. There, he found the infantry in appalling disorder, reduced to fending off volleys of musket fire by pressing up as close to the field fortifications built by the enemy.

Seeing this unfortunate state of affairs, Maréchal de Guiche made his way swiftly to join the Duc d'Enghien, who was with Maréchal de Turenne, supporting the infantry with a large number of men. De Guiche painted a vivid picture of the situation he had just witnessed explaining that it would be inhumane to leave an infantry, which instead of defending itself could only run for cover, be killed. The Duc d'Enghien agreed with him, but was also worried that if he ordered them to retreat before nightfall then the enemy cavalry would cut them to pieces as they retreated. Having seen the situation at first hand (and come under heavy fire at close quarters), and concluding that the field fortifications in place would stop the enemy cavalry from passing that way, Maréchal de Guiche assured the Duc d'Enghien of the contrary. And concerning the plain, de Guiche added that he would make sure that the enemy would not dare an attack through there. His advice was heeded and orders were immediately given to pull back the troops, and this was achieved without consequence. The losses suffered in soldiers and officers are difficult to number. Those of the enemy equally so: the general's brother, Baron de Mercy, was killed as well as many other officers of rank.

We stayed three days in our encampment and spent them transporting back to Brisach all the officers and soldiers wounded during the two great attacks. It was a terrible time because of all the dead bodies causing such infection that many men died of it. But it was inevitable: there was no other course of action possible. Once the wagons sent with the wounded had returned from Brisach, and with the enemy still posted in their positions, the option rejected at Brisach was chosen and Maréchal de Guiche marched the vanguard towards Langhendhentzeling.

Having to expose our flank so close to the enemy, the manoeuvre proved quite bold and hazardous, but the enemy took no action and let the two armies pass without hindrance. However, guessing that the plan was to cut off their supply lines, the enemy marched swiftly, but with some difficulty (due to the amount of equipment and large cannon they took with them), towards the San Peter Valley.

Early the next morning we left Langhendhentzeling to march on San Peter. That day the vanguard was led by Maréchal de Turenne accompanied by the Duc d'Enghien. They found the enemy above the abbey at San Peter. On seeing the advance, the enemy had abandoned the wagons, cannon, munitions and equipment that they could not take with them on the horses that they had beforehand unhitched from the wagons.

At first, the enemy's flight led the Duc

d'Enghien and Maréchal de Turenne to believe that they would be able to charge and engage the enemy's rearguard in combat whilst waiting for Maréchal de Guiche to reach them as he could only march in line. But things did not go according to plan: Mercy, who without a doubt was one of the greatest commanders of the century, charged them so violently that they were obliged to retreat swiftly before him in some disorder. He captured several standards from colonel Rosen, whom he beat soundly, and took many prisoners. Once he had the advantage, and seeing the king's army arriving, he lost no time and marched towards Philingen to avoid a battle he did not want to wage. Once all of our troops had arrived, we marched together so as not to repeat the same mistake as had just occurred. This gave Mercy two hours start on us and it did not prove possible, however hard we tried, to catch up with him. We returned to the abbey at San Peter to camp and the soldiers were able to recover from their exertions by plundering with great satisfaction the food that they found in the wagons that the enemy had left behind."

154

4 The battle of Allerheim or Nördlingen, on the 3 August 1645
✦ ... eyewitness accounts

The battle of Allerheim by Ramsay, in Turenne's memoirs:

"Mr de Mercy retired farther into the country towards Dinkefpuhel, where he left three or four hundred men, and encamped three or four leagues from thence behind the woods. A few days after, the king's army arrived near Dinkefpuhel,

and formed a design to attack it; a detachment of musketeers was ordered to advance among the ruins of some houses, where they opened some trenches: but before midnight, an officer that had been prisoner and had made his escape from the Bavarian army, came and told Mr de Turenne, that Mr de Mercy thinking that the king's army would be intent upon the siege of Dinkefpuhel, was marching by night, and was but two leagues off, behind the woods. Mr de Turenne went immediately to acquaint Mr d'Enghien with the news, who resolved to leave all the baggage with two or three regiments of cavalry, and to march presently with the whole army in quest of Mr de

Mercy. We set out an hour after midnight. Mr de Turenne had the vanguard and we crossed a wood. Mr d'Enghien was there, and had left Maréchal de Gramont with his army in the rear-guard. As we were going out of the wood we saw, for by this time there was daylight enough, a small troop of Bavarians; and a little after, as we were driving them back, we discovered some of the enemy's squadrons, who having seen the head of our vanguard, retired in all haste towards the body of their army, whereof these squadrons were the vanguard: so that if we had not set out too soon, we had found the enemy on their march, and consequently in a very bad posture. They halted behind several ponds, and presently drew up in order of battle, and having planted their cannon, began to make some works on their front, and entrench themselves.

The king's army, as they went out of the wood drew up likewise in order of battle; but could not march up to the enemy but through defiles. We brought up our cannon, which galled them pretty much; but theirs that were already planted, did us a great deal more mischief. The whole day was spent in gunning one another, with great loss on both sides. The next morning, two hours before daylight, the king's army retired by the same road it had come, which was by a defile in the wood. The enemy pursued only with some horse, and there happened but one skirmish, though they had once an opportunity to have defeated a part of our rear-guard. We repassed the wood, and went to join the baggage near Dinkefpuhel, where we encamped : but not judging it advisable to stop at so inconsiderable a place, we resolved to march to Nordlingen, and get there before the enemy; which was very easy to be done. The next day the army decamped early in the morning, and after a two or three hours march, arrived about nine o'clock in the plain near Nordlingen: no enemy appearing there, we resolved to halt, and had some thoughts of encamping, but no orders were yet given for unloading the baggage, or pitching the tents. As Mr de Turenne was advancing into the plain with a small guard, and while the prince was out not far off with another, he fell upon a German party that were marauding, and brought away two or three prisoners, who reported that the enemy's army was passing a rivulet a league from thence in order to draw near to Nordlingen. Mr de Turenne immediately joined the prince, and having learnt that there was no rivulet between the place where the enemy was passing and that where we were, orders were sent to the army that no man

should stir from his post. The prince and Mr de Turenne advanced still with a few men, in order to reconnoitre and have a greater certainty of what the enemy were a doing, and whether they continued their march. The plain is so open, and stretches so far, that there was no danger in advancing with a few men.

Mr de Mercy, who commanded the Bavarian army, to which a body of six or seven thousand imperialists, commanded by General Gleen, had joined, being come to the banks of a rivulet about nine o'clock in the morning; and judging, as it was true, that the king's army was encamped near Nordlingen, and that we intended to besiege it, thought that by passing that rivulet without baggage, he might with safety draw near Nordlingen, because of the hills and some advantages he might take with his army: he likewise imagined that we would not attack him that day, and so he should have time to entrench himself , which he was wont to do very expeditiously, having commonly following his army no other carriages but the ammunition wagons, and those in which were the tools and implements. He continued his march, and posted himself three or four hundred paces from the rivulet upon a hill (called Vineberg), which, at the place he stopped, was pretty high, but sloped insensibly towards a village (called Allerheim). In order to make the best use of the place, according to the strength of his army and the situation of the ground, he began to draw up his right wing, composed of a body of imperialists and some of his own troops, from that part of the hill which was nearest the rivulet, to the village, having two regiments of cavalry and his cannon in the place where his right wing began. From the place where the right wing terminated, the infantry extended in order of battle behind the village, and in the action almost all of them fought, in order to defend it; but at first it was possessed only by a detachment of musketeers in the church and upon the steeple. Next to the infantry, which was in two lines, as was the cavalry, the left wing, composed of the Bavarian cavalry, and commanded by Mr John de Wert, ended at a little castle (Pufendorf), situated upon a rising ground (the hill of Allerheim), round which there was some infantry that closed the left of the army, as the two regiments of infantry above-mentioned closed the right. The space between the village and the castle was a plain which might well contain twelve or thirteen squadrons. This was the disposition that Mr de Mercy made, as well for fighting, as for encamping, if we had not attacked him.

The prince having perceived that the enemy's army was passing the rivulet, sent orders to the troops to get themselves ready to march, and being confirmed by the scouts, and by what he himself saw, that the enemy was not unwilling to fight, he passed the place, behind which he would have had a great advantage, and sent orders for the whole army to march. About twelve o'clock the army advanced into the great plain, and about four o'clock the two armies came in sight of one another. It took up a good deal of time to extend and put ourselves in a posture of fighting. That village, which was before the enemy's army, justly made it doubtful, whether it were better to attack it, or march towards the two wings with the cavalry only: but as it is not very safe to attack wings, without at the same time charging the infantry posted in the centre, it was not judged proper, whatever difficulty there might be in attacking the village, to charge with the cavalry, without the infantry marching in the same front; and as the village was above four hundred paces more advanced than the place where the enemy's army was, it was thought best to halt with the two wings, while the infantry should attack and make themselves masters of the nearest houses of that village, or at least of some of them. For that end, our cannon were brought up, that we might not be annoyed by those of the enemy, without annoying them with ours: but as cannon that are planted have a great advantage over those that march, because the horses must always be put to the carriages in order to advance, whereby a great deal of time is lost, those of the enemy did a great deal more damage than ours.

In this disposition the infantry of the king's army marched straight to the village; the right wing being opposite to the enemy's left wing in the plain, and the left wing to the enemy's right, which was upon that hill, from which there was an insensible descent to the village. Our infantry found but little resistance at the nearest houses, but as they advanced farther, three or four regiments of the enemy (one, part of which possessed the churchyard, and the other had made holes for firing out of the houses) gave so great a fire, that they halted all of a sudden, and began to give way. We sent some regiments to their assistance; and Mr de Mercy, who was behind the village, caused his men to be sustained by other troops. Thus the fight became very obstinate, with great loss on both sides; but less on that of the enemy, because they were lodged in the houses;

and even while their first line was fighting in the village, the second was not idle upon the hill. These expedients did not succeed; but they showed a great deal of skill and presence of mind in the general. The prince came often into the village; he received a great many shots in his clothes, and had two horses wounded under him. He left Maréchal de Gramont on the right wing of his cavalry. Mr de Turenne also did what he could to make the infantry that were in the village near his wing to advance. Mr de Bellenave, major-general of his army was killed there. Mr de Castelaun, quartermaster general of that of the prince, was very dangerously wounded, as well as a great number of officers. In the heat, and about the end of this battle, Mr de Mercy, general of the Bavarian army, received a musket shot, of which he died on the spot; and I imagine, that when the enemy's left wing, commanded by John de Wert, advanced against the prince's cavalry, they knew nothing of his death: the battle having lasted above an hour in the village, where some squadrons were employed to sustain the infantry, the enemy's left wing began to march.

It has often been said, that there was a fault committed in passing a few ditches that were between the two wings, but I don't think there was any great matter in that; for the whole right wing of the king's army was in order of battle, and saw before it the left of the enemy, which advanced at a slow pace to engage and found but small resistance. Although Maréchal de Gramont did all that could be done, he was taken prisoner, not having been able to get either the first or second line to do their duty.

The prince, who was very near the village, went to the wing where Mr de Turenne commanded, who seeing that the attack of the village did not succeed, and that the cavalry of the enemy's left wing were marching up to the French cavalry, advanced with his wing towards the hill, and having discoursed a moment with the prince, told him, that if he would be pleased to sustain him with some squadrons of the second line and with the Hessians, he would go and charge the enemy: the prince having consented, Mr de Turenne continued his march up the hill at the head of Flextein's regiment. Being within a hundred paces of the enemy, and turning about, he saw that all the French cavalry – of the right wing – and the infantry that had been beaten out of the village, were entirely broke and scattered in the plain.

As Mr de Turenne was continuing his march up the hill with eight or nine squadrons abreast, the infantry, which the enemy had at the two extremities of the wing, gave a fire, and the cannon had time to give three or four discharges, the first with ball, and the last with cartridge-shot, with which Mr de Turenne's horse was wounded, and he himself received a shot in his cuirass, and the colonel and some of the other officers of Flextein's regiment were wounded before it attacked a regiment of cavalry that faced it. Notwithstanding this, the whole wing having marched abreast, broke the whole first line of the enemy, some squadrons making more, some less, resistance; and the enemy's second line sustaining the first that was broke, the fight was very obstinate. We had only one or two squadrons in the second line; and the Hessians, who made the body of reserve, were a little too far off: for which reason we were driven back a little, but without being routed; for our squadrons continued still in good order, and some of them had even the advantage of those of the enemy; but their numbers made them too strong for us.

The Hessians came up, and the prince at their head acted with no less courage than conduct. When the Weimarian cavalry saw the Hessians approach, they rallied, and we all at once charged the whole body of the enemy's cavalry, who had formed themselves into one line; we broke it; all the cannon upon the hill were taken; the regiments of infantry that were with the right wing were defeated, and Gleen, the general of the emperor's army, was made prisoner.

On the other hand, all the prince's cavalry, both of the first and second line, and even his reserve, commanded by the Chevalier de Chabot, and all the infantry, who being beaten out of the village, had fled to the plain, were entirely routed: John de Wert leaving the victory on that side to be pursued by two regiments, who drove our troops two leagues even to the baggage, returned to sustain his right wing, or to stop their flight. If, instead of returning by the place where he had been first posted, and leaving the village on the left hand, he had marched into the plain against the Weimarian and Hessian cavalry, we should not have been in a condition to have made the least resistance, and our left wing, thus hemmed in, would have been very easily put into confusion.

The sun was already set when Mr de Wert's cavalry began to return behind the village; and night coming on presently, the two wings that had beaten what was before them, flood in order of battle facing each other; and as the cavalry of the king's army was a little farther advanced than the village, some of the enemy's regiments that were in the churchyard and the church, surrendered to Mr de Turenne, and came forth without arms at twilight, not knowing that their own troops were not five hundred paces off.

The cavalry of both armies continued a part of the night very near one another in the plain, their advanced guards not being fifty paces from each other. About an hour after midnight, the enemy's army began to retire, without having any more reason for it than that of the king, except that they had lost their general. We heard no great noise, for they had no baggage. I believe they carried away but four small pieces of cannon; all the rest, which were twelve or fifteen, remained upon the field of battle. At break of day not one of the enemy was to be seen; we understood that they had retired towards Donawert, a small town (four leagues off) where there is a bridge upon the Danube. Mr de Turenne pursued them within fight of Donawert, with two or three thousand cavalry.

The whole right wing of the king's army was beaten, and all the infantry were put entirely into confusion, except three Hessian battalions that made the reserve, and I believe there were at least three or four thousand infantry killed upon the spot. Of the enemy's army, the whole right wing was beaten, three or four regiments of infantry, that were mixed with it, were routed, two surrendered in the church; a great many men were killed in the village, and almost all their cannon was taken. As for the loss of men, I believe, the king's army lost more than the enemy. On the one side, Maréchal de Gramont was taken, and on the other General Gleen, and a very great number of officers, and many standards. Our German cavalry of the old corps behaved exceedingly well, as also the regiments of Duras and Tracy.

It was some days before we could draw together above twelve or fifteen hundred of all the French infantry. After having stayed a day or two near Nordlingen, the prince knowing that the citizens were the strongest there, and that the garrison consisted but of four hundred men, resolved to attack it: the citizens desired to capitulate the very first night, and the garrison was sent to the enemy's army; but I think their arms were taken from them. We stayed seven or eight days at Nordlingen, which is a pretty large and fine town, where we greatly refreshed ourselves ; we found there some arms, harness, abundance of horses for the baggage, and plenty of medicine for the wounded."

158

The Battle of Allerheim by Maré-chal de Gramont:

"But, as the generals ate, we saw arriving at full gallop a Swedish reiter who came to announce that the enemy were no more than half a league away: this appeared so improbable, and so unlikely, that the company broke into laughter, and the Duc d'Enghien jokingly said: 'You will at least agree, my friend, that if these men were as wise and skilled as you tell us, they would have taken a position that puts the Vernitz river between us.'

'I'faith, Monseigneur,' replied the horseman, 'Your Highness may believe whatever you wish; but if Your Highness would come with me five hundred paces from here, on this small rising that is here on the left, I shall show him that I an neither blind nor poltroon; and Your Highness would agree with me that the army of Mercy is separated from his own only by a riverless plain as flat as the hand.'

The reiter spoke so positively and with such assurance that we began to fear that he spoke truly. The Duc d'Enghien, the two maréchals de France and the general officers mounted their horses with a few squadrons to appraise the situation for themselves, and the truth of such circumstantial news; and as they advanced they discovered the enemy arraying for battle and that they, having the higher ground, saw all the movements of our army. It was at this moment that Mercy and Gleen made a grave misjudgement; for if they had detached a large cavalry corps led by soldiers in open order to reach eight or ten plum-trees where the Duc d'Enghien and all the generals were placed to better observe the movement of the enemy, these would have found themselves engaged so far forward and so distanced from the rest of their troops, that they would inevitably have been taken or killed. But as it is impossible for a man to think of everything, this did not enter the heads of Mercy nor of Gleen; and they did not think, seeing that they were going to give battle, of anything other than taking the most advantageous position: which they succeeded to perfection, as they was none

better than that which they chose.

There was a village in the middle of the plain, in which they filled the houses and church with the infantry; and to defend it they raised a sort of entrenchment, where they placed their large infantry corps on the right and on the left. There were two small hillocks, on each of which was an old ruined château where their cannon was positioned: their first cavalry wing, composed of cuirassiers of the emperor, held the right side of the village up to just below the hillock on which the cannon was positioned; the left wing, composed of Bavarian troops, stretched up to the other hillock; and the second line was in the necessary distance. These positions of strong defence did not hinder the resolution to fight: and as it was a little late, the troops were urged strongly to form rank, realising that if they waited the following day, the affair would become more difficult, especially as the enemy would finish the entrenchment that they had already begun, and that it would then be unassailable.

Maréchal de Gramont had the right wing opposite that of Bavaria: and as it was believed to be impossible to attack their cavalry, which was flanked by the infantry from the village and the cannon of the two hillocks, without taking over the village, it was resolved to attack, although this appeared hard and difficult. Marsin and Castelnau were given this expedition. An officer of confidence had the order, with a few others, to reconnoitre a place which from a distance appeared to be a gulley between the left wing of the enemy and our right; but this passage was poorly observed by these gentlemen, who, without having seen it (the peril of approaching too close being manifest), reported that it was of considerable size, over which the squadrons could not pass: this was the source of much distress; and nearly caused the Duc d'Enghien to call a counsel of war, which the situation certainly merited.

In the meantime the attack of the village became terrible, and the Duc d'Enghien constantly pulled troops from the right wing to defend his infantry, which suffered greatly and which was nearly broken from time to time: Maréchal de Gramont, seeing this with distress, galloped as hard as he could to join the Duc and to inform him of the greatest inconvenience which could occur; for on returning to his position, he saw that the enemy had brought down infantry from the hillock on which their cannon was placed, which had already begun to cause much damage to the squadrons of our right; wishing to remedy this, he advanced the second line, the regiments of Fabert and the Irish Wal. During this lively skirmish, he received a musket shot to the middle of his helmet, by which he was so concussed that he fell on the neck of his horse as if dead; but he came to himself a little time after, and as the shot had not pierced him, he suffered only a serious contusion, which nevertheless did not prevent him from acting during the rest of the action, or from being wherever his presence was necessary.

At the same time, the two infantry regiments of Fabert and Wal pursued that of the enemy, which was troubling our cavalry; but at that moment, disorder and confusion began to appear in the village, and Baron de Marsin and the Marquis de Castelnau had been seriously injured and obliged to withdraw. The Duc d'Enghien, seeing that the affair of the village was not going well, and that the situation was nearly irremediable, passed to the left wing, which was composed of Hessian troops and commanded by Maréchal de Turenne, and found upon arriving that this general was impatient to sound the charge: and it was at this time that were made the impressive cavalry charges that made so much noise and of which so much has been spoken.

At that moment, the Bavarian left wing charged our right, and, in battle array, they crossed the place that had been reported to be a nearly impracticable gulley; which caused such surprise and fright to all our French cavalry, that it fled two leagues ahead, without waiting for the enemy to be within pistol range, an event which one would not have believed possible.

All Maréchal de Gramont was able to do was to place himself at the head of the two regiments of Fabert and Wal, which did not waver in the slightest from their positions, and when they were at point blank range they fired with such fury onto the enemy cavalry that it opened the charging squadrons, and Maréchal de Gramont took this opportunity to enter within, along with those men remaining around him: which did not serve him overmuch, as he found himself surrounded on all sides, and with four horsemen who were going to kill him, arguing together over who would do so. His captain of the guard killed one, and Hemon, his aide-de-camp, killed another, which gave him a little respite. He survived by good fortune:

a captain of the La Pierre regiment, named Sponheim, heard him named as Maréchal de Gramont, and rallied two or three officers from his friends, who diverted the company, pulled him from the intrigue and saved his life. The captain of his guards died there, the lieutenant was injured and taken prisoner with him, the cornette and the quartermaster were killed, and all the company of his guards, who were a hundred maîtres, with the exception of twelve who were also taken; four aides-de-camp were killed, three of his pages, and all his servants who had followed him were also killed at his side. Such is the result of affection for a much-loved master.

Another extraordinary occurrence happened to him: for the leading captain, wishing still to take him to General Mercy, unaware of his fate and not yet knowing that he had been killed by the first commanded musketeers upon the attack of the village, found a small Lorraine page of the Baron de Mercy, aged fifteen years; upon hearing that the general of the French had been captured, he wished to avenge upon him the death of his master: and as he had no pistols and Maréchal de Gramont was being led with the reins of his horse pulled back, he seized one of the maréchal's pistols and shot him in the head; but by good fortune it had been fired in the battle, and could not do harm. The Germans wished to inflict a serious punishment for such an evil action; but Gramont said that he was a child whom he wished to forgive, and prevented him from being shot then and there, the Germans being without pity in such situations.

While these things were happening on our right wing, the same could not be said for our enemy's, who, after a furious battle, were entirely defeated by the Duc d'Enghien and Maréchal de Turenne, who were on the left. General Gleen, who was in command, was injured and taken prisoner, as were a great number of senior officers and soldiers, as well as many cannon and standards. The battlefield was ours, with all marks of victory: upon seeing this, and with Mercy dead, Jean de Werth, who commanded the Bavarian army, thought only of withdrawing in the best possible order to a mountain near Donauwörth, named Schellenberg, which had been fortified since the time of the king of Sweden."

5

The Battle of Lens, on the 20 August 1648
✦ *... eyewitness accounts*

THE BATTLE OF LENS: MEMOIRS OF MARÉCHAL DE GRAMONT:

"In the evening, we halted the battle array and we gave three most important recommendations to all the troops: the first, to watch each other as they marched, so that the cavalry and the infantry would remain on the same line, and so that they could keep their distances and intervals; the second, to charge only at a walking pace; the third, to allow the enemy to fire first.

This was the arrangement of the army: the Prince de Condé took the right wing of the cavalry, which consisted of nine squadrons: one from his guards, two from His Royal Highness, one from the grand maître, one from Saint Simon, one from Bussy, one from Streiff, one from Harcourt 'le Vieux', and one from Beaujeu; Villequier was lieutenant general under him; the field marshals were Noirmoutier and La Moussaye; the Marquis de Fort was the battle sergeant, and Beaujeu was commander of the cavalry of this brigade.

The left wing was commanded by Maréchal de Gramont with the same number of squadrons: one carabin squadron, that of the guards; two from La Ferté-Senneterre, two from Mazarin, two from Gramont, and one from la Ferté's guards; La Ferté was lieutenant general; Saint Maigrin was field marshal; Linville was battle marshal, and the Comte de Lillebonne was the commander of the cavalry of this brigade.

The first line of infantry between the two wings was composed of two battalions of the Gardes Françaises, the Gardes Suisses and Ecossaises, the regiments of Picardie and his Royal Highness, and those of Persan and Erlach. The cannon marched at the head of the infantry.

Six gendarme squadrons protected the infantry: one each from the companies of the king, the queen, the Prince de Condé, the Duc de Longueville, the Prince de Conti, the chevau légers of his Royal Highness, and one from the Duc d'Enghien; this corps and the first line was under the orders of Châtillon, lieutenant general, and the battle sergeants, who were Villemesle and Beauregard.

The second line of cavalry, commanded by Field Marshal Arnault, was composed of eight squadrons: one from Arnault, two from Chappes, one from Coudray, one from Salbrich, one from Vidame and two from Villette.

The second line of the left wing was commanded by Le Plessis Bellière, field marshal, and composed of seven squadrons: one from Roquelaure, one from Gesvres, one from Lillebonne, two from Noirlieu, one from Meille and one from Chémerault.

The second line of infantry was composed of five battalions: one from La Reine with three hundred commanded men of the garrison of La Bassée, one from Erlach Français and Rasilly, one from Mazarin Italien, one from Condé and one from Conti.

The reserve corps was composed of six squadrons: one from Ruvigny, one from Sirot, three from Erlach and one from Fabri. It was commanded by Erlach, the lieutenant general, and Rasilly, field marshal.

We marched at dawn on the 19, in the same order, expecting to encounter the enemy at the position in which they had shown themselves the previous day with forty squadrons: but the surprise was extreme when, having passed beyond the said position, we saw the entire army arrayed for battle and positioned as thus: the right wing composed of Spanish troops, beneath Lens, of which they had taken control the previous night, having before them a number of ravines and ditches, and the infantry were in the brush, which provided natural entrenchment; and the left wing, composed of the Duc de Lorraine's cavalry, on a hill before which there were also a number of gullies.

The king's army being presented before that of the enemy, and the Prince de Condé, having recognized that if he wished to fight with a joyful heart it was unthinkable to attack the advantageous position the enemy occupied, contented to place himself before it; and the entire day passed with light skirmishes and a number of cannon shots fired from both sides.

The next day, the prince saw that in the place where they were there was neither forage nor water, and so he decided to march to Neus, a village two leagues from the place where he was encamped, in order to obtain supplies and victuals at Béthune, and in this way be in condition to follow the enemy wherever they went: and as he wished to show them his desire to fight, and that he did not fear them, he decamped from his position in front of them in broad daylight.

The reserve corps began the march, followed by the advanced guard; the second line followed by the first, in the same order and the same distance that had been observed the day before; but as the Price de Condé left ten squadrons for the rear guard a little too far from his line, led by Villequier and Noirmoutier, General Bec made use of this opportunity as the skilled captain he was, and charged them so vigorously with the cavalry of Lorraine that he broke them and put them in great disarray. Brancas, the mestre de camp, had his arm broken and was made prisoner, and many junior officers and horsemen were either taken or killed. And the Prince de Condé had great fortune not to be so; for he wished to remedy by his presence the disorder that he saw, but so great was the terror of his troops he was unable to do so, and he was pursued for a long time; and it was well that he had taken a good horse, for without it he would have suffered the same fate as his page, who was injured and taken behind him.

General Bec, proud of this success, and his natural pride increased by the success he had just won, together with the German braggery which made him despise our troops, ordered the Archduke and the Comte de Fuensaldagne to march at all haste, and gave his word that the French army would be defeated as soon as battle was engaged.

While our troops were being routed, Maréchal de Gramont's Captain of the Guard came to inform him that he saw the wing of the Prince de Condé in great confusion and making movement that did not bode well; which obliged Maréchal de Gramont to turn around all his troops whom he marched in battle array, leaving only small troops of thirty maîtres behind the squadrons marching alongside

the battalions for skirmishing, in the event that the enemy wished to follow. This done, he went at full gallop to the wing of the Prince de Condé, who embraced him and told him with much pain that his own regiment, which he had led, had abandoned him most shamefully, and that it would not have required much for him to have been killed or taken. The conversation they had together was of the shortest length; for seeing that the enemy was assembling and that they were already positioning their infantry and their cannon, they resolved to give battle then and there, knowing full well that on such occasions long discussion is neither prudent nor wise. The Prince de Condé said only to Maréchal Gramont that he asked for time to put the second line into the position of the first, because he found this line so terrified that it would certainly be defeated if he led it once more into the charge. And it was indeed his presence of mind and this perfect knowledge he had of men that put him always above the others in the most perilous and the greatest occasions; for everything he had to do came to him in an instant. Such men are a rare genius of warfare, a species of which there are only one in a hundred thousand.

Maréchal de Gramont left the Prince de Condé and returned to his wing; and passing to the head of the troops, he told them that battle had just been decided; he asked them to remember their valour, and what they owed the King, and also to observe well the orders they had been given; he said that this action was of such importance given the current state of affairs, that it was either victory or death, and that he was going to show them the example by entering first into the enemy squadron that would be opposite his own. This short and moving speech was infinitely pleasing to the soldiers; all the infantry shouted for joy and threw their hats in the air; the cavalry took their sword in hand and all the trumpets sounded fanfares with an inexpressible joy. The Prince de Condé and Maréchal de Gramont embraced warmly, and each thought of their own business.

Close to the wing commanded by Maréchal de Gramont was a small village, which broke nearly all his battle order: to allow the Prince de Condé to array for battle, this obliged him three times to withdraw a little to the left and for his troops to make a quarter-turn, then march along the high ground; after which he turned to the right and re-arrayed for battle. This manoeuvre was troublesome, and most dangerous in the presence of an alert enemy; but it was not possible to do otherwise. Finally, as he saw there was enough ground, he marched straight on the enemy at a slow pace, with such silence (most unusual for the French) that in his wing the only person that could be heard speaking was himself.

Maréchal de Gramont had the troops of Spain to fight; for as they had the right and he the left, they were opposite each other: the Comte de Bucquoy was at the head of the first line, and the Prince de Ligne at the second. They were positioned on a small hillock; and it can be said that it was a duel rather than a battle, as each squadron and battalion had their counterpart to fight.

The enemy held firm with the advantage of their higher ground. They were five or six paces behind the crest, so that if they were charged, the enemy cavalry would fall on them in disarray, while our cavalry would be able to counter-attack in order. They had no sword in hand; but like all the Spanish cuirassiers in Flanders, they carried mousquetons, which they held on the thigh when not fighting, the same as if they were lances. At twenty paces from them, Maréchal de Gramont sounded the charge, and informed the troops that they would have to withstand a furious discharge; but after this he promised them that they would easily have the advantage of their enemy. This discharge was so close and so terrible that one would have said Hell opened: there were hardly any officers at the head of the corps that they commanded that were not killed or injured; but it can be said that the return from the charge was worthy of Matins; for our squadrons entered theirs, and resistance was practically non-existent. We had little mercy, and many were killed.

The second line came to defend the first; but they were so violently charged by ours that they hardly held at all and were broken. Our infantry had the same advantage over theirs; and we lost few men, except in the regiment of the guards who had been charged on the flank by a number of squadrons, and lost six captains and many officers.

The reserve corps commanded by Erlach defended marvellously the wing of the Prince de Condé, who broke the first and second enemy lines, after having charged ten times in person, and carried out actions worthy of this valour and capacity that are so well known.

Never has there been a victory more complete; General Bec was fatally injured and taken prisoner, as were the Prince de Ligne, general of the cavalry,

all principal German officers, all Spanish and Italian mestres de camp, thirty-eight pieces of cannon, their pontoons and all the baggage train.

The battle was well and truly won, but, as Maréchal Gramont reformed his squadrons which found itself a little in disorder having charged many times, one of the enemy squadrons which was fleeing as fast as possible fell on him at the moment he expected the least; and he would have been taken or killed had they not been in such a hurry to flee, for he found himself in the middle of them. Nevertheless, they fired a discharge as they passed, which killed one of his aides-de-camp at his side: a most strange episode.

The two wings continued to pursue victory, and the prince and the maréchal met beyond the gulley of Lens; and with sword in hand, the prince came to the maréchal to embrace him and congratulate him on what he had achieved; but there was such a furious fight between their two horses, which before had been as gentle as mules, that they nearly ate each other, and they nearly endangered the lives of their masters more than the battle itself.

The number of prisoners increased to five thousand; and as they needed to be sent to France under an escort sufficient to lead such a large number, the order was given to Villequier, with two cavalry regiments and one infantry regiment; in consequence, the army was obliged to remain close to the battlefield for seven or eight days to await the return of the troops and for our horses to lead all the captured soldiers to Arras and La Bassée, which required a number of journeys."

THE BATTLE OF LENS,
ACCOUNT BY LA PEYRÈRE:

162

"The Prince was delighted by the presence of the archduke. His plan had succeeded; it seemed that his retreat had simply been a feint to engage the enemy in battle. This was indeed a subtle trap for the greatest captains of Spain, for which the archduke fell. The illusion which confused him was bizarre; he raced to victory and did not have time to take breath for the battle. The prince was ready, the archduke was not; the French hastened to array themselves for battle, to surprise the Spanish in their disorder. (...)

It was around eight o'clock in the morning when the army began to march in excellent array to the sound of trumpets, drums and cannon. The prince called a halt from time to time to redress the lines and to maintain distances and, the cannon of the Comte de Cossé was so well and so diligently used that it fired while marching, which is a significant feat; they had the advantage that, by firing from the plain onto the hillock of the enemy position, all shots reached either the squadrons, or the battalions, and created great confusion for them to array themselves for battle. Their cannon, which fired from the top of the hill to the foot, did not have the same effect as ours, although the numbers were unequal, with the archduke having 38 and the Prince 18.

The enemy was impatient to fight; they looked brave and marched resolutely towards us. However they were attempting two things at the same time, marching and arraying for combat, which is a hindrance when marching to a decisive battle (...)

The two armies were at 30 paces from each other when three shots were fired from the left wing of the enemy into our right wing. Condé, who feared the precipitation of his soldiers, halted them and forbade the musketeers from opening fire before the enemy had fired; fire should not begin until at point-blank range. This halt had three good effects; it tempered the ardour of our troops, readjusted the battle array and confirmed the soldier in the resolution to withstand the enemy discharge.

The prince of Salm advanced at a trot with his first line of Walloon and Lorraine soldiers against Condé's first line, who advanced at a walk to receive them. The two lines met horse to horse, pistol to pistol, and remained in this position for a fairly long time, awaiting who would fire first, with neither side wavering.

The enemy was more impatient and opened fire; it was as though the gates of Hell had opened! All our front line officers were killed, injured or unseated. Condé gave the signal to fire, then, leading the Gassion regiment with his sword held high, he crushed the squadron facing him. His six other squadrons followed him, and, on his example, charged the first enemy line so violently that it was overwhelmed. (...)"

ACCOUNT OF THE BATTLE OF LENS, ON THE 20 AUGUST 1648, BY ONE OF CONDÉ'S OFFICERS.

MANUSCRIPT MS933 PRESERVED AT THE CHÂTEAU OF CHANTILLY

"After the Prince de Condé took Ypres, he led his army back to Bethune, where he set up camp. Between Lillers and this town he summoned Erlach to join him, to repair by the junction of their troops the great loss of his cavalry (...) who had been greatly inconvenienced during the siege of Ypres by the hindrance caused to convoys and foraging parties.

Archduke Leopold during this time had taken Courtrai, and marched to Lillers: one of our parties took a company of Croats in the war with the commanding captain who was garrisoned in Gère; the prince generously sent him back to the archduke with his corps trumpeter, and ordered him to pay his respects to the archduke. He did so while General Beck was in the tent of the archduke. But this prince received this honour with a stupid arrogance and responded with such words that it would be shameful to repeat what the trumpeter reported, and Beck, to go further than the impoliteness of the prince, said such idiotic things that he revealed the character of the low gentlemen that he was, calling the Prince de Condé a young leveret that he threatened to take by the ears to Luxemburg. As the trumpeter replied in a similar style, he was threatened with prison, and finally was dismissed, very poorly satisfied. The man who told us this was in the suite of the prince who, awaiting the return of his trumpeter, read Dante in Italian and interpreted to a few assistants a word that many did not know, which was 'Vespaio', meaning a swarm of wasps; Mr de la Moussaye brought the gazette from Brussels, in which the enemy, proud of their success in the seizing of Ypres, had published a rather uninspired gibe, saying that his Imperial Highness sought everywhere the army of the Prince de Condé and that he would give wine to the man who could find this army and bring him news of it; as the prince turned the affair to mockery, the trumpeter arrived and related the content of his embassy to Condé so heatedly that his master who, out of all the heroes of his century is the most sensitive to glory, changed his tone and swore that he would spare him the trouble of searching if he was hardy enough to leave the woodland where he had entrenched his army.

In the meantime, this army arrived at Estaires.

There was a château on the Lys where we had forty or fifty men garrisoned. The archduke took it the same night and from there, covered all the way by the river, he marched on Lens.

Lens is outside the marsh that this river makes, which is called Watergangs. There is on the plain which goes to Arras a small stream, which has its source near to this town and it was occupied by the Spanish army who camped there at the top of the Rideau of Lens and positioned its cannon in two small spinneys on the Rideau.

And brave as they were in their gazette, the Spaniards entrenched without reflecting that they had thirty five thousand men. Hearing the cannon fire to the south of Lens, the Prince de Condé rejoiced to see his enemies on a plain and that same hour commanded Maréchal de Châtillon to prepare a guard corps positioned on a bridge they had won. He had woodcuts brought, and charged those facing him with his guards and the guards he found there so brusquely that the enemy abandoned the passage (...) to their army which was only two leagues from there.

The Prince crossed the Lys and left the baggage train beneath Béthune; I have never seen anyone cross with such impetuosity; one

hour before dawn we arrived at the edge of the gullies. This great Prince was naturally content when the artillery was advanced.

The narrator of this account found himself in an orchard of fruit trees, on the edge of which was our hero, who saw the pieces of cannon go by which increased as they passed. Our hero cut a switch from which he made an implement to throw apples, and began to throw against the Marquis of Normanville; the prince found this entertainment pleasing, and he took one also.

This pleasant prelude to battle continued, with each man taking part until Mr de Cossé passed with the last piece of artillery under his command.

Then Maréchal d'Erlach came to greet the prince, to whom he had brought eight thousand good men (author's note: in fact he brought less than four thousand). The sun was already high in the sky, and the enemy generals came with twelve hundred horses to see if it was all of our army or a part that was already downstream of the river; to remove their doubt, His Highness marched his artillery at the first line; they saw it clearly and returned to their entrenchments, leaving the entire plain free for us.

While marching, His Highness formed his troops into three lines, which together made at the most twenty thousand men and at least eighteen thousand; he placed the guards, Picardie and the regiments of the army of Erlach in the first line, and for the cavalry, all the gendarmes of both the king and the princes and all the companies of the guards of the generals; the second line was arrayed in the same way and our light cavalry commanded by Guiche; Mr d'Erlach was the third line and the reserve corps; Mr de Cossé led a band of artillery. At the first line he marched them as fast as the troops; in this array we went to show our army to the archduke, who was well covered by his lines, in front of which we halted a stone's throw away, and remained there all day (...)

It is to be noted that the prince had spoken so much of the German troops that never fired first and obliged their enemies to discharge their weapons then flee before them that each officer had this in mind, and while this was said only with regard to the cavalry, nevertheless nearly the entire infantry made it a point of honour not to fire at all.

Night came and the army had not eaten;

they could not fast until the following day when they would have to fight, particularly the horses. The prince resolved that at daybreak they would withdraw to a village named Loo which our rearguard touched in order for the soldiers to fill their stomachs, and said aloud that he was ready to fight the archduke whenever he desired, and this public remark contributed to the beginning of battle the following day.

That night, the enemy brought out of their entrenchment the regiment of Croats, but they were much astonished when they encountered our artillery, and they returned in haste.

Dawn came, and to show the enemy that they would not emerge covertly, His Highness waited until the sun had risen, and then he ordered a volley from six pieces by Monsieur de Cossé, and then marched without breaking his battle array, but sending only to the right the companies of gendarmes and chevau légers and those of the guards of the generals retreating in the same order that they were to make the advanced guard.

The Lorraine troops of the Spanish army and a few other squadrons, seeing the small number of unregimented companies, fell on them with their entire cavalry wing, broke them easily and pressed them so closely that they were only able to rally with the support of the regiment of Picardie that had the right wing of the first line.

This happy commencement caused Lorraine to cry victory. Beck, who thought he could gain precious time, led the Archduke out of the lines and showed him our infantry dispossessed of cavalry in the middle of one of the largest plains in the world; the archduke said that he had given the express order that no risks should be taken. Beck insisted and said that there was no more risk, and he offered his head in answer to their (oath?) of the battle; the Spanish reproaching him that he gave up an opportunity to redress their affairs and to rewrite the history of Rocroi, jumped the entrenchment, arrayed their regiments for battle and ran to us.

This was this master stroke of our hero (...)

He did nothing but fill the place of the fallen by the cavalry which was in the second line to defend it. And he sent the troops towards the left, marching straight on the enemy, where each soldier was ready for battle and the columns were formed, but were not yet in battle array

The regiment of the guards that had been the first to fire its volley was cut to pieces, and the regiment of Picardie which did not wish to fire broke seven regiments, among which was that which had killed the regiment of the guards; the regiments that Erlach had led which were Nettancourt, Vaubecourt and others did not fire either.

Our cavalry suffered greatly, for the enemy still had three squadrons against one, but when they were broken, they always came to rally behind Picardie; (author's note: three names of unidentified officers are listed here), after having charged twenty times and breaking the corps that they fought, came here to refresh themselves, and Streif came here to die.

Your gazetteer found Maréchal d'Aumont here, whom the Spanish brought as prisoner after having (...) to kill him in cold blood with a pistol shot in his order, while he was prisoner.

History shall tell the rest (...) suffice to say that we took more than six thousand prisoners and did not kill one hundred (...) men; all their cavalry fled. Beck was injured and captured by a lieutenant of the Aumont regiment; Mr d'Arnault wished to reproach him for something relating to the death of Monsieur de Feuquières, and Beck responded very brutally. We took him as a prisoner to Arras, where he died as brutally as he had lived; the prince, far from taking his revenge on him, lent him his carriage to take him there.

Through the account of a Jesuit reverend father of the group (...) which followed the archduke, we learnt that as soon as he had given the generals and the three Spaniards the permission to join the battle under their insistence, he armed himself, confessed, and fled."

P. 166-167 :
Bohemians and soldiers at rest
circa 1640-1643 by Sébastien
Bourdon (1616-1671).
Montpellier, Fabre museum.

[APPENDIX III : SCULPT AND PAINT FIGURINES FROM THE PERIOD OF THE THIRTY YEARS' WAR]

Sculpt and paint a bust of Richelieu

"On the 4th of December 1642, France lost this powerful genius who governed the kingdom so comprehensively, and the king himself, of whom he was the companion, if not the master, rather than the minister, who had revived all the power of the former palace masters, leaving the king with only his name and usurping all authority. Whether this minister survived through terror, as his enemies claim, or whether he lasted through his influence borne of his great qualities and superior mind, I cannot say: perhaps a mixture of both." In *Histoire de France sous le règne de Louis XIV*, 1718, by Mr de Larray, councillor of the Court and Embassies of His Majesty the King of Prussia.

"It was very dangerous to cross his path to stand in his way as death was the certain outcome, especially when the State was involved, the grandeur of which was of great importance to him, inseparable from his own interests, wanting to retain its reputation at any cost, which he believed was based on his master's glory and the prosperity of his affairs, of which he was in charge. He performed this task gloriously, as he had placed France in its highest position since the reign of Charlemagne, having defeated the Huguenot party who had stood up to five kings, humiliated the house of Austria, who wanted to rule over the entire Christendom, and established the king's authority so much so that nothing in his kingdom could resist him: he had done this by reducing the princes' authority and elevating the nobility and gentlemen whom he liked and esteemed." in *Mémoires de François de Paule de Clermont, marquis de Monglat*, Paris, 1838.

Cardinal Richelieu remains the artisan of the French army's renewal, which is why this major character in French history deserves some attention. To do this, we shall use an original approach, by letting two great artists, Luca Piergentili and Jean-Paul Dana, do the talking.

Figuralia bust of Armand-jean du Plessis, Cardinal de Richelieu (1585-1642).
Sculpture by by Luca Piergentili, oil painting by Jean-Paul Dana.

Sculpt a bust of Richelieu
... by Luca Piergentili

I am a casual sculptor. I mean I do not sculpt for living and from an artistic point of view I do not have any kind of academic background. I just sculpt for hobby and only when something really catchs my interest. Also, I am not a big fan of historical miniatures, what I really like are superheroes and comics-based characters, but in spite of this some time ago an article on an art book made me thinking about the not so obvious meaning that some things could have. The article was about how the cardinal Richelieu got portayed by Philippe de Champaigne (1602 - 1674), the French painter who did the well known three-views painting of Richelieu. Basically Philippe de Champaigne portrayed the Cardinal Richelieu as a triangle, used the pyramidal shape as a metaphor for the power embodied by the Cardinal. It is the same concept expressed by Gianlorenzo Bernini (1598-1680) on the Richelieu bust he sculpted, which I took as a reference to sculpt my own.

Sculpting is a tricky thing and there is a big difference between sculpting for your own pleasure and sculpting for an audience. I do not think that things have an absolute meaning, and most in general I think one will never know about the exact meaning of any kind of art. Even considering the miniature sculpting as a form of art, getting an agreement about what should be considered art is really hard. Are you judging the piece as an historical miniature ? Or are you thinking of it as a medium to express something ? It is all up to you. Personally I do not care at all about that, I simply do what I like, the way I like without thinking to much about the audience. To be honest I finished this little bust only thanks to the advices of a friend. I got sort of sculpting block and I was unable to follow with it. When I showed it to a friend of mine he told me "finish it no matter how it will turn, just take it as a sculpting exercise", so I did it that way and looking at it now I must admit is one of my preferred pieces. For the torso I tried to reproduce the same shape and folds sculpted by Bernini while for the face I did it in my own style, trying to render a tired but still fierce expression.

Paint a bust of Richelieu
... by Jean-Paul Dana

My passion for painting and history, lead me naturally into the world of historical miniatures. I met up with many other people sharing the same hobbies, who collectioned metal or resin miniatures who took great pleasure in painting them. From meeting to meeting and exhibitions to exhibitions, I took my first steps into this world. Ever since, I have painted a variety of miniatures of different sizes (54mm, 75mm, 90mm.....). On this occasion I met Luca Piergentili, who, at the time, had just started his own business of miniatures. Luca Priergentili, proposed to me, to paint some of his pieces, including the Richelieu bust.

The bust that I own, is not the original, but a copy made from a mould. Luca possesses his very own company of miniatures [http://www.figuralia.com/index.html] and molds his creations that are destined for sale. It is most important for a professional like Luca to protect his original sculpture from the start. Incase of deterioration or damage to the mold he can always start again with fresh molds made from his original sculpture. When I opened the box of the bust, I was taken by the high level of skill. I could not

see one trace of the mold or any air bubbles in the resin which is exceptional for a copy. Luca is careful and meticulous which is highly appreciated. The bust comes in one piece and includes a pedestal.

Before painting, I carefully washed the pieces in soapy water, with the help of a tooth brush. This stage is extremely important. Each miniature that has been molded will carry residues, of vasaline, talc and various other products in order for the resin not to stick to the mold. These residues get into all the folds and stop the paint from sticking to the miniature. When all the pieces are dry they can be glued together and the painting can commence.

I paint in oils, as have artists for centuries. This medium is ideal for a superb rendition of the bust. The paint will not stick directly to the resin and so needs to be undercoated. There are many forms of undercoat available, from acrylic, thinner based paint, spray paint, etc... I used "Humbrol" known as modelers paint, applied with an airbrush.

When painting the miniature the small scale of detail needs to be taken in consideration and so the paint needs to be applied thinly to avoid loosing fine details. The paint needs to be pulled out and spread as much as possible for a fine finish effect. The techniques for painting on a flat surface, for example canvas are similar. Thick on thin, blending and washes are examples of what can be done or used, just as I did on this bust. The colors I used and mixed are relatively standard. My painted version was used for the official box art for the bust, in 2006 for Lucas miniatures better known as Figuralia. You can take a look at his web site for more photos and details in painting.

171

BIBLIOGRAPHY

CONTEMPORARY DOCUMENTS

Abrégé de la vie et de la mort détestable de monsieur le duc de Rohan, chef des rebelles en France, Lyon, 1622

Assaut donné contre la ville de Montauban par monsieur le duc de Mayenne, le 26 juillet 1621, Lyon, 1621

Commission du roi à monsieur le maréchal de Themines pour commander son armée en Languedoc, Lyon, 1625

Congé général de l'armée du Roy, Lyon, 1620

Congé général de l'armée du Roy, Lyon, 1622

Déclaration du roi sur la cessation d'armes, licenciement des gens de guerre, Paris, 1619

État général de la puissante armée du Roy, sous la conduite de monsieur le maréchal de La Force, Lyon, 1633

L'estat du siège contre Montauban, par l'armée royale de Sa Majesté contre ceux de la rébellion, Lyon, 1621

L'ordre établi en France pour le service du Roy, avec le nombre de gens de guerre loués, Lyon, 1622

La défaite des troupes de monsieur de Favas, La Noue et Bessay au bourg de Saint-Benoît en Bas-Poitou, par messieurs les mareschals de Praslin, duc d'Elbœuf et comte de La Rochefoucault, Lyon, 1621

La réduction et triomphante entrée du roi en la ville de Montpellier, Lyon, 1622

La seconde défaite des rebelles de Montauban, par l'armée du roi commandée par le duc d'Espernon, Lyon, 1625

La victoire emportée en champ de bataille contre le marquis de La Force par monseigneur le duc d'Elbœuf, Lyon, 1622

Les heureux progrès des armées du roi très chrétien Louis XIII, au Piémont et Montserrat (1630), Lyon, 1631

Ordonnance du roi pour la paix, Lyon, 1616

Récit véritable de ce qui s'est passé à la Valteline depuis le 3 mars 1625 jusqu'au mois de mai dernier, Lyon, 1626

Réduction de la ville de Privas à l'obéissance du roi par monsieur le duc de Montmorency, Lyon, 1620

Relation ample et véritable de la descente en l'Isle de Ré, de monsieur le maréchal de Schomberg, Lyon, 1627

Véritables mémoires de ce qui s'est passé de jour en jour au voyage du roi depuis son départ de Paris le 7 juillet jusqu'à son retour du pays de Béarn le 7 novembre 1620, Paris, 1620

ARTAGNAN (d'), *Mémoires de M. d'Artagnan, capitaine lieutenant de la première compagnie des mousquetaires du roi*, Cologne, 1701

AUMALE (duc d'), *Histoire des princes de Condé*, Paris, 1886

BACHET, *Recueil des diverses relations des guerres d'Italie des années 1629, 1630 & 1631*, Bourg-en-Bresse, 1632

BESSÉ (de), sieur de la chapelle Milon, *Relation des campagnes de Rocroi et Fribourg*, Paris, 1826 (première édition : 1675)

BILLON (de), *Les Principes de l'art militaire*, Paris, 1613

COUSIN (V.), *La Jeunesse de madame de Longueville*, Paris, 1859 (on y trouvera un appendice de 50 pages sur la bataille de Rocroi qui contient la relation de la bataille par Lenet, les mémoires du baron de Sirot, ainsi qu'un extrait de celles du marquis de La Moussaye)

DANIEL (G.), *Histoire de la milice française*, Paris, 1721

HAMY (E.T.), *Correspondance du cardinal Mazarin avec le maréchal d'Aumont*, Monaco, 1904

ISAMBERT et TAILLANDIER, *Recueil général des anciennes lois françaises, ordonnances des Bourbons*, Paris, 1829

GASTON (duc d'Orléans), *Mémoires*, collection des mémoires relatifs à l'histoire de France, Paris, Petitot, 1824

GRAMONT (duc de), *Mémoires*, nouvelle collection des mémoires pour servir à l'histoire de France, Paris, 1839

GUISE (duc de), *Mémoires*, nouvelle collection des mémoires pour servir à l'histoire de France, Paris, 1839

LARRAY, *Histoire de France sous le règne de Louis XIV*, Rotterdam, 1718

PAULE DE CLERMONT (de), marquis de Monglat, *Mémoires*, collection des mémoires relatifs à l'histoire de France, Paris, Petitot, 1838

PLESSIS (maréchal de), *Mémoires*, collection des mémoires relatifs à l'histoire de France, Paris, Petitot, 1827

RAMSAY, *Histoire du vicomte de Turenne, maréchal général des armées du Roy*, Paris, 1735

RICHELIEU, *Mémoires*, collection des mémoires relatifs à l'histoire de France, Paris, Petitot, 1821

RICHELIEU (attribué à), *Relation fidèle de ce qui s'est passé en Italie en l'année 1630*, Paris, 1631

RICHEMONT (de) (?), *Siège de La Rochelle*, Paris & La Rochelle, (d'après un manuscrit contemporain de Richemont), 1872

ROHAN (duc de), *Le Parfait Capitaine, et Traité de la guerre*, Paris, 1636

ROHAN (duc de), *Mémoires*, collection des mémoires relatifs à l'histoire de France, Paris, Petitot, 1822

VAL (du), marquis de Fontenay-Mareuil, *Mémoires*, collection des mémoires relatifs à l'histoire de France, Paris, Petitot, 1826

WALHAUSEN (J.-J), *Art militaire pour l'infanterie*, 1615

SUMMARY BIBLIOGRAPHY : 19TH AND 20TH CENTURY WORKS

ANDRÉ (L.), *Michel Le Tellier et l'organisation de l'armée monarchique*, Paris, 1906

BÉRENGER (J.), *Turenne*, Paris, Fayard, 1987

BOGDAN (H.), *La Guerre de Trente Ans 1618-1648*, Paris, Perrin, 1997

CARMONA (M.), *Richelieu*, Paris, Fayard, 1983

CHILDS (J.), *Warfare in the Seventeenth Century*, Cassel & Co, 2001

CORVISIER (A.), *Histoire militaire de la France, tome I*, Paris, Puf, 1997

DANSKIN (N.), *The French Army in the Thirty Year's War*, The Pike and Shot Society, 1995

DUCCINI (H.), *Histoire de la France au XVIIe siècle*, Paris, Sedes, 2000

GERRER (B.), PETIT (P.), SANCHEZ-MARTIN (J.-L.), *Rocroi 1643, Vérités et controverses sur une bataille de légende*, 2007

HENNINGER (L.), *Les Grandes Batailles de l'histoire : Rocroi 1643*, Socomer, 1993

LÉOMY (F.), *Les Grandes Destinées : Louis II de Bourbon dit le Grand Condé*, Socomer, 1994

LIMM (P.), *The Thirty Year War*, Longman, 1984

NAPOLÉON Ier, *Précis des guerres du maréchal de Turenne*

PERINI (de), *Batailles françaises* volumes III et IV, Paris, Flammarion, 1895

SCHILLER (von), *Histoire de la guerre de Trente Ans*, Paris, 1881

172

Aknowledgements & Photographic copyrights

Publisher : Stéphane Thion
Page layout by Valérie Liu
Typeset in Dutch Medieval
Originated by Daniel Tallet
Translated by TranslatNation
Printed in Singapore through Tien Wah Press Ltd

Legal deposit : June, 2008
ISBN : 978-2-917747-01-8